Abstracts
of
HENRY COUNTY VIRGINIA
Deeds
(Books 3 *and* 4)

- *1784-1792* -

Compiled by:
Lela C. Adams

Southern Historical Press, Inc.
Greenville, South Carolina

Copyright 1978
By: Lela C. Adams

Copyright Transferred 1983
To: Southern Historical Press, Inc.

All rights reserved. No part of this publication may be reproduced, stored in a retrieval system, transmitted in any form, posted on to the web in any form or by any means without the prior written permission of the publisher.

Please direct all correspondence and orders to:

www.southernhistoricalpress.com
or
**SOUTHERN HISTORICAL PRESS, Inc.
PO BOX 1267
Greenville, SC   29601**
southernhistoricalpress@gmail.com

ISBN #0-89308-359-3

Printed in the United States of America

TABLE OF CONTENTS

Deed Book 3   1
    Aug 1784 to Sept 1788

Poll for the Election of Delegates
    for Henry County April 1787   71

Deed Book 4
    Sept 1788 to June 1792   76

Name Index   122

Creeks, Rivers, Roads, Mountains

Slave Index

INTRODUCTION

In 1776, Patrick County was cut out of Pittsylvania County and was named for Patrick Henry. When first formed, Henry County embraced the whole of what is now Patrick County, and the greater portion of present Franklin County, Virginia.

These deeds include many bills of sale; trust deeds; powers of attorney; dower right releases; names of counties and states where the grantor has taken up residence or plans to reside; leases; damage suits; inquisitions into death; deeds of gifts; bonds and contracts.

Page 1: 26 Aug 1784. WILLIAM DAVIS to ANDREW THOMPSON (FARGEMAN) both of the County of Henry state of Virginia, for the sum of one hundred pounds said DAVIS conveys a parcel or tract of land on the South Branch of Story Creek containing 139 acres more or less with the lines of DILLINGHAM. Signed: WILLIAM DAVIS. . .RUTH DAVIS, the wife of the said WILLIAM DAVIS hereby relinquishes her right of dower. Proved: 26 Aug 1784 at a Court held for the County of Henry.

Page 2: 26 Aug 1784. ELISHA HARBOUR to PETER LEAK both of Henry Co., Va., in consideration of the sum of two hundred forty pounds sells 243 acres on the branches of Marrowbone Creek adjoining the lands of JOSIAH SHAW, it being the place whereon said ELISHA HARBOUR now resides. Signed: ELISHA HARBOUR. Witness: JAMES PITTMAN, JESSE WITT. . .MARY HARBOUR wife of ELISHA HARBOUR relinquishes her right of dower. Proved: 26 Nov 1782, Henry County, Va.

Page 3: 20 Aug 1784. JAMES ACTON of the County of Washington state of North Carolina to JAMES TAYLOR of the county of Henry state of Virginia sells and conveys land on the branches of No Business fork of the Mayo River for the sum of seventy pounds containing by estimate 171 acres joining the lands of SAMUEL SMITH and crossing Yeallow Bank Branch. Signed: JAMES (X) ACTON. Proved: 26 Aug 1784, Henry County, Va.

Pages 4-5: 26 Aug 1784. RICHARD COLYAR (COLLIER) of Henry Co., Va. to GEORGE DODSON of Pittsylvania Co., Va. for the sum of one hundred eighty pounds convey land on both sides of Praythors fork of the Mayo River containing by estimate 229 acres, beginning at an oak on Lockhart's mill path, Pulliam's millpath. Signed: RICHARD (X) COLLIER. Proved: Henry Co., Va. 26 Aug 1784.

Pages 6-7: 25 Aug 1784. WILLIAM EDWARDS, SR. to DUTTON LAYNE both of Henry Co., Va., for the sum of one hundred fifty pounds sells land on the west side of Smith River whereon the said LAYNE now lives. Lines: a box oak on the Indian Grave Ridge, being the dividing line between WILLIAM EDWARDS and THOMAS EDWARDS and near the shole branch of the River, it being 200 acres. Signed: WILLIAM EDWARDS. Proved Henry Co., Va. 26 Aug 1784.

Page 8: 25 Aug 1784. WILLIAM EDWARDS to THOMAS

EDWARDS JR. both of the County of Henry, Va. for the consideration of fifty pounds sells and conveys land on the west side of Smith River, where the said THOMAS EDWARDS, JR. now lives it being 100 acres more or less. Signed: WILLIAM EDWARDS. Proved: 26 Aug 1784, Henry Co., Va.

Page 9: 25 Aug 1784. AMOS RICHARDSON of the county of Henry to MOSES BROCK for sum of fifty pounds sells 100 acres on the north side of Snow Creek adjoining WILLIAM VINCENT'S line. Signed: AMOS RICHARDSON. Proved: 26 Aug 1784 Henry Co., Va.

Pages 10-11: 26 June 1784. HUGH MCWILLIAMS of Henry Co., Va. to THOMAS CRAIG of the same for the sum of forty pounds conveys land being 150 acres more or less, beginning at the road on the top of the Ridge. Signed: HUGH MCWILLIAMS, MARY (X)MC-WILLIAMS. Proved: Henry Co., Va. 26 Aug 1784.

Pages 11-12: 5 June 1784. JOHN ELLIS of the county of Henry state of Virginia to ALLEN RIDLEY YOUNG of the same for the sum of thirty pounds sells 100 acres on the Bull Run of Turkey Cock and Jacks Creeks, beginning at JOHN SMITH'S. Signed: JOHN ELLIS. Wit: WILLIAM YOUNG, MELLON YOUNG, ELIZABETH SOUTHERLANE. Proved: Henry Co., Va. 26 Aug 1784.

Pages 12-13: 25 Aug 1780. JAMES MELTON and his wife ANN MELTON of Henry Co., Va. to JESSE DELOZEAR for the sum of one hundred pounds conveys 270 acres of land being a part of a land grant to the said JAMES MELTON by patent bearing the date 1 March 1781. Signed: JAMES (X) MELTON. Proved: 26 Aug 1784 Henry Co., Va. . .NANCY, the wife of JAMES MELTON relinquishes her right of dower.

Pages 13-14: 3 May 1784. EUSEBUS HUBBARD to JAMES PRUNTY both of Henry Co., Va. for the sum of sixty six pounds sells land by estimate 100 acres more or less on Snow Creek joins THOMAS BOLTONS and CHOICE'S lines. Signed: EUSEBUS HUBBARD. Wit: AMOS RICHARDSON, JAMES ROGERS, ROBERT PRUNTY. Proved: 26 Nov 1784 Henry Co., Va.

Pages 14-15: 22 July 1784. HUGH MCWILLIAMS to JAMES YOUNG both of Henry Co., Va. for the sum of fifty pounds sells land by estimate 150 acres that crosses Reedy Creek with the lines of

THOMAS CRAIG, JAMES YOUNG and Snow Creek. Signed: HUGH MC WILLIAMS. Wit: JOHN JAMESON, THOMAS CRAIG.

Pages 15-16: 23 Apr 1771. Deed of Trust. I, GEORGE LUMPKIN of the county of Pittsylvania state of Virginia am bound unto SILVANUS WHITT of Chesterfield Co., Va. in the sum of one hundred pounds. The Condition of the said obligation is that said GEORGE LUMPKIN make a good and lawfull rite either by deed or pattent to a sartain tract of land in Pittsylvania Co. on Ironmonger branch of Horsepasture Crk, it being land said LUMPKIN purchased of EDWARD YOUNG containing 300 acres more or less. Signed: GEORGE LUMPKIN. Wit: JOSHUA MABRY, JOHN CHILDRESS, DAVID WITT. Proved: 26 Aug 1784, Henry Co., Va.

Pages 16-17: 13 May 1784. BENJAMIN MURRELL to JOHN SNEAD both of Henry Co., Va. for the sum of sixty pounds sells a tract of land containing 154 acres on both sides of Beards Creek. Signed: BENJAMIN MURRELL. Proved: 26 Aug 1784, Henry Co., Va.

Pages 17-18: 26 Feb 1784. WILLIAM SMITH of Henry Co., Va. to WILLIAM ARNOLD of the same, for the consideration of ninety four pounds conveys land being 200 acres more or less being on Russell's Creek joining JAMES MC KINSEY...Being part of WILLIAM SMITH'S tract of 353 acres on the South Mayo River. Signed: WILLIAM SMITH. Wit: JOHN STAPLES, JOHN DILLARD, WILLIAM GRAVES, JAMES MAY. Proved: 26 Aug 1784, Henry Co., Va.

age 19: .. Nov 1784. JAMES MELTON of Henry Co., Va. to THOMAS WILKINS for the sum of thirty pounds sells land in the amount of 50 acres more or less, joins JONATHAN SWAN and MELTON'S own land. Signed: JAMES (X) MELTON. . .NANCY, wife of JAMES MELTON relinquishes her right of dower. Proved: 26 Aug 1784 Henry Co., Va.

Page 20: 5 Dec 1783. Power of Attorney. JANE HAWKINS of Henry Co., Va. parish of Patrick, appoints JAMES COWDEN of the same to be her lawfull attorney to act for her. Wit: WILLIAM GRAVES, MILLEY THOMAS, WILLIAM WOODS, ROBERT WOODS. Proved: 26 Aug 1784, Henry Co., Va.

Pages 20-21: 4 June 1784. JOHN SHIELDS of the County of Pittsylvania state of Virginia to SAMUEL JOHNSON of Henry Co., Va. for the sum of one hundred sixty pounds sells land in Henry County on both sides of Turkey Cock Creek containing by estimate 400 acres with JOHN CUMMINGS and EDWARD SMITH'S lines. Signed: JOHN SHIELDS. Wit: EDWARD SMITH, JOHN CUNNINGHAM, KILLIS BALLINGER, JOSEPH CUNNINGHAM. Proved: 26 Aug 1784, Henry Co., Va.

Pages 22-23: 26 Aug 1784. JOHN WIMBISH of Pittsylvania County to ARCH. HUGHES of Henry County, Virginia. Said WIMBISH and HUGHES being partners and holding joint accounts now agree to an equal division of said lands. WIMBISH grants, releases all claims to a tract in Henry County containing by estimate 697 acres, whereon the said HUGHES now lives. 497 acres of this was purchased by WIMBISH and HUGHES of GEORGE WALTON by deed recorded in Pittsylvania County and 200 acres purchased of JAMES ROBERTS also in Pittsylvania County. The said land lies on the south side of the South Mayo River and joins HENRY FRANCE and FONTAINE. Signed: JOHN WIMBISH. Wit: JOHN COX, JOSEPH COOPER, JOHN WILLS, WILLIAM RYAN. Proved: Henry County, Va. 26 Aug 1784.

Page 24: 12 Jan 1783. JOHN NOWLAND of Washington County, North Carolina to PETER GILLIAM for the sum of two hundred pounds sells and conveys a parcel of land containing 370 acres more or less and being on the south side of Blackwater River. Signed: JOHN NOWLIN. Wit: JESSE HEARD, JOHN SHARP, JOHN LUMSDEN, JR. Proved: At a Court held for Henry County, Va. 27 Mar 1783.

Pages 26-27: 26 Aug 1784. Agreement. JOHN WIMBISH of Pittsylvania County and AR. HUGHES of Henry County as partners have mutually agreed to equally divide their jointly held lands. Therefore, to ARCHELAUS HUGHES a tract of land being in Henry County on both side of Mill Creek of the Mayo River containing 437 acres it being the land purchased partly of NICHOLAS LANKFORD and partly of ROBERT LANKFORD. Signed: JOHN WIMBISH. Wit: none recorded. Proved: 26 Aug 1784.

Pages 28-29: 20 Aug 1784. AMOS RICHARDSON and his wife MARTHA to JAMES ROGERS both of Henry County for the sum of thirty pounds sells 100 acres of land that joins ABRAHAM ARDEN'S Oldfield. Signed: AMOS RICHARDSON. Wit: none recorded. Proved: 26 Aug 1784.

Pages 29-30: 13 March 1784. RALPH SHELTON, SENR. to JAMES SHELTON, his son both of Henry County for the sum of five pounds conveys 400 acres of land on both sides of the south fork of the Mayo River joining JAMES LANKFORD. Signed: RALPH SHELTON. Wit: JESSE REYNOLDS, HALL (X) HUDSON, ELEPHAZ SHELTON. Proved: At a Court held for Henry Co., Va. 23 Sept 1784.

Page 31: 3 Aug 1784. THOMAS FLOWERS of Botetourt County, Va. to WILLIAM GARDNER of Henry County for the sum of eighty pounds part of a tract of land that was 930 acres by survey bearing date of 15 Nov 1772 on both sides of Flat Creek of Smith River. The part being conveyed is by estimate 300 acres, it being the lower part of the survey and crosses Rich Run. Signed: THOMAS FLOWERS. Wit: JOHN KINDRICK, HENRY (X) GUFFEE, MARTIN LAWRENCE. Proved: 23 September 1784 at a Court held for Henry Co., Va.

Pages 32-33: 3 April 1784. JOHN LINDSAY of Henry County, Va. to JOHN READ of Ninety Six District of South Carolina for the consideration of the sum of one hundred pounds sells 100 acres of land in Henry Co. on the north fork of the Mayo River to the mouth of Horsepasture Creek. Signed: JOHN LINDSAY. Wit: GREGORY DURHAM, ELIZABETH LINDSAY, MARY LINDSAY. Proved: not noted in the deed book. . . . Memorandum: That if the said JOHN LINDSAY his heirs, etc. shall well and truly has to JOHN FOSTER on negro girl 12 years old last Christmas that is well groon, heathey and sumable on or before the 1st day of July next, insuing then the within indenture to be null and void, otherwise to remain good and valid. Signed: JOHN READ. Wit: GREGORY DURHAM, ELIZABETH LINDSAY, MARY LINDSAY. Proved: At a Court held for Henry Co., Va. 23 Sept 1784.

Page 34: 23 Sept 1784. JACOB ADAMS of Henry County to CHARLES COLLIER of the same for the consideration of twenty five pounds conveys land on Bowins Creek one of the waters of Smith River, beginning at the whole tract patented to sd ADAMS for 295 acres; this part being conveyed is 73 and 3/4 acre with ANGLIN'S old line. Signed: JACOB ADAMS (X). Wit: CHARLES HIBBER, CHARLES HASTEN, RALPH MITCHELL. No date of being recorded.

Pages 35-36: 15 Aug 1784. JOHN KINDRICK of Henry Co. to NICHOLAS COGER (KOGER) of the same for the sum of twenty pounds sells land on

Smith River beginning at THOMAS HUFF'S line, crosses Buffalow Creek to THOMAS HARBOUR'S corner on Smith River containing more or less 250 acres. Signed: JOHN KINDRICK. Wit: none recorded. Proved: 23 Sept 1784.

Pages 36-38. .. Sept 1784. JOSIAH SMITH of the county of Henry to JOHN STAPLES of the same for the sum of five hundred pounds sells and conveys three tracts to wit: (1) containing 216 acres on the branches of Horsepasture Creek adjoining the land of JAMES SHELTON, deceased, SAMUEL SHELTON and JAMES SPENCER, deceased, it being the place JOSIAH SMITH now lives. (2) by patent 189 acres on the branches of Horsepasture Creek. (3) containing by estimate 150 acres on the south side of the North Mayo River adjoining the lands of HAMON CRITZ, it being part of a tract purchased by WILLIAM FRENCH of THOMAS M. RANDOLPH and conveyed to said SMITH, it joins Mill Creek and this tract is now in the possession of said JOHN STAPLES. Signed: JOSIAH SMITH. Wit: SAMUEL CRUTCHER, JOHN DILLARD, JOHN HUNTER. . .JAMIMA SMITH, wife of JOSIAH SMITH relinquishes her right of dower. Proved: 23 Sept 1784.

Pages 38-39: 23 Sept 1784. WILLIAM SMITH of Henry County and THOMAS LOCKHART of the same for the sum of thirty pounds sells land on both sides of the south fork of the Mayo River containing by estimate 180 acres more or less crosses Russell's Creek and with lines according to courses and tenor of the patent. Signed: WILLIAM SMITH. No witness recorded. Proved: 23 Sept 1784.

Pages 39-40: 15 Sept 1784. THOMAS CREWS of Henry County to ANTHONY BITTING of the same for the sum of six pounds sells 81 acres by survey bearing date of 17 May 1780 on a branch of Marrowbone Creek joining HAMMONS line. Signed: THOMAS CREWS, SUSANNAH CREWS, wife of THOMAS CREWS. Wit: ROBERT STOCKTON, JAMES ANTHONY, THOMAS COOPER. Proved: 23 Sept 1784, Henry County, Va.

Page 41: 23 Sept 1784. JACOB ADAMS of Henry County to JOHN PRESTON for the sum of seventy a parcel of land on a branch of the Mayo River called Roundabout being part of tract containing 971 acres, this deed for 500 acres more or less. Signed: JACOB ADAMS. Wit: RALPH MITCHELL, CHARLES HIBBERT, DANIEL RICE. Proved: 23 Sept 1784.

Pages 42-43: 10 Sept 1784. WILLIAM MAVITY of Henry County to JAMES CALLAWAY for the sum of one hundred pounds a tract of land containing 146 acres on the branches of Pigg River with the lines of THOMAS JONES and RENTFRO'S. Signed: WILLIAM MAVITY. Wit: none recorded. . . .MARY MAVITY the wife of WILLIAM MAVITY relinquishes her right of dower. Proved: 23 Sept 1784.

Pages 43-44: 23 Sept 1784. JOHN HENDERSON of the county of Henry to FRANCIS TURNER of the same for and in consideration of the sum of two hundred fifty pounds sells land on both side of Smith River beginning at the mouth of Flat Creek where it emties into said River, thence on a dividing line between MARY HUFF and said FRANCIS TURNER to an old line on the southside of the River containing 150 acres. Signed: JOHN HENDERSON, ELIZABETH HENDERSON. Wit: WILLIAM AMOS, DANIEL (X) CASEY. Proved: 23 Sept 1784.

Page 45: Power of Attorney. I, HARRIS WILSON of Henry County hereunto moving appoint COL. JAMES LYON of Henry County my true and lawful attorney to make title to a tract of land that is all the lands to me belonging on the waters of Russell Creek, a branch of the Mayo River, particular the land I live on and others adjoining, to make title to STEPHEN LYON and to do all that is necessary. Signed: HARRIS (X) WILSON. Wit: JOSEPH CLOUD, HENRY SMITH, JAMES MANKIN, MILLER WOODSON EASLY, HARVEY FITZGERRALL. Proved at a Court held for Henry County 23 Sept 1784.

Pages 46-47. 30 Nov 1783. HENRY TATE of Henry County to THOMAS NUNN of the same for the sum of forty pounds conveys a tract of land on a branch of the Smith River containing 172 acres that was granted said TATE by patent bearing date 1 February 1781 at Richmond, Va., joins RANDOLPH'S land. Signed: HENRY TATE. Wit: NEWSOM PACE, WILLIAM HARDMAN, INGR. NUNN. 23 Sept 1784, proved at a Court held for Henry County.

Pages 48-49: 19 June 1784. JOHN MARCUM of Henry County to JOSIAH MARCUM of the same for the sum of fifty pounds sells a parcel of land on the Blackwater River...joins PETER HOLLAND, HUMPHREY EDMONSON, WILLIAM HEARD'S old line, HOLLAWAY'S corner and crosses Poplar Camp Creek...containing 170 acres more or less. Signed: JOHN (X) MARCUM. Wit: JAMES MASON, ELUTRUS (X) HARDING, WILLIAM (X) HARDING.

Proved 23 Sept 1784 at a Court held for Henry County.

Pages 49-51: 22 February 1780. MARTIN KEY of Fluvanna County an attorney for JOHN HARMER of the Kingdom of Great Britian to THOMAS BUSH of the county of Henry. Whereas JOHN HARMER by his certain letter of Attorney bearing date of 1770 did empower MARTIN KEY to sell and dispose of certain lands. Among these lands on Little Marrowbone Creek in Pittsylvania County (now Henry), KEY did covenant to said BUSH ca. 25 June 1777 about 100 acres belonging to the said HARMER lying on the south side of Little Marrowbone Creek for the sum of fifty pounds with the plantation whereon THOMAS BUSH now lives. Signed: MARTIN KEY. Wit: NICHOLES SPEARES, JOHN ALEXANDER, DANIEL REAMEY. . .Notation that this 22nd Feb 1780 THOMAS BUSH had paid in full for the above property.

Pages 52-53: 9 Aug 1784. RICHARD FARRER of Pittsylvania County to MOSES HODGES of Henry County for the sum of sixty pounds sells a parcel of land containing 200 acres more or less, being part of a 400 acre tract surveyed for WILLIAM RICKLE on the south side of the southfork, South Branch of Sandy River. Signed: RICHARD FARRER. Wit: WILLIAM TUNSTALL, HENRY JONES, FELDING JONES, EA. ROBERTS. Proved 28 Sept 1784 at a Court held for Henry County.

Page 54: 22 April 1784. Agreement. An agreement between WALTER KING COLE and JAMES BAKER both of Henry County. W. K. COLE for the sum of fifty pounds sells to JAMES BAKER a negro girl not under 13 years old nor more than 16 be likely well grown, healthy, of sound mind and clear of infirmities to be delivered by the 25th of November next. Should there be a dispute, refer it to MORDICAI HORD and JOHN BARKSDALE. Should COLE refuse to deliver said girl, he is to pay fifty pounds of 100 acres of land to be chosen by said BAKER. Signed: WALTER K. COLE, JAMES BAKER. Wit: WILLIAM ALEXANDER, EDMUND LYNE. Proved at a Court held for Henry County 28 Oct 1784.

Pages 55-57: 28 Oct 1784. THOMAS MEDKIFF of Henry County, Virginia to WOODY BURGE of Scurry County, North Carolina for the sum of one hundred pounds sells two parcels of land on both sides of Peters Creek; 1 tract containing 64 acres it being the tract on which MEDKIFF now lives and the 2nd containing 129 acres more or less. Signed: THOMAS

MEDKIFF (X). Wit: none...RUTHY MEDKIFF, wife of THOMAS MEDKIFF relinquishes her right of dower to the above transaction. Proved: 28 Oct 1784 at a Court held for Henry County.

Pages 57-58: 25 Nov 1784. JOHN DICKENSON of Henry County to JOHN WILLS of the same for the sum of one hundred pounds conveys land on the LEATHERWOOD Creek, adjoining lines of said WILLS own land containing 306 acres. Signed: JOHN DICKENSON. Wit: none. Proved 25 Nov 1784, Henry County, Va.

Pages 58-59: 9 Nov 1784. ROBERT MASON of Henry County to ROBERT HALLADY of the same for the sum of fifty pounds sells land on the south fork of the north fork of Chestnut Creek, it being the tract whereon the said HALLADY now lives containing 443 acres...beginning at an oak on Briery Mtn. Signed: ROBERT MASON. Wit: none. Proved 25 Sept 1784 Henry Co., Va.

Pages 60-61: 25 Nov 1784. JACOB STALLINGS of Henry County to DANIEL RAMEY of the same for the sum of one hundred pounds sells two tracts of land on both sides of Balls Creek of Smith River. The 1st tract containing 204 acres beginning with MORRAH (MERRY) WEBB'S line; the 2nd, being 90 acres and adjoining the aforementioned tract on the River and now being in the possession of DANIEL RAMEY. Signed: JACOB STALLINGS. Wit: none....ANN STALLINGS, wife of JACOB STALLINGS relinquishes her right of dower. Proved at a Court held for Henry County 25 Sept 1784.

Pages 62-63: 21 Aug 1784. WILLIAM HIGGENBOTTOM of Henry County to JAMES GOWING of the same for the sum of five pounds sells and conveys land on both sides of the Dan River by estimate to be 201 acres. Signed: WILLIAM (X) HIGGENBOTTOM. Wit: EDWARD TATUM, JAMES LYON, ELIPHAZ SHELTON, JACOB MANES...MARY HIGGENBOTTOM, wife of WILLIAM HIGGENBOTTOM relinquishes her right of dower. Proved: 25 Nov 1784 at a Court held for Henry Co.

Pages 64-65: 12 Nov 1784. GEORGE SUMPTER of Henry County to BENJAMIN POSEY of the same for forty pounds sells land on both sides of Smith River, beginning at WILLIAM COX'S on the South side of the River containing 106 acres. Signed: GEORGE SUMPTER. Wit: RALPH MITCHELL, JAMES BAKER, THOMAS PRUNTY. Proved 25 Nov 1784 at a Court held for Henry

County, Va.

Pages 65-66: 27 Oct 1784. CHARLES COLYAR of Henry County to GEORGE SUMPTER of the same for ninety pounds sells all that part of a tract on Bowen's Creek, one of the orders of the Smith River, beginning at the whole tract patented by JACOB ADAMS for 295 acres and deeded out of the said 295 acres. This deed for 73 and 3/4 acres and joins the old line of ANGLIN'S. Signed: CHARLES (X) COLLIER. Wit: JOHN SALMON, JAMES BAKER, ABSALOM ADAMS. Proved: Henry County, 25 Nov 1784.

Pages 67-68: 12 Feb 1784. WILLIAM HASKINS of Henry County to JOHN DAVIS of the same for two hundred pounds sells land on both sides of Mountain Creek, it being 329 acres more or less. Signed: WILLIAM HASKINS. Wit: JOSEPH KING, JOHN KERBY, JESSE KERBY. Proved: At a Court held for Henry County 25 Nov 1784.

Pages 69-70: 10 March 1784. JOHN HELTON of the county of Montgomery, state of Virginia to THEODRICK WEBB of Bedford County, Va., for the sum of four hundred pounds sells 200 acres on the waters of Blackwater River, beginning on the north side of the River at RANDOLPH'S corner. Signed: JOHN HELTON. Wit: MOSES GREER, JOHN RENTFRO, JOHN (X) ANDERSON, THOMAS DOGGETT, CHATTEN DOGGETT, ISHAM FITGERALD, JACOB (X) WEBB. Proved at a Court held for Henry County 25 Nov 1784.

Page 71: 23 Dec 1784. Bond. Bond of ABRAHAM PENN who is sheriff of Henry County along with bondsmen GEORGE WALLER and THOMAS NUNN.

Page 72: 23 Jan 1785. Deed of Gift. AMOS RICHARDSON of Henry County gives, grants and conveys unto AARON RICHARDSON a tract of land on the Buck Branch of Snow Creek containing by estimate 75 acres. Signed: AMOS RICHARDSON. Wit: none. Proved 27 Jan 1785, Henry Co., Va.

Page 73: 22 Nov 1784. AMOS RICHARDSON of Henry County to DANIEL RICHARDSON of the same for the sum of forty pounds land on the Buck Branch of Snow Creek being 50 acres more or less. Signed: AMOS RICHARDSON. Wit: none. Proved 27 Jan 1785, Henry Co., Va.

Page 74: Deed of Gift. I promise to give up all my

right and property of one sixth part of all my father
JOHN RAMSEY'S (deceased) estate in land and other
personal property which was my part of the said estate. I give it to my mother, MARY RAMSEY to dispose
of. Signed: GEORGE (X) RAMSEY. Wit: SAMUEL (X)
BIRD, JAMES (X) BIRD, THOMAS (X) JONES. Proved: 17
Jan 1785, Henry Co., Va.

Pages 74-75: 29 July 1782. ANDREW REA and his wife
SALLY REA of Henry County to JOHN SIM-
MONS of the same for the sum of sixty pounds sells
land on Grassey Creek a branch of the Smith River
being by estimate 202 acres more or less joins JESSE
WILLINGHAM and STEPHEN RENNO. Signed: ANDREW REA,
SALLY REA. Wit: REUBIN PAYNE, JOHN SALMON, DAVID
LANIER. Proved: 28 Jan 1785, Henry Co., Va.

Pages 76-77: 8 Feb 1785. TULLEY CHOICE of Henry
County to BENJAMIN COOK of the same for
one hundred eighty pounds sells land on Snow Creek
containing by estimate 200 acres...lines: Musterfield
branch at the Path, WILLIAM ESTES now BENJAMIN COOK'S
line. Signed: TULLY (X) CHOICE. Wit: HUGH INNES,
DANIEL RICHARDSON, DAVID WILLIS. Proved: 24 Feb
1785, Henry Co., Va.

Page 78: 24 Feb 1785. JOHN RENNO of Henry County
to WILLIAM MULLINS of the same for one
hundred twenty pounds sells land on the branches of
Reedy Creek being 100 acres more or less with the
lines of HENRY VAUGHAN and JURDENS. Signed: JOHN (X)
RENNO. Wit: none. Proved: 24 Feb 1785, Henry Co.,
Va.

Pages 79-80: 24 March 1785. ROWLAND CHILES of
Henry County to ABRAHAM ROWDIN of the
same for thirty five pounds sells land beginning at
JEREMIAH CLANCHES to RICHARD COLLIER'S corner and
with WILLIAM MARTIN'S line. (no acreage given).
Signed: ROWLAND CHILES. Wit: none recorded. Proved:
24 March 1785, Henry Co., Va.

Pages 80-81: 24 March 1785. ROWLAND CHILES of Henry
County to RICHARD COLLIER of the same
for thirty pounds sells 50 acres of land...lines:
BARTLETT FOLEY'S survey line and WILLIAM MARTIN'S
corner. Signed: ROWLAND CHILES. Wit: none. . . .
NANCY CHILES, the wife of ROWLAND CHILES relinquishes
her right of dower. Proved: 24 March 1785, Henry
Co., Va.

Pages 81-82:   24 March 1785. ROWLAND HORSLEY BIRKS (BURKE) of Henry County to RICHARD COLLEAR (COLLIER) for the sum of one hundred pounds sells land containing 100 acres, it being the land where the said BURKE now lives and joins the land of WILLIAM WALDIN. Signed: ROWLAND HORSLEY BIRKS. Wit: none. . .SARAH BIRKS, wife of ROWLAND HORSLEY BIRKS relinquishes her right of dower. Proved: 24 March 1785 at a Court held for Henry Co., Va.

Pages 83-84:   24 March 1785. SAMUEL JOHNSTON of Henry County to DAVID WATSON of the same for one hundred pounds sells land containing by estimate 450 acres on the branches of Leatherwood Creek beginning at GARROT BIRCHES corner and LOMAX & CO., also part of another tract or parcel of land to make out the 450 acres more or less, this with SHORT'S corner and HOOKER'S old line. Signed: SAMUEL JOHNSTON. Wit: none. Proved: 24 March 1785, Henry Co., Va.

Pages 85-86:   21 March 1785. SAMUEL JOHNSTON of Henry County to FRANCIS HILL of Prince Edward Co., Va. for the sum of fifty pounds sells land containing by estimate 326 acres on both sides of the Baretree fork of Chestnut Creek beginning at WEAKLEY'S old line (now WOODS). Signed: SAMUEL JOHNSTON, BETTY JOHNSTON. Wit: JOHN CUNNINGHAM, BELLY (X) CONWAY. Proved: At a Court held for Henry County 24 March 1785.

Pages 87-88:   24 March 1784. EDMUND EDWARDS and his wife ELIZABETH EDWARDS of the parish of Patrick and County of Henry to ANDREW RAY of the same for eighty pounds sells land containing 263 acres on Stewarts Creek. Signed: EDMUND EDWARDS. Wit: none. Proved: 24 March 1785, Henry Co., Va.

Pages 88-89:   24 March 1785. SAMUEL JOHNSTON of Henry County to MATHEW WELLS of the same for twenty five pounds conveys 272 acres by estimate on the branches of Leatherwood Creek with DICKENSON'S corner and a spur of Turkey Cock Mountain. Signed: SAMUEL JOHNSTON. Wit: none recorded. Proved: 24 March 1785, Henry Co., Va.

Pages 90-91:   20 March 1785. JAMES SHARD of Henry County to MORRIS HUMPHREY of the same for the sum of five pounds sells a parcel of land containing 216 acres by estimate on the waters of the

North Mayo River, it being part of a tract surveyed by the said JAMES SHARD...beginning at an old road called the Critz Road and with GEORGE TAYLOR'S land. Signed: JAMES SHARD. Wit: none recorded. . .HANNAH SHARD, the wife of JAMES SHARD relinquishes her right of dower. Proved: Henry Co., Va. 24 March 1785.

Pages 91-92: 16 Feb 1785. THOMAS HAMMON of Henry County to NATHANIEL PARIOTT for the sum of twenty pounds sells 100 acres on both sides of Jack's Creek. Signed: THOMAS HAMMONS. Wit: RICHARD PERRYMAN, ISHAM (X) HALL, JEREMIAH EARLY, JOHN RENTFRO, HUGH INNES. Proved: 24 March 1785, Henry Co., Virginia.

Pages 92-93: 23 Sept 1784. WILLIAM COCKRAM of Henry County to REUBEN NANCE of the same for ten pounds sells 176 acres on the branches of Leatherwood Creek. Signed: WILLIAM COCKRAN. Wit: ALEYGOND MAGWIER, SALLY NANCE, JOHN MINTER. Proved at a Court held for Henry County 24 March 1785.

Pages 93-94: 24 March 1785. SAMUEL BIRD of Henry County to WILLIAM DILLINGHAM of the same for sixty pounds sells land on the south side of Chestnut Creek, being land whereon the said DILLINGHAM now lives and contains by estimate 74½ acres. Signed: SAMUEL (X) BIRD. Wit: none. Proved: 24 March 1785, Henry Co., Va.

Pages 95-96: 31 July 1784. JOHN VAN MEAPOLL of Pittsylvania Co., Va. to JACOB KINGERY of the same for the sum of one hundred and four pounds and ten shillings conveys land containing 140 acres more or less in Pittsylvania County on the fork of Blackwater River beginning at JOHN RENTFRO'S. Signed: JOHN (X) VAN MAPLE, JEAN (X) VAN MAPLE. Wit: JOHN KELLY, WILLIAM KELLY, WILLIAM KELLY, JAMES STOUT.

Pages 96-97: 12 July 1782. GEORGE HEARD of Henry County to HENRY TRENT of the same for forty pounds sells a certain tract acquired by patent bearing date 10 Nov 1779...land begins at HEARD'S old line, to a gray rock marked J.D. 1779 and crosses SIMMON'S Creek contains 250 acres more or less. Signed: GEORGE HEARD. Wit: WILLIAM TRENT, WILLIAM BLANKENSHIP, JAMES MASON. Proved: At a Court held for Henry Co., Va., 24 Mar 1785.

Page 98: 5 Feb 1785. JAMES MASON of Henry County to

SAMUEL DILLON of the same for thirty pounds sells land on Popler Camp Creek beginning where BEHELERE ride path crosseth the Wagon Road on STEPHEN HEARD'S line...100 acres more or less. Signed: JAMES MASON. Wit: JOHN HEARD, BRYANT TRENT, WILLIAM HARDING. Proved 24 March 1785, Henry County, Va.

Pages 99-100: 26 Jan 1785. JOSEPH ANTHONY and his wife ELIZABETH ANTHONY to GEORGE HAIRSTON for the sum of four hundred pounds sells and conveys one tract of land on Marrowbone Creek which said ANTHONY purchased of ARCHIBALD ROBERTSON containing more or less 345 acres. Signed: JOSEPH ANTHONY, ELIZABETH ANTHONY. Wit: THOMAS COOPER, THOMAS GLASS, JAMES ANTHONY. Proved at a Court held for Henry County 24 March 1785.

Pages 101-102: 26 Jan 1785. JOSEPH ANTHONY and his wife ELIZABETH ANTHONY to GEORGE HAIRSTON both of Henry County for the sum of fifty pounds sells land on the branches of Marrowbone Creek, containing by patent 372 acres. Signed: JOSEPH ANTHONY, ELIZABETH ANTHONY. Wit: THOMAS COOPER, THOMAS GLASS. Proved: 24 March 1785, Henry Co., Va.

Page 103: 3 Feb 1785. RICHARD BAKER of Henry County to CHARLES COLLIER for the sum of forty pounds sells land on both sides of Bowen's Creek, being 218 acres by survey. Signed: RICHARD (X) BAKER. Wit: none. Proved 24 March 1785, Henry Co., Va.

Page 104: 23 Jan 1785. AMOS RICHARDSON of Henry County to BENJAMIN RICHARDSON of the same grants land on Bucks Branch of Snow Creek, being 75 acres with the lines of WILLIAM LONG and JOHN RICHARDSON. Signed: AMOS RICHARDSON. Wit: none. Proved: 24 March 1785, Henry Co., Va.

Pages 105-106: 5 Feb 1784. JOHN MARR of the county of Henry to RODHAM MOORE of the same for fifty pounds sells land on each side of ARARAT Creek containing 180 acres, it being part of our order of council formerly claimed by BILL, the same is land whereon the said MOORE now lives adjoining SAMUEL CANNON. Signed: JOHN MARR. Wit: ROBERT HUDSPETH, WILLIAM COOKSAY, JOHN PRYOR. Proved: 24 March 1785, Henry Co., Va.

Pages 106-107: 5 Feb 1784. JOHN MARR of Henry County to RODHAM MOORE of the same for two hundred pounds sells land on Stoney or Story Creek containing 370 acres, whereon the said MOORE now lives. Signed: JOHN MARR. Wit: ROBERT HUDSPETH, WILLIAM COOKSAY, JOHN PRYOR. Proved: 24 March 1785, Henry Co., Va.

Pages 107-108: 3 Aug 1784. THOMAS FLOWERS of Botetourt County, Va. to JOSEPH HURT of Henry County for the sum of sixty pounds sells part of a tract of 930 acres by survey bearing date of 15 Nov 1772 being on both sides of Flat Creek of Smith River; this deed is for 150 acres by estimate. Signed: THOMAS FLOWERS. Wit: WILLIAM GARDNER, JOHN KINDRICK, HENRY (X) GUFFEE.

Pages 109-110: 9 April 1785. RICHARD KEARBY of Henry County to LEWIS HANCOCK of Fluvanah County for the sum of one hundred fifty pounds sell land on Sycamore Creek beginning at THOMAS MORRISON'S and LUKE FOLEY'S. Signed: RICHARD KEARBY (KERBY), SARAH KERBY. Wit: THOMAS MORROW, JESSE CORN, JOHN HENDERSON. Proved: Henry Co., Va. 28 April 1785.

Page 111: 9 April 1785. RICHARD KERBY of Henry County to THOMAS MORROW of the same for four pounds sells and conveys a parcel of land being on Little Sycamore Creek containing 30 acres. Signed: RICHARD KERBY. Wit: JOHN HENDERSON, JESSE CORN, DAVID HARBOUR. Proved: 28 April 1785, Henry County, Va.

Page 112: 24 Nov 1785. Deed of Gift. THOMAS FEE of Henry County to RACHEL FEE of the same for and in consideration of the natural affection I have for my grandfather's wife, RACHEL FEE, who is the widow of THOMAS FEE, deceased. do give her land on the south Mayo River, the tract whereon she now lives agreeable to the lines conveyed to my grandfather by deed. Signed: THOMAS (X) FEE. Wit: GEORGE TAYLOR, WILLIAM FEE, HENRY (X) FEE. Proved: 28 April 1785, Henry Co., Va.

Page 113: 25 April 1785. JOSEPH DAVIS of Henry County to JOHN HARRIS of the same for twelve pounds sells tract containing 178 acres on Nicholas Creek on Nicholas Knob, being part of a survey belonging to the said DAVIS. Signed: JOSEPH DAVIS. Wit: none. Proved: 28 April 1785.

Page 114: 26 April 1785. FREDERICK FULKERSON to AUGUSTINE THOMAS both of Henry County, for the sum of twenty pounds sells land containing 100 acres more or less on the north side of Mayo River (South Mayo River) it being the land whereon the said AUGUSTINE THOMAS now lives near the mouth of Green Creek thence down the river to near the wagon ford, thence to the Big Road beginning at THOMAS LAW'S corner. Signed: FREDERICK FULKERSON. Wit: A. HUGHES, HENRY THOMAS, JAMES FULKERSON. Proved: 28 April 1785, Henry County, Va.

Page 115: 21 April 1783. JAMES COOLY of Henry County to ISHAM CHOAT of the same for twenty five pounds sells land on the north branch of the north fork of Chestnut Creek containing 150 acres more or less, with WARREN'S corner. Signed: JAMES (X) COOLY, ANN (X) COOLY. Wit: ROBERT MASON, WILLIAM WARREN, DAVIS WARREN, ELIZABETH WARREN. Proved: 28 April 1785 at a Court held for Henry County.

Pages 116-118: 8 April 1785. JOSEPH STREET of Henry County to JAMES INGRUM of the same for thirty pounds sells land on both sides of Goblingtown Creek beginning at a corner in ROWLAND H. BIRKS line, HARBOUR'S and FOLEY'S survey. Signed: JOSEPH STREET. Wit: none. . .MILLEY STREET, the wife of JOSEPH STREET relinquishes her right of dower. Proved: 28 April 1785.

Page 118: 27 April 1785. SAMUEL BIRD of Henry County to JAMES MC WILLIAMS for the sum of forty pounds conveys a parcel of land by estimate being 100 acres more or less on Reedy Creek joining the land of WILLIAM HERD. Signed: SAMUEL BIRD. Wit: none. Proved: 28 April 1785 at a Court held for Henry Co., Va.

Pages 119-120: 27 April 1785. SAMUEL BIRD of Henry County to JOHN BIRD of the same for the sum of twenty pounds sells land on Reedy Creek by estimate containing 75 acres adjoining: JOHN HERD, HENRY HARRIS and JAMES MCWILLIAMS. Signed: SAMUEL (X) BIRD. Wit: none. . .MARY BIRD, wife of SAMUEL BIRD relinquishes her right of dower. Proved: Henry County, Va. 28 April 1785.

Pages 120-121: 25 Dec 1784. WILLIAM EVANS of Washington County to ROBERT PRUNTY of Henry County both state of Virginia for the sum of fifty pounds EVANS sells land containing by survey 130 acres and was granted said EVANS patent dated

11 Dec 1780, it being on both sides of Chestnut Creek the north fork beginning at ROBERT MASON'S line. Signed: WILLIAM EVANS. Wit: THOMAS DYER, JAMES ROGERS, DURRETT HUBBARD, ELIZABETH RICHARDSON. Proved: At a court held for Henry County, Va. 28 April 1785.

Page 122: 28 May 1785. WALTER KING COLE to JAMES BAKER both of Henry County, for the sum of seventy four pounds COLE sells land on both sides of Blackberry Creek containing 120 acres, being a part of a larger tract with HUNTER'S line. Signed: WALTER KING COLE. Wit: AL. HUNTER, THOMAS NUNN, MARTHA HUNTER. Proved in Henry Co., Va. 28 June 1785.

Pages 123-124: 24 May 1785. WILLIAM STANDEFER of Henry County to JESSE RENTFRO of the same, for seventy pounds sells all messuages, tenements and land on both sides of Pigg River containing 50 acres in one tract and 54 acres in the other. Lines: HUGH JONES, ROBERT JONES, THOMAS JONES, BARTON and RYON. Signed: WILLIAM STANDEFER. Wit: none recorded. Proved: 26 May 1785, Henry Co., Va.

Pages 124-125: 4 November 1784. Power of Attorney. State of Georgia, County of Wilkes. I, JOSEPH COOK of Wilks County, Georgia nominate and appoint my friend BENJAMIN COOK of the County of Campbell and state of Virginia to be my lawful attorney to sell and dispose of a certain parcel of land in Henry County, Virginia on the grassy fork of Snow Creek containing 444 acres. Signed: JOSEPH COOK. Recorded in Henry County, Va., 26 May 1785.

Pages 125-126: 25 March 1785. WILLIAM MEAD of the county of Bedford to JOHN DAVIS of the county of Henry for the sum of eight thousand pounds sells said DAVIS 650 acres of land whereon he now lives on Simmons Run, beginning on Blackwater River. Signed: WILLIAM MEAD. Wit: BEN. PERRYMAN, JESSE KIRBY, RICHARD PERRYMAN, MEREDITH WALKER. Proved: Henry County, Va., 26 May 1785.

Pages 127-128: 31 Oct 1782. JOSEPH COOK executor of JOHN COOK, deceased, late of the state of North Carolina to DANIEL RICHARDSON of Henry County conveys for the sum of eight hundred twenty five pounds land on Snow Creek and the Crabtree fork thereof; it being land whereon JOHN COOK formerly lived. There is a mill and the part that lies on the Crabtree Fork being part of the land he bought of HUGH INNES containing in the whole 590 acres. This said tract DANIEL RICHARDSON had bargained for some years past with the said JOHN COOK and his bond to make him a right to the same has been in possession of the land ever since. Beginning on Snow Creek above the Mill, to a line which divides and lays off that part of a tract which JOHN COOK gave his son BENJAMIN COOK. Signed: JOSEPH COOK. Wit: HUGH INNES, DAVID WILLIS, SAMUEL (X) BOLLING, ELKANAH HUCHERSON. Two dates are shown for proving and recording: 23 May 1783 and 26 May 1785.

Pages 129-130: 1 April 1785. ABRAHAM PENN and his wife RUTH PENN of Henry County to GEORGE WALLER of the same for the sum of one hundred eighty pounds sells one certain tract of land in Henry County on the south side of IRVIN (alias) SMITHS River containing 290 acres being that part purchased by PENN of THOMAS MAN RANDOLPH, GEORGE HARMER and WALTER K. COLE as appears by deed executed 7 Oct 1783. Begins at the mouth of Jourdons Creek. Signed: ABRAHAM PENN. Wit: SAMUEL STAPLES, JOHN WALLER, JOHN COX. Proved: 27 April 1785, Henry County, Va.

Page 131: 30 April 1785. INQUEST. Inquisition on the body of MORDECAI STEWART indented on the road in the County of Henry with JOHN SALMON Coroner. The body of MORDECAI STEWART then and there lying dead on the 29 April 1785. The following men to inquire as to the manner of his death: JOSEPH ANTHONY, ROBERT STOCKTON, THOMAS COOPER, JOHN REDD, JOHN HEARD, JOHN BIRD, JOHN BARKSDALE, HENRY CLARK, JACOB FARRIS, JOHN HUNTER, WILLIAM MULLINS, JOESPH KING and JOHN CUNNINGHAM. The said STEWART was found dead and he had no marks of violence appearing on his body and died by the visitiation of God in a natural way and not otherwise. Proved: 28 May 1785 at a Court held for Henry Co., Va.

Page 132: 30 April 1785. Inquest. Inquisition indented at WILLIAM HUNTER'S in Henry County on the body of GEORGE HUNTER then and there lying dead. Inquiry by: SABERT STONE, WILLIAM HEARD, JOHN REDD, JOSEPH KING, JOHN HEARD, JOHN BIRD, JOHN BARKSDALE, HENRY CLARK, JACOB FARRIS, STEPHEN STONE, JOHN HUNTER and WILLIAM MULLINS to ascertain how and after what manner said GEORGE HUNTER came by his death. One WILLIAM HUNTER appearing to have the fear of God before his eyes and not moved by the instigation of the devil neither with malice fore thought or assalt that the said WILLIAM HUNTER with a riffle gun made of iron and held in his right hand and at a distance of 60 yards my mischance did kill with aim to kill a wild turkey which glancing shot in and upon the face of said GEORGE HUNTER did enter of which wound said GEORGE HUNTER then and instantly died. At the death WILLIAM HUNTER appeared to be in perfect love, peace and friendship towards the said GEORGE HUNTER. Returned at Court held for Henry Co., Va. 26 May 1785.

Page 133: 25 May 1785. Agreement. RICHARD REYNOLDS of the one party and his wife MARY REYNOLDS of the other part. The said RICHARD REYNOLDS hath allowed his wife MARY the following articles: a tract of land that joins the east side of the land he now lives on with the plantation and orchards thereon to have peaceful possession during her lifetime if she will live thereon, also five pounds in gold or silver to be paid her yearly during her lifetime, also one hundred pounds to be valued to her in stock and house goods. MARY REYNOLDS agrees for her part to give the said RICHARD REYNOLDS all the best of the estate belonging to them to have it in peaceful possession and all other properties to him and his heirs, never to claim anything belonging to the said RICHARD REYNOLDS. Signed: RICHARD (X) REYNOLDS, MARY (X) REYNOLDS. Proved and recorded 25 May 1785.

Page 134: 20 April 1785. WILLIAM SMITH, SR. to HARBOURD SMITH for the sum of five shillings gives him 139 acres by survey dated 10 Oct 1789 being on Little Peters Creek. Signed: WILLIAM SMITH. Wit: D. LANIER, THOMAS EDWARDS, DANIEL REAMY. Proved: 26 May 1785 at a Court held for Henry County, Va.

Pages 135-136: 23 June 1785. JOHN HOLLAND and SARAH HOLLAND his wife of Henry County to GEORGE HAIRSTON for the sum of fifty pounds land on the north side of Smith River containing by patent 200 acres. Signed: JOHN HOLLAND, SARAH (X) HOLLAND. Wit: none recorded. Proved: 23 June 1785 Henry Co., Va.

Pages 136-137: 9 April 1785. RICHARD KERBY of Henry County to MARY OLDHAM of the same for sixty pounds sells land on Sycamore Creek joining THOMAS MORROW and JOHN FARROLL being 368 acres, part of a survey purchased of JOHN FARRELL. Signed: RICHARD KERBY, SARAH KERBY, JOHN FARREL. Wit: JOHN HENDERSON, THOMAS MORROW. Proved: 28 June 1785, Henry Co., Va.

Page 138. Power of Attorney. GEORGE ROWLAND, SENR. of Henry County, we hereunto moving have made, ordained and appointed BALDWIN ROWLAND, BRICE MARTIN and JOHN COX to be my lawful attorneys to receive from the executors of JOHN ROWLAND, deceased, such judgement as may be recovered. Signed: GEORGE ROWLAND. Wit: JOHN SALMON, JOHN CUNNINGHAM, DANIEL TAYLOR. Proved: 23 June 1785, Henry Co., Va.

Page 139: 17 March 1785. WILLIAM MATLOCK of Henry County to JOHN PHILPOTT of the same for the sum of fifty pounds sells land on the north side of Smith River being 20 acres more or less. Signed: WILLIAM MATLOCK. Wit: SAMUEL PHILPOTT, BENNETT POSEY, CHARLES MATLOCK, RICHARD (X) BAKER. Proved: 23 June 1785, Henry Co., Va.

Pages 140-141: 13 Dec 1784. JAMES PHIPS (FEPS) of Brunswick County, Va. to DAVID BARTON of Henry County for the sum of eighteen hundred pounds sells the whole tract of land contained by patent granted PHIPS 16 June 1783 containing 335 acres on both sides of Meadow Creek, a north branch of the Pigg River. Signed: JAMES FEPS. Wit: SWINFIELD HILL, JOHN (X) GREMET, MILLEY (X) MENEFEE, SR., MILLEY (X) MENEFEE, JR. Proved: Henry Co., Va. 28 July 1785.

Page 142: 23 July 1785. JOHN WELLS of Henry County to RICHARD CORNWELL of the same for twenty two pounds sells 132 acres of land on Rugg Creek. Signed: JOHN WELLS. Wit: none. Proved: 28 July 1785.

Page 143. Deed of Gift. I, JOSIAH SMITH of the county of Henry, Parish of Patrick for the pure love and good will I have to my dutiful son ISAAC SMITH bequeath unto him land on the south side of Stone's Creek on the waters of the Mayo River, adjoining the lines of JOHN COGO (KOGER) containing 303 acres more or less. Signed: JOSIAH SMITH. Wit: SAMUEL HARRIS, WILLIAM FRENCH, JAMES EAST, JOHN STAPLES. Proved: 28 July 1785.

Pages 144-145: 7 Dec 1784. WILLIAM HARRIS of Henry County to PETER STORM of the same for one hundred pounds sells a tract of land containing 111 acres on both sides of Shooting Creek. Signed: WILLIAM (X) HARRIS. Wit: NATHAN HALL, WILLIAM HARRIS, CORNOOLD (X) STORM. . .SARAH HARRIS, the wife of WILLIAM HARRIS relinquishes her right of dower. Proved: 28 July 1785 and recorded.

Pages 145-146: 10 March 1785. Power of Attorney. I, JOHN HARDMAN of Henry County do impower my son WILLIAM HARDMAN to sell my land on Grassey Creek or trade it to any advantage that suits him to discharge my debt with him. Also to pay him the twenty pounds I owe him. Signed: JOHN (X) HARDMAN. Wit: JAMES EAST, WILLIAM ELKINS. Recorded 28 June 1785.

Page 146-147: 28 July 1785, ISHAM CHOAT of Henry County to JOHN GALLASPY (GILLESPIE) for the sum of twenty five pounds convey land on the north branch of the north fork of Chestnut Creek being 154 acres. Signed: ISHAM (X) CHOAT. Wit: none. . . ANN CHOAT, the wife of ISHAM CHOAT relinquishes her right of dower. Proved 28 July 1785.

Page 147: 28 July 1784, SAMUEL COLEMAN MORRIS of Henry County to GREGORY DURHAM of the same for the sum of one hundred pounds sells 120 acres more or less on the waters of Little Horsepasture Creek, on a branch known as Ironmonger, joins WILLIAM SHELTON, JESSE WITT and the aforesaid DURHAM, it being the place whereon PETER LEAK now lives. Signed: SAMUEL COLEMAN MORRIS. Wit: none. Proved 28 July 1785.

Page 148: 28 July 1785. Whereas, ROBERT STOCKTON hath obtained authority from the County of Henry to officiate and perform the duties of a preacher and minister of the gospel. Bondsmen: PETER SAUNDERS, GEORGE WALLER, JOHN RENTFRO.

Page 149: 28 July 1785. RANDOLPH HALL has received authority to perform the duties of a Minister of the Gospel. Bondsmen: RANDOLPH HALL, NATHAN HALL, JOSEPH SHOWERS PRICE.

Page 149: 28 July 1785, WILLIAM LOVELL has received authority to perform the soleminzation of marriages. Signed: WILLIAM LOVELL, J.S. PRICE, JOHN RENTFRO.

Page 150: 28 July 1785, WILLIAM STEVENS has received authority to perform the duties of a preacher. Signed: WILLIAM STEVENS, JOHN REY, REUBIN NANCE.

Page 150: 27 July 1785, JOSEPH ANTHONY has received authority to solemize marriages. Signed: JOSEPH ANTHONY, JAMES ANTHONY, WILLIAM WHITRITTS.

Page 151: 27 July 1785, JESSE RENTFRO shall celebrate the rites of matrimony according to forms and customs of the Church to which we belong agreeable to the Act of the Assembly past in 1780. Signed: JESSE RENTFRO, JOHN RENTFRO, JAMES LYON.

Page 152: 8 July 1785, ROBERT JONES shall well and truly perform the soleminzation of marriages. Signed: ROBERT JONES, JOSEPH S. PRICE, ISAIAH WILLS, THOMAS PRUNTY.

Pages 152-153: 28 July 1785, GREGORY DURHAM of the county of Henry to JESSE WITT of the same for thirty eight pounds sells to WITT 50 & 2/3 acres on both sides of Ironmonger branch joining WITT'S own land, DURHAM and SAMUEL C. MORRIS. Signed: GREGGORY DURHAM. Wit: none. Proved 28 July 1785.

Page 154: 25 Feb 1785, WILLIAM BAYS of Washington County, Va. to JOHN DOYAL, heir of FRANCES DOYAL, for the sum of twenty five pounds sells him 52 acres of land joining JEREMIAH CLANCHAS and SAMUEL CRITCHFIELD. Signed: WILLIAM BAYS. Wit: ROWLAND CHILES, WILLIAM BRISTOW, SAMUEL CRITCHFIELD. Proved 28 June 1785, Henry Co., Va.

Page 155: 25 Feb 1785, WILLIAM BAYS of Washington Co., Va. to SAPHANIAH TENASON for the sum of sixty pounds sells 100 acres joining JOHN DOYAL'S line. Signed: WILLIAM (X) BAYS. Wit: SAMUEL CRITCHFIELD, ROWLAND CHILES, WILLIAM BRISTON. Proved 28 July 1785.

Pages 156-157: 29 July 1785, MILES HICKS of the county of Henry to GEORGE HAIRSTON of the same sells and conveys for forty five pounds land on the south side of Marrowbone Creek a branch of the Smith River, 76 acres. Signed: MILES HICKS. Wit: none. Proved 28 July 1785.

Pages 157-158: 29 June 1785, ROBERT DALTON of Pittsylvania County, Va. to HARMON COOK of Henry County for the sum of sixty pounds sells a tract containing by patent dated 20 Oct 1785 109 acres more or less on Turkey Cock Creek on the south branch of Irvin (Smith) River. Signed: ROBERT DALTON. Wit: THOMAS DYER, JOHN WRIGHT, HUNDLEY VAUGHAN. Proved Henry Co., Va. 28 July 1785.

Pages 159-160: 26 June 1785, SAMUEL ALLEN of Henry County to WILLIAM HARRIS, SENR. of the same for twenty six pounds six shillings sells land on both sides of the north fork of Tacks Creek, being 112 acres. Signed: SAMUEL ALLEN. Wit: ISAAC MABRY, JOHN (X) STAMPS, PARTHANEY (X) STAMPS. Proved 28 Aug 1785, Henry Co., Va.

Pages 161-162: 25 Aug 1785. DAVID WITT of Henry County to JOHN STAMPS of the same for two hundred pounds sells land on both sides of the south fork of Goblington Creek containing by estimate 313 acres. Signed: DAVID WITT. Wit: none. Proved 25 Aug 1785, Henry Co., Va.

Pages 162-163: Bill of Sale. JOHN COLLEY of Henry County have sold and delivered unto HENRY FRANCE two negroes, a girl JUDE about 8-9 years and a boy LOTT about 7 years for the sum of twenty pounds 3 shilling 1 penny. Which negroes were liabe to be sold by an execution of JAMES SPENCER, deceased. Signed: JOHN COLLEY. Wit: JOHN DILLARD, JOHN STAPLES, BRETT STOVALL. Proved 28 Aug 1785, Henry County, Va.

Pages 163-164: 20 May 1785, JOHN WILLIS of Henry County to THOMAS MILLER of the same sells for seventy pounds a tract of 222 acres on the branch of Blackwater River beginning at FRANCIS BIRDS. Signed: JOHN WILLIS. Wit: none. . .PHEBE WILLIS, wife of JOHN WILLIS relinquishes her right of dower. Proved 28 Aug 1785, Henry Co., Va.

Page 165: Bill of Sale, JOHN LINDSAY sells and conveys unto WILLIAM MOORE a negro man named MINGO for the sum of forty pounds. Signed: JOHN LINDSAY. Wit: JARRETT PATTSON. Proved Henry Co., Va. 28 Aug 1785.

Page 166: 25 Aug 1785, JOEL ESTES and his wife ANN to WILLIAM HUTCHERSON and CHARLES HUTCHERSON for the sum of sixty pounds sell and convey land on both sides Grassey Fork of Snow Creek being 200 acres more or less with lines of: WILLIAM RYAN, CHRISTOPHER SKILMAN, SAMUEL PATTERSON, CHARLES PINKERD and BENJAMIN COOK. This is the land JOEL ESTES bought of SARAH HUTCHERSON. Signed: JOEL ESTES. Wit: none. Proved 25 Aug 1785, Henry Co., Va.

Page 167: 27 Oct 1785, PALATIAH SHELTON of Henry County to JAMES MAC BRIDE for the sum of twenty pounds sells 250 acres on Widgon Creek joining JONES and WARD. Signed: PALATIAH SHELTON. Wit: none. Proved 27 July 1785.

Pages 168-169: Deed of Gift. I, JAMES STANDEFER for good cause, me hereunto moving as well as the natural love I bear my son JACOB STANDEFER (in two other places it lists this son as ISRAEL STANDEFER) I give and grant ISRAEL STANDEFER a certain dividend of land on the south side of Blackwater River being part of a tract whereon JEREMIAH SALESBURY now lives and known by the name of the Mine old fields, granted by patent to JAMES STANDEFER in 1763 then being called Luningburgh County. Signed: JAMES STANDEFER (X). Wit: none. Proved 27 Oct 1785.

Pages 169-170: 27 Oct 1785, THOMAS EDWARD to BONER CUMPTON both of Henry County, for the sum of one hundred twenty pounds sells and conveys 100 acres more or less, being part of a tract of land that DUTTON LAIN now lives on, Shoot Branch of the Smith River. Signed: THOMAS EDWARDS. Wit: none. Proved 27 Oct 1785.

Pages 171-172: 27 Oct 1785, JOHN BRISCOE and ANN his wife, to ELIZABETH NUNN for the sum of one hundred pounds sells 289 acres more or less on the south side of Irvine (Smith) River on the waters of Marrowbone Creek. Signed: JOHN BRISCOE, ANN BRISCOE. Wit: none. Proved 27 Oct 1785, Henry Co., Va.

Pages 172-173: 19 Nov 1785, LEWIS JENKINS of Henry County to FREDERICK RIVES of the same for twenty pounds sells land on both sides of the Pigg River, being land whereon Rives now lives containing 400 acres more or less...beginning at the mouth of Jack's Creek on the north side of Pigg River, joins THOMAS POTTER. Signed: LEWIS (X) JENKINS. Wit: BURWELL RIVES, PEYTON GRAVES, ISHAM (X) HALL. Proved 24 Nov 1785, Henry Co., Va.

Pages 174-175: 16 April 1785. DUTTON LAYNE of Henry County to JAMES MAY of the same for thirty pounds sells 400 acres more or less on both sides of Horsepasture Creek adjoining Randolph & Co. it being part of a tract surveyed by DUTTON LAYNE also joins JAMES EAST. Signed: DUTTON LAYNE. Wit: JOHN TAYLOR, JOHN MAY, JAMES EDWARDS, WILLIAM MAY. Proved 24 November 1785.

Pages 175-176: 10 Aug 1785. Dower release. To the Commonwealth of Virginia...Justices of the Peace of Wilks County, Georgia, JOHN CUNNINGHAM, JOHN FERGUS and STEPHEN HEARD, Esq. attest that JUDITH COOK widow of JOHN COOK releases her right of dower in the transaction whereas JOSEPH COOK as executor of the estate of JOHN COOK, deceased, by his indenture did convey unto DANIEL RICHARDSON of Henry County, Virginia a parcel of land containing 599 acres. Signed: JOHN CUNNINGHAM, J.P., JOHN FERGUS, J.P. Recorded Henry Co., Va. 24 Nov 1785.

Page 177: 21 Nov 1785, DANIEL SPANGLE, SENR of Henry County to DANIEL SPANGLE, JR of the same for fifty pounds sells land being 180 acres on Blackwater River, crosses Pounding Mill Run and Grave Yard Knob. Signed: DANIEL SPANGLE, SR. Wit: none. Proved 24 Nov 1785.

Page 178: 26 Nov 1785, Bond of ABRAHAM PENN who is Sheriff of Henry County.

Page 179: 24 Nov 1785, Bond of JAMES LYON, appointed sheriff of Henry County.

Page 180: 25 Oct 1785, JOHN HELTON of the county of Montgomery, state of Virginia to MOSES RENTFRO of Henry County. HELTON sells and conveys a parcel of land on the waters of Haikil (?) Run being 78 acres for the sum of one hundred pounds. Signed: JOHN HELTON. Wit: THOMAS MILLER, JR., THOMAS MILLER SR., DANIEL SPANGLE, JR., DANIEL SPANGLE, SR. Proved at a court held for Henry County 24 Nov 1785.

Pages 181-182: 15 Sept 1785, ARTHUR EDWARDS and his wife NANCY EDWARDS of Henry County to HENRY ROGERS of the same, for the sum of eighty pounds sells land on a fork of Crabtree fork of Snow Creek containing 100 acres by survey, it being part of a tract of 1500 acres granted EDWARDS. Signed: ARTHER EDWARDS, ANN EDWARDS. Wit: BENJAMIN COOK, DANIEL RICHARDSON, FRED. REIVES. Proved 24 Nov 1785, Henry County, Va.

Pages 182-184: 4 June 1785, MATHEW TALBOT of North Carolina to THOMAS PRUNTY of Henry County for the sum of three hundred pounds sells two surveys of land containing 236 acres more or less on both sides of Pigg River, one corner joined by THOMAS JONES. Signed: MATHEW TALBOT. Wit: JOHN HARRIS, ISAAC TAYLOR, JOHN KINSEY. Proved 24 Nov 1785, Henry County, Va.

Pages 184-185: 5 Nov 1785. NICHOLAS ALLEY and ANN, his wife of Henry County to JOSEPH S. PRICE of Buckingham County, Va., for the sum of six thousand five hundred pounds sells a parcel of land containing 300 acres more or less with all that is on it, being on the south fork of Blackwater River. Signed: NICHOLAS ALLEY. Wit: none. Proved Henry Co., Va. 25 Nov 1785.

Pages 186-187: 24 Nov 1785, JOSEPH COOPER and SARAH his wife of Henry County to JOSEPH ANTHONY of the same, for the sum of four hundred fifty pounds sells land on Beaver Creek joining AMBROSE JONES containing 370 acres more or less. Signed: JOSEPH COOPER, SARAH COOPER. Wit: none. Proved 25 Nov 1785 at a Court held for Henry Co., Va.

Pages 188-190: 24 Nov 1785, ANTHONY BITTING and MARTHA BITTING his wife of Henry County to GEORGE HAIRSTON of the same for the sum of thirty pounds sells land on the branches of Marrowbone Creek being by estimate 81 acres. Signed: ANTHONY BITTING, MARTHA BITTING. Wit: JOHN SALMON, GEORGE WALLER, JAMES ANTHONY. Proved 22 Dec 1785, Henry County, Va...MARTHA BITTING, wife of ANTHONY relinquishes her dower right.

Page 191: Bill of Sale. WASHINGTON LANIER sells to DAVID LANIER both of Henry County, one negroe girl known by the name of Tazey, for the sum of fifty seven pounds. Signed: WASHINGTON LANIER. Wit: BENJAMIN HICKS, ALEXANDER JOYCE, THOMAS JAMISON. Proved 22 Dec 1785, Henry Co., Va.

Pages 191-193: 19 January 1786. JOHN HORD of Henry County to JOSHAWAY DILLINHAM of the same for one hundred pounds sells a tract of land on both sides of Ready Creek containing more or less 180 acres. Signed: JOHN HEARD. Wit: none. . . SUSANNAH HORD wife of JOHN HORD relinquishes her right of dower. Proved Henry Co., Va. 26 Jan 1786.

Pages 193-194: 3 Oct 1785. JAMES EAST, SENR and EUSSAN or EUSSHAN his wife of Henry County to JOHN WATSON of the same, sells part of a tract of land, it being part of a tract granted EAST 11 April 1780 which contained by survey 670 acres on Horsepasture Creek now laid off to be 400 acres more or less and joins JOSEPH EAST and WATSON'S own line for the consideration of one hundred fifty pounds. Signed: JAMES EAST (X). Wit: JOSEPH MORRIS, DANIEL FRANCE, JOHN WRIGHT WATSON.

Page 194: 16 Jan 1786. Bill of Sale. Received of

JOHN LINDSEY, by the hands of MAJOR JOHN MARR, one negro girl named LUCY and one mare it being in full for what said LINDSEY owes me, also in full for JOHN FOSTER'S judgement against JOHN LINDSAY. Signed: JOHN REED. Wit: ABRAHAM PENN, JOHN PRYOR. Proved and recorded 25 March 1786, Henry Co., Va.

Pages 195-196: 2 Dec 1785, WILLIAM HARDMAN attorney for JOHN HARDMAN of Henry County sells to JOHN SALMON for the sum of thirty five pounds land conveyed by deed from JOHN MANNION and JOHN SIMMONS to JOHN HARDMAN, which tract contains 100 acres joins ARCHIBALD ROBERTSON. Signed: WILLIAM HARDMAN, attorney for JOHN HARDMAN. Wit: THADDEUS SALMON, GEORGE WALLER, BRICE MARTIN. Proved 25 March 1785, Henry Co., Va.

Pages 196-197: 29 Aug 1785, I, MARY DAUGHORTY of Green County (no state recorded) do appoint my brother-in-law JAMES GREEN, he being my nearest and trusty friend, my lawful attorney and authorize him to recover the legacy left me by my father MICAEL DOUGHTORY'S will also the legacy left me by my grand-father HUGH DAUGHORTY. Signed: MARY (X) DAUGHORTY. Wit: WILLIAM LOWEL or SOWEL, ELIZABETH LOWEL or SOWEL, SARAH (X) DAUGHORTY. Proved 24 March 1786, Henry County, Va.

Page 197: Power of Attorney, I, SARAH DAUGHTORY of Henry County, Va. do appoint my brother-in-law JAMES GREEN my lawful attorney to recover the legacy left me by my father MICHAL DAUGHORTY'S will also the legacy of my grandfather HUGH DAUGHORTY. Signed: SARAH (X) DAUGHORTY. Wit: JOHN DILLARD, SARAH DILLARD, WILLIAM (X) ELKINS. Proved 24 Mar 1786, Henry Co., Va.

Page 198: 21 March 1786, Deed of Gift. I, MARY ROWLAND of Henry County to the children of my daughter OBEDIANCE RYAN, for the love and affection I bear unto these grandchildren and the sum of five shillings, give to these grandchildren all my whole estate (except my desk which I give to JOSEPH NUNN after my decease) consisting of two negroes Will and Betty, all my hoggs, cattle, household and kitchen furniture and every other commodity that is now in my possession. To be under the direction of OBEDIANCE RYAN until the said children arrives to full age. Signed: MARY (X) ROWLAND. Wit: JOHN COX, MARY COX. Proved 24 March 1786 at a court held for Henry Co., Va.

Pages 199-200: 24 Oct 1785, ZACHARIAH SMITH of Guilford County, North Carolina to WILLIAM HAYS of Henry County for the sum of ten pounds sells land on the waters of the Mayo River containing 75 acres and joins PHILIP ANGLIN and JOHN GARNOGAN. Signed: ZACHARIAH SMITH. Wit: JAMES TAYLOR, JAMES PITTMAN, PHI. ANGLIN. Proved 23 March 1786 at a court held for Henry Co., Va.

Pages 200-201: 18 Nov 1785, BENJAMIN HAWKINS of Surry County, North Carolina to WILLIAM COOKSEY of Henry County for the sum of seventeen pounds sells 209 acres of land on the branches of Stone's Creek joining WILLIAM TAYLOR, RICHARD WELCH, it being part of a tract surveyed by ROBERT HOOKER and by him conveyed to BENJAMIN HAWKINS. Other lines: KOGER'S old Road and DRURY SOLLOMAN line. Signed: BENJAMIN HAWKINS. Wit: WILLIAM TAYLOR, JOHN TAYLOR, JOHN DILLARD. Proved 23 March 1786, Henry County, Va.

Pages 202,203: 22 August 1785, JOHN LINDSAY of Henry County to PHILIP PENN of the same for one hundred pounds sells 200 acres more or less on the north side of the North Mayo River, beginning on the north side of a branch of the Horsepasture Creek. Signed: JOHN LINDSAY. Wit: JACOB PEREGAN, GEORGE FLETCHER, GEORGE PENN, JOSIAH FARRIS. Proved 23 March 1786 and recorded Henry Co., Va.

Pages 203-104: 20 Oct 1785, JOHN HELTON of Montgomery County, Va. to THOMAS MILLER, JR. of North Carolina for the sum of eighty pounds 12 shillings sells 100 acres in Henry County on the waters of Hatchets Run...crosses two small branches of Blackwater River. Signed: JOHN HELTON. Wit: WILLIAM MILLER, THOMAS DOGGIT, JOSHUA WILLSON, THOMAS TERRY, THOMAS (X) MILLER, WILLIAM GIBSON, DANIEL SPANGLER, DANIEL SPANGLER, JR. Proved and recorded 23 March 1786 Henry County, Va.

Page 205: 22 Feb 1786, EDWARD BAKER of Henry County to SAMUEL PERRY of the same for forty pounds sells 25 acres of land on the south side of Smith River beginning at Cair (?) Branch on BAKER'S old lane. Signed: EDWARD (X) BAKER. Wit: JOSEPH STREET, WILLIAM ADAMS, THOMAS TENISON. Proved 23 March 1786, Henry County, Va.

Page 206: Inquest. Inquisition taken at the plantation of ELISHA ESTES, SENR of Henry County

11 Nov 1786 before JOHN SALMON coroner of Henry County to view the body of a negro man slave named MAJOR, property of THOMAS TERRY, then and there lying dead and upon the Oaths of HUGH INNES, SPENCER CLACK, JAMES MAJORS, JAMES BEAVERS, ELISHA ESTES, CHRISTOPHER SKELMON, AMOS RICHARDSON, JAMES PRUNTY, ROBERT PRUNTY, JOHN WILKES, BOTTOM ESTES, ELISHA ESTES, JR. being charged to inquire into the manner of the death of the said JAMOR. He came to his death from the explosion of a gun made of iron held in the hands of JAMES HUBBARD, which gun is of value 20 shillings, said negro shot in the left side of which wounds he died then and instantly. Entered into record 28 March 1786, Henry Co., Va.

Pages 207-208: 21 Aug 1785, JOSEPH STOUT and his wife CATHERINE of Henry County to WILLIAM ANDERSON of Buckingham Co., Va. for the sum of seven hundred pounds sells land in Henry County on both sides of the south fork of the Blackwater River containing 540 acres more or less with lines of WILLIAM KELLY and JOSEPH SHORES PRICE. Signed: JOSEPH STOUT, CA. (X) STOUT. Wit: JOSEPH SHORES PRICE, P. GUERRANT, SHADRACK WILSON, SHOWERS PRICE. Proved Henry County, Va. 23 March 1786.

Pages 209-210: 22 April 1786, JOHN BIRD of Franklin County, Va. to JOHN NORRIS of Henry County sells for the sum of forty pounds land in Henry County containing 70 acres more or less on Ready Creek, joins JOHN HEARD. Signed: JOHN BIRD. Wit: none. . .MOLLY BIRD, wife of JOHN BIRD, relinquishes her right of dower. Proved and recorded 27 April 1786, Henry Co., Va.

Page 210: 28 April 1786, Bond for JAMES LYON as Sheriff of Henry County. Bondsmen: GEORGE HAIRSTON, JOHN SALMON and HENRY LYNE.

Pages 211-121: 27 April 1786, GEORGE HAIRSTON of Henry County to STARK BROWN of the same for fifty pounds sells land on the north side of Smith River being 50 acres more or less joins land of CHRISTOPHER BOLING, SR. old line, where he did live. Signed: GEORGE HAIRSTON. Proved and recorded 27 April 1786.

Pages 212-213: 23 Jan 1786, MATHEW WELLS of Pittsylvania County to JAMES HALEY of Henry County for seventeen pounds sells 140 acres more or less, being part of a tract WELLS purchased of SAMUEL

JOHNSON on Leatherwood Creek to Turkeycock Mtn. Signed: MATHEW WELLS. Wit: JOHN WELLS, THOMAS DICKERSON, JR., NATHAN RYAN, and BARNABA WELLS. Proved 27 April 1786, Henry Co., Va.

Page 214: 27 April 1786, GEORGE HAIRSTON of Henry County to JOSEPH CHANDLER for the sum of one hundred twenty seven pounds sells 250 acres of land beginning at HENRY MAYSE'S dividing line, MCKLEAN'S line and Marrowbone Creek. Signed: GEORGE HAIRSTON. Wit: none. Proved and recorded 27 April 1786 Henry County, Va.

Page 215: 28 April 1786, WILLIAM WOODS produced a commission from the Masters of William & Mary Collage appointing him surveyor for the County of Henry. Bondsmen: JOHN WELLS, ABRAM. PENN.

Pages 215-216: 28 April 1786, WILLIAM ALEXANDER of Pittsylvania County, Va. to CHARLES FOSTER of Henry County for one hundred pounds sells 100 acres more or less with lines of: WALTER K. COLE, W. MAXEY and CHARLES FOSTER, JR. Signed: WILLIAM ALEXANDER. Wit: none. Proved and recorded 28 April 1786, Henry County, Va.

Pages 216-217: 27 April 1786, WILLIAM ALEXANDER of Pittsylvania County, Va. to JOHN PACE of Henry County for one hundred eighty pounds sells more or less 204 acres on Smith River. Signed: WILLIAM ALEXANDER. Wit: JAMES EAST, JAMES (X) PHIFER, JOHN HORD. . .JEAN ALLEXANDER, wife of WILLIAM relinquishes her right of dower. Proved and recorded Henry Co. Va., 28 April 1786.

Page 218: 22 June 1786, RICHARD ADAMS of Henry County to ISAAC ADAMS of same for two hundred pounds sells land containing by estimate 426 acres lying on the Long branch of Mill Creek beginning at THOMAS ADAMS line, old line of RICHARD ADAMS, it being part of a larger tract whereon MADAM STOVALL now lives. Signed: RICHARD ADAMS. Wit: none. Recorded 22 June 1786, Henry Co., Va.

Page 219: 22 June 1786, RICHARD ADAMS of Henry County to WILLIAM ADAMS of the same for one hundred pounds sells 162 acres on Mill Creek of the Mayo River joining THOMAS ADAMS, THOMAS SMITH, WILLIAM BANKS, it being part of a larger tract whereon MADAM STOVALL now lives...the land laid off by JAMES YOUNG. Signed: RICHARD ADAMS. Recorded 22 June 1786, Henry Co. Va.

Page 220: 22 June 1785, JOHN SALMON and ELIZABETH his wife of Henry County to SAMUEL CROUCH of the same, for sixty pounds sells land on the Grassy fork of Warf Mtn Creek containing 363 acres. Signed: JOHN SALMON, ELIZABETH (X) SALMON. Wit: WILLIAM WATTS, THADDOUS SALMON, GEORGE PENN. Proved & recorded Henry Co., Va. 22 June 1786.

Pages 221-222: 22 May 1786, CHARLES BURNIT of Henry County to JOHN MASTERS of same for thirty five pounds sells land on the south fork of Mulberry Creek being 146 acres, part of a tract granted CHARLES BURNIT as Assignee of SHOCKLY SIMMONS, by patent 1 Feb 1781. Signed: CHARLES BURNET. Wit: none. . .CATHERINE, wife of CHARLES BURNET relinquishes her right of dower. Recorded 22 June 1786, Henry Co., Va.

Pages 222-223: 26 July 1786, WILLIAM STEPHENS of Henry County to GEORGE BRITTON of the same for five pounds sells land on Home Creek containing 45 acres, starts STEPHEN'S old line, BREATON'S Spring Branch...WALTON'S line. Signed: WILLIAM (X) STEPHENS, ANN (X) STEPHENS. Wit: MATHEW RAINEY, WILLIAM (X) RICKELS, GEORGE FULLER HARRIS. Recorded Henry County, Va. 27 July 1786.

Pages 224-225: 30 Nov 1784, JOSIAH SMITH of Henry County to ABRAHAM PENN of same for thirty pounds sells land on both sides of the North Mayo River containing by patent 343 acres. Signed: JOSIAH SMITH. Wit: PHILLIP PENN, GEORGE PENN, JOHN DILLARD, JOHN LINDSAY. Proved and recorded Henry Co., Va. 27 July 1786.

Pages 225-226: 24 May 1786, EDWARD COCKRUM of Henry County to PRESTON KINDRICK of same for fifteen pounds sells land on the south side of Smith River containing 50 acres more or less with EDWARD'S line. Signed: EDWARD (X) COCKRUM, MARY (X) COCKRUM. Wit: GABREEL ROBERTS, JOSEPH GOODWIN. Proved and recorded 27 July 1786.

Page 227: 27 July 1786, LUCY RICHARDSON wife of AMOS RICHARDSON, SENR. relinquishes her right of dower to 250 acres land sold BENJAMIN COOK.

Page 228: 27 July 1786, JOHN CUNNINGHAM and ANN his wife of Henry County to GEORGE HAIRSTON of the same for eighty pounds sells 225 acres by estimate on Reed Creek near the old Baptist Meetinghouse.

Signed: JOHN CUNNINGHAM. Wit: none. Recorded 27 July 1786.

Pages 229-230: 28 Nov 1785, ISAAC SMITH and MARY his wife, to ABRAHAM PENN both of Henry County, for the sum of twenty five pounds sells a parcel of land on the branches of Stone's Creek, it being 302 acres more or less and joins JACOB COGAR. Signed: ISAAC SMITH, MARY SMITH. Wit: BRETT STOVALL, JOHN STAPLES, WILLIAM HAMMOTT, GEORGE PENN. Proved 27 Jan 1786, Henry Co., Va.

Pages 231-232: 29 Oct 1785, DANIEL RICE and JUDY his wife, of the County of Henry and Parish of Patrick to SAMUEL CROUCHER for the sum of forty five pounds sells and conveys land on both sides of Gray's fork, joins PENN and NEAL in the amount of 206 acres. This is the land whereon said RICE now lives. Signed: DANIEL RICE, JUDY RICE. Wit: ABRAHAM PENN, JOHN CAMERON, GEORGE PENN, BARTLET EADS. Proved and recorded 27 July 1786, Henry Co., Va.

Pages 233-234: 24 March 1786, JAMES EAST, SR. of Henry County to BENJAMIN KENNON of the same for fifty pounds sells parts of different tract, the first at WOODSON'S now WATSON'S beginning on the south side of Horsepasture Creek containing 117 acres, another part of a tract patented on 10 April 1781, the other 1 June 1782. The other part on Camp Branch with JOSEPH EAST'S line and REDMON'S being 320 acres more or less. Signed: JAMES EAST, SR. Wit: WILLIAM HUNTER, THOMAS PRUNTY, JOHN DICKERSON. Proved and recorded 27 July 1786, Henry Co., Va.

Pages 235-236: 27 July 1786, RICHARD ADAMS and HANAH his wife of Henry County to MARY STOVALL and BRETT STOVALL of the same for two hundred pounds sells land on both sides of Mill Creek beginning at WILLIAM BANKS corner on the north side of the creek thence joining WILLIAM ADAMS, THOMAS ADAMS, ISAAC ADAMS and JACOB CRITZ, containing by estimate 261 acres, it being the land where RICHARD ADAMS formerly lived. Signed: RICHARD ADAMS, HANAH (X) ADAMS. Wit: none. Proved & recorded 27 July 1786, Henry Co., Va.

Pages 236-237: 27 July 1786, MATHEW RAINEY of Henry County to WILLIAM ROBERTSON HAMMONS for the sum of seventeen pounds sells 100 acres more or less on the Long Branch to the mouth of Back Creek, GEORGE HARRIS corner, GIBSON'S spring. Signed:

STEPHEN RAINEY. Wit: none. Proved and recorded 27 July 1786, Henry County, Va.

Pages 238-239: 27 May 1786, ISAIAH WATKINS of Pittsylvania County to MATHEW RAINEY of Henry County for fifty pounds sells land on Saville Creek joins G. T. NORRIS and CLAY'S lines being by estimate 411 acres. Signed: ISAIAH WATKINS. Wit: THOMAS EDWARDS, WILLIS (X) WATKINS, WILLIAM (X) STEPHENS, GEORGE FULLER HARRIS, WILLIAM R. HAMMONS, WILLIAM RICKEL, SAMUEL ROBERTS. Proved and recorded 27 July 1786, Henry Co., Va.

Pages 239-240: 18 July 1786, EDWARD BAKER to ROBERT FRASHUR both of Henry County for the sum of fifty pounds sells land on both sides of Smith River, 150 acres. Signed: EDWARD BAKER (X), ELIZABETH (X) BAKER. Wit: SAMUEL PERRY, HOLDEN MEGEE, ALEXANDER FRASHEER. Recorded and proved 27 July 1786, Henry Co., Va.

Page 241: 28 April 1786, WILLIAM ALEXANDER and his wife JANE of Henry County to CHARLES FARRIS of the same for fifty pounds sells land on Little Marrowbone Creek, joins W. K. COLE and JOHN PACE, it being 25 acres. Signed: WILLIAM ALEXANDER. Wit: GEORGE HAIRSTON, JOSEPH STOVALL, JOHN WITT, ISIAS SHAW. Proved 27 July 1786, Henry Co., Va.

Pages 242: 8 Feb 1786, THOMAS FLOWERS of Botetourt County to HENRY MC GUFFEY of Henry County for one hundred pounds sells land it being 110 acres on the waters of Smith River on Buffalo Creek joins BENJAMIN STINET and JOHN KENDRICKS. Signed: THOMAS FLOWERS. Wit: ADAM LACKEY, WILLIAM ISAM, SAMUEL ALLEN. Proved and recorded 27 July 1786, Henry Co., Va.

Page 243: 28 Dec 1785, CHARLES MATLOCK of Pittsylvania County to HARRISON HOBART of the other part, for thirty pounds sells land in Henry County on the south side of Smith River being 20 acres more or less. Signed: CHARLES MATLOCK. Wit: JOHN PHILPOTT, GEORGE REEVES, RICHARD (X) BAKER. Proved and recorded 28 Sept 1786, Henry County, Va.

Pages 244-245: 24 Aug 1786, JOHN FUSON of Henry County to SAMUEL DURST of the same for one hundred pounds sells land on both sides of Story Creek with lines of PHILLIP SPERIDAN. Being 220 acres. Signed: JOHN FUSON. Wit: THOMAS PRUNTY, JOHN FUSON, JR., ALEXANDER HUNTER, RACHAEL HALE, JOHN

TURNER, TUNSTALL COX. Proved and recorded 28 Sept 1786, Henry Co., Va.

Pages 245-246: 25 April 1786, THOMAS RICHARDSON of Henry County to ISHAM BRAWDER TATUM of same for the sum of eighty five pounds sells 250 acres by survey date 27 Nov 1755, land on both sides of the south fork of Sandy River. Signed: THOMAS RICHARDSON, MARY (X) RICHARDSON. Wit: FRANCIS COX, ELISHA WALKER, PAUL (X) PIGG. Proved 28 Sept 1786, Henry County, Va.

Pages 247-248: 9 Oct 1784, WILLIAM TACKETT of Henry County to SYLVESTER ADAMS of Pittsylvania County for fifty pounds sells land containing by estimate 100 acres more or less on the north side of the Smith River. Signed: WILLIAM TACKITT. Wit: EDWARD COCKRAM, JOHN ROSS, JOHN MORGAN, SAMUEL TOMPKINS. Proved 28 Sept 1786, Henry Co., Va.

Page 249: 28 Sept 1786, JAMES ELKINS of Henry County to NATHAN HALL of the same for ten pounds sells 100 acres being part of a tract surveyed by JAMES POTEET for said JAMES ELKINS and sold by said POTEET to ABNER BARNETT being on the north side of Smith River. Signed: JAMES ELKINS(X). Wit: none. CATY ELKINS wife of JAMES relinquishes her right of dower. Proved 28 Sept 1786, Henry Co., Va.

Page 250: 15 Sept 1786, PALETIAH SHELTON of Henry County to BLIZARD MAGRUDER for four hundred pounds sells land and all that is on it; land being 309 acres on the middle fork of the Little Dan River. Signed: PALETIAH SHELTON. Wit: STEPHEN LYON, JOSEPH JOYCE, EDMOND (X) HOLT. Proved 28 Sept 1786, Henry County, Va.

Pages 251-252: 7 ___ 1785, CHARLES COX of Henry County to EDWARD COCKRAM of the same for one hundred pounds sells land containing 135 acres on Turkey Pen branch, where the said CHARLES COX now lives being 135 acres. Signed: CHARLES COX. Proved 28 Sept 1786.

Pages 252-253: 15 April 1786. Deed of Trust. FRANCIS GILLEY, SENR. of Henry County to JAMES TARRANT. FRANCIS GILLEY being indebted to said TARRANT in the amount of twenty one pounds seven shillings sells him one soril mare 18 years old, 1 gray horse 9 yrs old and 1 soril horse 10 years old. Signed: FRANCIS GILLEY, SENR. Wit: JOHN DOYAL, JOHN

TARRANT, THOMAS CHOWNING. Proved 28 Sept 1786, Henry Co., Va.

Pages 254-255: 6 April 1786. Deed of Trust. THOMAS EDWARDS, SENR. of Henry County to JAMES TARRANT of the same; EDWARDS being indebted to TARRANT in the amount of forty four pounds 3 shillings 9 pence, sells him a negro boy named ANDREW about 10 years old and a bed. Signed: THOMAS EDWARDS. Wit: JOHN TARRANT, THOMAS CHOWNING, JACOB DILLENDER (X). Proved & recorded 26 Sept 1786 Henry Co., Va.

Pages 256-257: 27 Sept 1786, PALATIAH SHELTON of Henry County to STEPHEN LYON of the same for fifty pounds sells whereon the said SHELTON now lives on the north side of Big Russell Creek with JAMES LYON'S former lines, it being 50 acres more or less. Signed: PALATIAH SHELTON. Wit: none. . . . ANN SHELTON the wife of PALATIAH releases her right to dower. Recorded and proved 28 Sept 1786, Henry County, Va.

Pages 257-258: 21 Oct 1786, SAMUEL MORRIS, JOSEPH MORRIS and WILLIAM SHELTON of Henry County to ALEXANDER HUNTER of the same for the sum of two hundred pounds sells land on the Waters of Horsepasture Creek it being 400 acres more or less. Signed: SAMUEL C. MORRIS, JOSEPH MORRIS, WILLIAM SHELTON. Wit: JAMES EAST, JACOB PERAGEN, JESSE WITT. Proved 26 Oct 1786, Henry Co., Va.

Page 259: 31 March 1786, TABITHIA DEPRIEST of Henry County to JOHN NORTON of the same for thirty pounds sells 250 acres on both sides of Jinnings Creek joins EDMUND WINSTON, JOHN LINDSAY, JOHN NICULS. Signed: TABITHIA (X) DEPRIEST. Wit: JACOB PERAGON, PETER LEAK, GEORGE FULCHER. Proved 26 Oct 1786, Henry County, Va.

Pages 260-261: 26 Oct 1786, JOSIAS SHAW of Henry County to GEORGE HAIRSTON of the same for one hundred fifty pounds sells land on Marrowbone Creek, it being 2 acres more or less with the mill and mill seat waters and watercourses. Signed: JOSIAS SHAW and his wife. Wit: none. Proved 26 Oct 1786, Henry Co., Va.

Pages 262-263: 13 Oct 1786, JOSIAS SHAW of Henry County to GEORGE HAIRSTON of the same for five hundred fifty pounds sells land on Marrowbone Creek being 619 acres with lines of MC CAINS,

TAYLOR, to the falls in HICK'S line and the school house branch. Signed: JOSIAS SHAW. Wit: THOMAS COOPER, JOHN DILLARD, THOMAS STOVALL, THOMAS ADAMS, JR., THOMAS JAMISON. Recorded & proved 26 Oct 1786, Henry Co., Va.

Pages 264-265: 12 Oct 1786, GEORGE HAIRSTON of Henry Co. to THOMAS STOVALL of the same for two hundred fifty pounds sells land on the north side of Marrowbone Creek beginning at the mouth of Sinking Creek with lines of SAMUEL LANIER and SHAW, it being 300 acres more or less. Signed: GEORGE HAIRSTON. Wit: ALEXANDER JOYCE, JOHN KING, JOHN DILLARD, THOMAS COOPER. Proved 26 Oct 1786, Henry County, Va.

Pages 266-267: 17 Oct 1786. EDWARD COCKRAM of Henry County to JOHN GROGAN of Rockingham County, North Carolina for the sum of one hundred fifty pounds sells 170 acres of land, it being the tract of land and plantation where the said EDWARD COCKRAM now lives on beginning at PRESTON KINDRICKS on the river. Signed: EDWARD (X) COCKRAM. Wit: HENRY GROGRAM, JOHN ALEXANDER, DANIEL (X) ALEXANDER. Proved at a Court held for Henry County, Va. 26 Oct 1786.

Pages 267-269: 24 Oct 1786. GEORGE REYNOLDS and his wife of Pittsylvania County to THOMAS RICHARDSON of Henry County for the sum of seventy five pounds sells parcel of land containing 600 acres more or less in Henry County on Muster Branch of Leatherwood Creek beginning at Lomax & Company. Signed: GEORGE REYNOLDS. Wit: WILLIAM STEPHENS, RICHARD PIGG, ELIZA (X) PIGG. Proved 26 Oct 1786, Henry Co., Va.

Page 270: 11 Sept 1786. Power of Attorney. MORDECAI HORD of Henry County appoints my trusty friend MAJ. JOHN DILLARD my lawful attorney to recover from WILLIAM CAMPBELL a negro boy named RANDALL 11 years of age which said CAMPBELL got from me in a decitful manner. Signed: MORDECAI HORD. Wit: JOHN HALL, JOHN COX, ROBERT WILLIAMS, RICHARD VENABLE. Proved Henry County Court held 24 Nov 1786.

Pages 271-272: 11 Sept 1786. MORDECAI HOARD of Henry County, Virginia and WILLIAM CAMPBELL of Winham, state of Connecticut sells to said CAMPBELL a tract of land and plantation where said HORD now lives containing 900 acres more or less, 11 slaves, viz: MARGERY and her seven children, LUCY, LATT, BETSY,

PEGGY, PETER, ANTHONY and MANDREY also MILLEY and HENRY children of WINNEY and RANDOLPH son of BESS; 50 head horned cattle, 600 bu. Indian corn, 1 wagon and gear, 5 horses, ten thousand weight of tobacco for the sum of Two Thousand Nine Hundred and Seventy Pounds to be paid 1st of January next at which time the said CAMPBELL to have full possession. One Thousand to be paid 1st January, One Thousand Seven Hundred and eighty eight and the residue of nine hundred seventy pounds on the 1st of January 1789, with legal interest. Signed: MORDECAI HORD, WILLIAM CAMPBELL. Wit: JOHN HALL, JOHN COX. At a Court held for Henry Co., Va. 24 Nov 1786, above agreement proved.

Pages 273-274: 18 July 1785. MICHAEL DUNN of Boteourt County to JASPER TERRY of Henry County for the sum of ten pounds sells land on Snow Creek on Bucks Run and Guttorys Run. Signed: MICHAEL DUNN. Wit: SAMUEL EASON, THOMAS GOODSON, JOHN GOODSON, THOMAS GOODSON, SR., JOHN NICKHAM. Proved at a Court held for Henry Co., Va. 24 Nov 1786.

Pages 274-275: 22 Feb 1787. ALEXANDER HUNTER of Henry County to EUSEBOUS STONE of the same for the sum of one hundred fifty pounds sells land on the east side of Smith River, it being part of the HORSHAW Tract known as TATE'S place containing by estimate 100 acres joins NUNN'S land. Signed: ALEXANDER HUNTER. No witnesses. Proved 22 February 1787.

Pages 276-277: 27 Sept 1786. DENIS TRAMELL being indebted to SAMUEL TARRANT in the amount of Twenty Four Pounds 3 shillings and to settle said claim this Deed of Trust for 6 head cattle, 4 feather beds, with furniture, 6 pewter plates, 7 basons, 3 dishes, 2 pots, 1 dutch oven and all my stock of hogs, corn and fodder on my plantation, one case of bottles, one trunk on a chest, 3 chairs. Signed: DENIS TRAMELL. Wit: JOSEPH GRAVELY, ENNNIS BAKER TRAMMELL, JOSIAH DENNIS. Proved 22 February 1787, Henry Co., Va.

Page 278: Dower Release. State of Frankland, County of Washington, whereas WILLIAM COX and BEN. HOLLAND, Justices for Washington County state of Frankland have examined said WINIFRED COX and she does relinquish her right of dower to land sold by her husband JAMES COX to SAMUEL TARRANT in Henry County, Virginia. Recorded Henry County, Va. 22 Feb 1787.

Page 279: 9 Dec 1786. Inquisition taken at the home of THOMAS NUNN, an infant here lying dead and upon the oaths of JOSEPH ANTHONY, MIKEL DILLINGHAM, JOSEPH KING, EUSEBUS STONE, JACOB FARRIS, HENRY CLARK, JOHN WEAVER, STARK BROWN, JOHN HOLMNS, JOHN STOCKS, JAMES ANTHONY, AMBROSE JONES, JOHN PYRTLE, ALEXANDER HUNTER, WILLIAM HURD, THOMAS NUNN charged to inquire as to how the infant died. The above say that one MARY LUCK not having God before her eyes, but being moved and seduced by the instigation of the devil 7 Dec in the 11th year of the Commonwealth felonously, volentary and of her mature affore thought took her infant born of her own body and carryed it in the woods where the said infant was found wounded on the right cheek. Recorded Henry County, Va. 22 Feb 1787.

Page 280: 1 October 1786. Inquisition at the house of JOHN CUNNINGHAM in the 10th year of the Commonwealth on the body of JOHN JONES then and there lying dead upon the oaths of HENRY LYNE, BRICE MARTIN, MORDECAI HORD, GEORGE WALLER, THOMAS COOPER, DANIEL SMITH, JOSEPH KING, JOHN CUNNINGHAM, JOSEPH FIPHER, THOMAS PRATER, HENRY BUTLER and JOHN PYRTLE. That on Saturday the 30th of September said JONES accidently falling from a house together with some part of the timber of which the house he was building, pressed on the body of the said JONES of which fall and bruises he instantly died. Recorded Henry County, Va. 22 Feb 1787.

Pages 281-282: 22 Jan 1787. LEONARD VANDERGRIDD, SR. of Henry County to NATHANIEL SCALES of the same, for the sum of two hundred pounds conveys to SCALES 200 acres of land on the north side of the South Fork of the Mayo River, being part of a larger tract granted ROBERT WALTON'S Heirs consisting of 100 acres. Signed: L. LEONARD VANDERGUFF, EDEY (X) VANDERGUFF. Wit: P. SCALES, THOS. PILGRIM, EDWARD JAMES. Proved 22 Feb 1787.

Pages 282-283: 27 Nov 1787. JESSE MAUPIN of Henry County to STEPHEN KING of the same for the sum of four hundred pounds sells 300 acres of land more or less on Reedy Creek, which I purchased of WILLIAM ESTIS and it being the land whereon I now live. Signed: JESSE MAUPIN. Wit: JOHN WALLER, STANWIX HORD, SAMUEL READ, HENRY LYNE, HEZEKIAH SALMON, JOHN SALMON, AUGUSTINE LAWLESS. Proved 22 Feb 1787, Henry Co., Va.

Pages 285-286: 22 Feb 1787. The bond of JAMES LYON to be Sherif for the year 1786. His securties were: JAMES LYON, JOHN SALMON, HENRY LYNE, JOHN DILLARD.

Page 287: 1786. Expenses for Henry County 1786.
County of Henry by the Overseers of the Poor 1786.

Payments to:	Tobacco
CHARLES FOSTER for the support of ELLINOR BAYS	1,000#
SARAH BROCK, as formerly	2,000
ADAM CHAVERS	500
WIDOW BOWMAN (under Vol. LYON & CAPT SHELTON)	1,000
WIDOW CARTER (under direction of THOMAS COOPER)	500
DR. JOHN WATSON for visits and physick to JOHN MC MILLION	160
ABRAM PENN for burial and maintaining JOHN MC MILLION	840
JOHN SALMON, Clerk, 1 year	1,500
WIDOW BISHOP	1,000
A deposition	500
Sheriff for collecting	930
By 1822 tythe, tobacco and pole	16,398
Sheriff	32

Signed: A. PENN, THOMAS COOPER, JAMES TAYLOR, JOHN WELLS, RICHARD STOCKTON, JOHN SALMON. C. O. P.

Pages 288-289: 22 Feb 1787. JAMES POTEET of the county of Henry to NATHAN HALL of the same for the sum of twenty pounds sells land 45 acres more or less on Smith River with HALL'S line, land that he purchased of JAMES ELKINS. JAMES NOWLING, ABNER BARNET, it being part of the tract JAMES POTEET sold to JAMES NOWLING the land and plantation that JAMES POTEET sold ABNER BARNET containing 50 acres. Signed: JAMES POTEET. Wit: JOHN HALL, THOMAS ROW. HALL, SARAH HALL.

Pages 289-290: 22 Feb 1787. ROWLAND SALMON of Henry County to JOHN BRAMMER, JR. of the same for the sum of thirty pounds sells 120 acres land, it being where the said ROWLAND SALMON now lives, lying on a branch of Smith River, beginning at BENJAMIN HUBBARD'S line to a tree in SILAS RATLIFF'S line. Signed: ROWLAND SALMON. Wit: NATHAN HALL, WILLIAM PERKINS, SR., JAMES MCBRIDE. Proved Henry County, 22 Feb 1787.

Page 291: 2 Feb 1787. JOHN SMALL of Henry County to CHARLES BARNARD of the same, for ten pounds sells land on the south side of Gills Creek it being 50 acres more or less. Signed: JOHN SMALL. Wit: WILLIAM AMOS, GEORGE MABRY, JAMES DENNY. Proved

9 April 1787.

Page 292: 9 April 1787. JOHN ACUFF of Henry County to CAIN ACUFF of the same for the sum of fifty pounds sells 100 acres of land it being part of a tract granted and patented by JOHN ACUFF with the lines of JOHN NANCE and the LOMAX & CO. Signed: JOHN ACUFF. Wit: none. . .SARAH ACUFF,wife of JOHN relinquishes her right of dower. Proved 9 April 1787.

Pages 293-294: 9 April 1787. WILLIAM SHARP of Henry County to JOHN SHARP of the same for one hundred pounds sells land on the Middle Fork of Mayo River containing by est 93 acres as may appear by pattent. Signed: WILLIAM (X) SHARP. Wit: EDWARD TATUM, GEORGE DOTSON. Proved 9 April 1787.

Pages 294-295: 1 Oct 1786. BENJAMIN STENNET of Montgomery Co., Va. to WILLIAM ISAM of Henry County for fifty pounds sells land in Henry County by estimate 100 acres more or less, it being the upper part of the survey of land that was formerly JOHN HENDRICK...to a dividing line between JOHN HENDRICK and STENNET on Buffalow Creek that said STENNET purchased of JOHN HENDRICK...line: Still Branch. Signed: BENJAMIN STENNET. Wit: ADAM LACKEY, SAMUEL ALLEN, DAVID HARBOUR, SR. Proved 9 April 1787.

Pages 295-296: 29 Dec 1786. JOHN ACUFF and his wife SARAH of Henry County to JOHN ACUFF, JR. for five pounds sell 100 acres more or less on the branches of Leatherwood Creek, being part of a tract granted JOHN ACUFF by patent. Signed: JOHN ACUFF, SR., SARAH (A) ACUFF. Wit: RALPH ELKINS, JAMES SANFORD, CAIN ACUFF, WILLIAM NANCE. Proved 9 April 1787.

Pages 296-297: 13 Dec 1786. THOMAS LOWE of Henry County to HENRY FRANCE of the same for the sum of two hundred pounds sell land containing 134 acres by survey on the Mayo River near the mouth of Green Creek. Signed: THOMAS LOWE, ALICE (X) LOWE. Wit: GEORGE TAYLOR, JAMES SHARD, RALPH MITCHELL, JESSE ATKISSON. Proved 9 April 1787, Henry Co., Va.

Pages 298-299: 16 Jan 1787. JOHN FREDERICK RICKELS and WILLIAM RICKELS to SAMUEL SHEWMATE for twenty pounds sell land on both sides of a branch of the lower South Fork of Sandy River...joins: HENRY JONES, JOHN BROWN, CLAY AND MOSELY, being 190 acres more or less. Signed: JOHN FREDERICK RICKELS (X), WILLIAM (X) RICKELS. Wit: HENRY JONES, MATHEW RAINEY, WILLIAM R. HAMMON, SAMUEL MOSLEY, ARMSTED JONES. Proved 9 April 1787.

Pages 299-300: 2 Feb 1787. JOHN SMALL of Henry County to JAMES DENNY of the same for the sum of forty five pounds sells land on both sides of Gills Creek beginning at a poplar on Haw Branch, 290 acres. Signed: JOHN SMALL. Wit: WILLIAM AMOS, GEORGE MABRY, CHARLES BARNARD. Proved 9 April 1787.

Pages 301-302: 27 April 1784. DARBY RYAN of Henry County to SAMUEL HAIRSTON of the same for one hundred pounds sell all tenaments, land, etc on Nichol's Creek containing 127 acres, joins ROBERT JONES. Signed: DARBY RYAN. Wit: JOHN BRAMMER, JOSEPH JONES, WILLIAM DUNN, JOHN (X) BATES. Proved 9 April 1787.

Pages 302-303: 2 Sept 1786. WALTER KING COLE of Henry County to REUBIN PAYNE of the same for fifty pounds land on the branches of Little Marrowbone Creek...lines: JOHN HARMER, WILLIAM ROBERTSON, JOHN ROWLAND, Main County Road as it now runs that crosses Marrowbone Creek and Smith River at Rowland's Ford, (so called). Signed: WALTER K. COLE. Wit: D. LANIER, WATERS DUNN, DANIEL GOLDSBAY. Proved 9 April 1787.

Pages 303-304: 17 Feb 1787. JOHN ACUFF and SARAH his wife of Henry County to WILLIAM ACUFF for the sum of twenty five pounds conveys 100 acres of land more or less on the branches of Leatherwood Creek being part of a tract granted JOHN ACUFF. Joins RALPH ELKINS, JOHN ACUFF, JR. Signed: JOHN ACUFF, SARAH ACUFF. Wit: CAIN ACUFF, JOHN ACUFF, JR. Proved 9 April 1787.

Page 305: 10 April 1787, proved. Power of Attorney. MARY HAMELTON of the County of Henry appoints her friend THOMAS ADAMS to sell and dispose of certain negro wench now my property by the name of ROSE as I would do if I were present personally. Signed: MARY HAMILTON. Wit: GEORGE HAMILTON, THOMAS STOVALL. Recorded 10 April 1787.

Pages 305-307: 11 Jan 1787. JOSEPH FARGUSON of Henry County to GEORGE HAIRSTON of the same sells for two hundred pounds land on Wine Creek of Read Creek containing 625 acres joins COPLAND'S lines.

Signed: JOSEPH FARGUSON. Wit: REUBIN PAYNE, ALEXANDER HUNTER, WILLIAM W. WARD, RICHARD (X) WILSON.

Pages 307-308: 9 April 1787. GEORGE HAIRSTON of Henry County to EUSEBOUS STONE of the same for one hundred twenty five pounds money paid by ALEXANDER HUNTER...land on the east side of SMITH River part of the HORSHAW tract known by the name of TATE place, joins NUNN'S lines being 100 acres more or less. Signed: GEORGE HAIRSTON. Recorded 9 April 1787.

Pages 308-309: 16 Oct 1787. AARON WALDEN of Henry County to ANTHONY STREET of Halifax County for forty pounds conveys 100 acres land joins EDWARD BAKER and JOHN DORRELS old line. Wit: ABRAM E. ROWDEN, WILLIAM BRISTOW, PETER BAYES. Proved 9 April 1787.

Pages 310-311: 21 Nov 1786. AARON WALDON of Henry County to ROBERT WARDON for twenty two pounds sells 180 acres land...lines: WOLF PIT, Falling Branch and NATHAN WALDEN. Signed: AARON WALDEN. Wit: WILLIAM BRISTOW, WILLIAM (X) WALDEN, ROBERT (X) WARDEN. Proved 9 April 1787.

Pages 311-312: 1787. GEORGE HAIRSTON of Henry County to DAVID CHADWELL of the same for ... ... sells land that joins CHADWELL on Smith River containing by patent 200 acres. Signed: GEORGE HAIRSTON. Recorded 9 April 1787.

Page 313: 9 April 1787. WILLIAM WALDEN of Henry County to MOSES WALDEN of the same for eighteen pounds sells 30 acres land joins: WILLIAM MARTIN, BOMAN MARTIN, JOSEPH STREET and JOHN INGRAM. Signed: WILLIAM (X) WALDEN. Wit: ABRAM ROWDEN, JOSEPH STREET, JOSEPH WALDEN. Proved 9 April 1787.

Pages 314-315: 14 May 1787. JAMES DICKERSON of Henry County to SAMUEL CLARKE for the sum of one hundred fifty pounds conveys 160 acres on both sides Spoon Creek, it being the land granted SAMUEL HARRIS by patent 22 Sept 1786. Signed: JAMES DICKERSON. . .JEAN DICKERSON, wife of JAMES relinquishes her right of dower. Proved at a Court held for Henry County at the House of ABRAM PENN the 14 May 1787.

Page 316: 10 May 1787. ABRAHAM MAYS of Rockingham County, North Carolina to DAVID MAYSE of Henry County for the sum of fifty pounds sells 100 acres land beginning at Marrowbone Creek at the mouth of the Long Branch at ANDREW RAY'S corner to the mouth of Hurricane Branch, joins ALEXANDER JOYCE. Signed: ABRAM. MAYES. Wit: D. LANIER, JOHN EAST, THOMAS ADAMS, JR. . .SARAH MAYES, the wife of ABRAHAM relinquishes dower right. Proved 14 May 1787 at a Court for Henry County held at ABRAM PENN'S house.

Pages 317-318: 14 May 1787. JAMES DICKERSON of Henry County to SAMUEL CLARKE of the same for the sum of fifty pounds sells and conveys 361 acres on Spoon Creek with the lines of WILLIAM POORS and WILLIAM WILSON. Signed: JAMES DICKERSON. . .JEAN DICKERSON, the wife of JAMES relinquishes dower right. Proved 14 May 1787 at ABR. PENN'S house.

Pages 318-319: 24 Feb 1787. Dedimus for relinquishment of dower. EDEY GILLIAM, wife of DEVERIX GILLIAM relinquishes dower right to a deed of 250 acres to WILLIAM BANKS. Proved 14 May 1787 at AB. PENN'S.

Pages 319-320: 5 June 1787. JACOB ADAMS of Henry County to RICHARD BAKER of the same for the sum of sixty pounds sells 295 acres of land on both sides of Bowen's Creek beginning at ANGLIN'S old line. Signed: JACOB (X) ADAMS. . .MARY ADAMS, the wife of JACOB relinquishes dower right. Proved 11 June 1787.

Pages 321-322: 20 Nov 1786. Deed of Trust. WILLIAM PRICE to WILLIAM BARBER PRICE in the amount of thirty pounds which the said WILLIAM PRICE is endebted to WILLIAM B. PRICE and places in trust 600 acres of land on the south side of Smith River at the mouth of Puppy Creek, likewise eleven Virginia born slaves named as: JAMES 21 yrs, SAM 17 yrs, HENRY 15 yrs, GEORGE 12 yrs, JACK 7 yrs, SET 40 yrs, SAL 35 yrs, OLD JUDE 35 yrs, DIANER 17 yrs, JINNEY 10 yrs, CHLO 6 months; likewise 3 head horses, 4 neat cattle, 8 head hogs, 3 feather beds with all furniture, household furniture and plantation utensils. Signed: WILLIAM PRICE. Wit: ROWLAND CHILES, QUILA BLACKLEY, _____ INGRUM. Proved 11 June 1787.

Page 323: 1780. ROBERT CAVE of Henry County to JOSEPH HARDIE for the sum of _____ pounds sells and conveys 50 acres of land (no description). Signed: ROBERT CAVE, ENIE CAVE. Wit: JACOB HICKEY, JAMES (X) KEATH, RICHARD BRADBERRY. Proved 11 June 1787.

Page 324: 13 Aug 1787. Bill of Sale. I, DAVIS BROWN, sell to WILLIAM MOORE for the sum of two hundred pounds one waggon and hind gear, two bay horses, one purchased of JAMES BLANTON, one black horse which I purchased of JOHN LAWSON, one set pewter moles, two feather beds and furniture and all other household furniture of every kind. Signed: DAVIS BROWN. Wit: PHIL. RYAN, ALEXANDER MOON. Proved 13 Aug 1787.

Page 325: 2 Feb 1787. Power of Attorney. JOHN SMALL of Henry County gives power of attorney to JAMES DENNY (also spelled DOONLY) to sell a tract of land in Amherst on the east side of Rockfish River under the Pilate Mtn. that joins the land of JAMES WOODS. Signed: JOHN SMALL. Wit: WILLIAM AMOS, GEORGE MABRY, CHARLES BARNARD. Proved 13 Aug 1787.

Page 326: 5 Dec 1785. JOHN ROBERTSON of Henry County sells to SAMUEL PATTERSON for forty pounds land under the north side of Turkacock Mtn on the brances of Beaver Creek joins ALEXD. GARDINS. (No acreage given). Signed JOHN (X) ROBERTSON. Wit: JOEL ESTES, DANIEL RICHARDSON, NATHAN RYAN, WILLIAM RYAN, THOMAS DUNAVANT. Proved 13 Aug 1787.

Page 327: 22 Dec 1786. JOSEPH COOPER of the state of Georgia to THOMAS COOPER of Henry County for seventy pounds sell land on both sides of Beaver Creek being 2 acres more or less. Signed: JOSEPH COOPER. Wit: JOHN STOKES, JAMES COOPER, JAMES ANTHONY. Proved 13 Aug 1787.

Pages 328-329: 12 Jan 1787. WALTER MAXEY of Henry County to JOHN PACE of the same, for sixty pounds sells 228 acres on Smith River joins JOHN RICE. Signed: WALTER MAXEY. Wit: PHIL. RYAN, JOHN EAST, SANFORD REAMEY. Proved 13 Aug 1787.

Pages 330-331: 29 May 1787. EDWARD BAKER of Henry County to SAMUEL HAIRSTON of the same for two hundred pounds sells land on Smith River being 150 acres lying operset to SAMUEL PERRY'S in the bend of the River, to a branch on RICHARD TUCKER MANENS lines with all houses, etc. Signed: EDWARD (X) BAKER. Wit: SPENCER JAMES, JAMES JAMES, RICHARD (X) COLLIER, KELLEY (X) PILSON. Proved 14 Aug 1787.

Pages 332-333: 13 Aug 1787. MICHAEL ROWLAND of Henry County being indebted to GEORGE MICHAEL ROWLAND in the amount of one hundred fifty pounds offers as security...6 negros, NED, a milatto man, BOB, CLOE, JESSIE, a yellow boy, the girl AGGY, one bay horse, all stocks, cattle, hogs, kitchen furniture, three feather beds and furniture, chairs, tables, desk, pewter potts, skillets, all crops of corn now growing. This indebtedness may be redeemed until 25 Dec 1788. Signed: MICHAEL ROWLAND. Wit: SAMUEL HAIRSTON, JOHN STAPLES, JACOB MC CRAW. Proved 15 Aug 1787.

Pages 334-335: 11 Aug 1787. Inquisition taken at the Delivery House of JOHN FORSIL (?) on Leatherwood to view the body of CHARLES SPROUSE, late of Henry County then and there being dead and upon the oaths of JOHN WELLS, foreman, SAMUEL JOHNSON, EDWARD SMITH, JAMES MORTON, JOHN BOOTH, JOHN ACUFF, FRANCIS COX, THOMAS LETCHWORTH, ALEXANDER MC CULLOCK, REUBIN NANCE, JOSIAH DENNIS, JOHN MINTER, THOMAS CHAPMAN, JOHN PHILLIPS, JOHN HALEY, WILLIAM ACUFF, JOHN ACUFF, JR., WILLIAM MITCHELL, THADDEUS SALMON, JOHN OLDHAM, JOSEPH MARTHELY, JAMES BOWLING, HENRY JONES and JAMES HALEY to determine how CHARLES SPROUSE came by his death. That one, J. FORISICE JR. late of Henry County not having God before his eyes but being seduced by the instigation of the devil on the 10th of August, felloniously, vollintary and of his malice forethought, with a gun made of iron of a value of thirty shilling, held in his right hand in and upon the belly of said CHARLES SPROUSE below the navel shot a brace of lead, of which wound the said CHARLES SPROUSE died instantly. The Jurors do say that the said J. FORSICE at the time of committing the murder had goods and chattels contained in the inventory following: Nine negroes, HARRY, KADRICK, KATE, HENRY, WILL, JUDAH, MILDRED, PETER, DINAH (infirm), 7 horses, 15 head cattle, 12 sheep, 22 hogs, 2 feather beds and furniture, 3 plows, 7 hoes, 3 axes, 10 pewter basins, 9 pewter dishes, 18 plates, spoons, a crop of corn and tobacco growing, a quantity of wheat, rye and oats. Recorded 11 Aug 1787.

Pages 336-337: 25 Oct 1781. Bill of Sale. To all Christian People...Whereas JAMES CALLAWAY of Bedford County and JEREMIAH EARLY late deceased in his lifetime seized and possessed of an estate both real and personal in the County of Henry known and called by the name of WASHINGTON IRON WORKS as joint tenants in fee, did by his will 29 March 1779 devise his son JOSEPH EARLY now deceased one third of morety of said joint estate and said JOSEPH in his lifetime did sell his third to JOHN EARLY. JAMES

CALLAWAY now moving sells to JOHN EARLY. Signed: JAMES CALLAWAY. Wit: STEPHEN SMITH, BARTLET WADE, JEREMIAH EARLEY, WILLIAM STRODE. Proved 25 Oct 1781.

Pages 337-338: 20 Dec 1780. THOMAS MAN RANDOLPH of Goochland County to THOMAS NUNN of Henry County for the sum of one hundred pounds sells land in Henry County on the north side of Smith River being 240 acres joins PATRICK HENRY. Signed: THOMAS M. RANDOLPH. Wit: P. HENRY, GEORGE HAIRSTON, PETER SAUNDERS.

Pages 330-340: 10 Sept 1787. JESSE CAMERON and CASA his wife of Henry County sell to JOHN STAPLES for one hundred pounds 400 acres of land, except the third of his Mother's, SUSANNAH CAMMERON, in the said tract of land for her natural lifetime. Land being on the branches of Horsepasture Creek, joins HARMER'S order line and JOHN DILLARD. Signed: JESSE CAMMERON, CASSENERH (X) CAMMERON. Proved 10 Sept 1787.

Pages 340-342: 8 Sept 1780. THOMAS RICHARDSON and his wife ____, of Henry County to DANIEL RAIMEY of the same for the sum of eighty pounds sells and conveys 2 tracts of land adjoining each other, one being 100 acres formerly in Pittsylvania County on Muster Branch of Leatherwood Creek, the other joins LOMAX & CO, 600 acres. Signed: THOMAS RICHARDSON. . .MARY RICHARDSON, the wife of THOMAS relinquishes dower right. Proved 10 Sept 1787.

Pages 342-343: 10 Sept 1787. JAMES ELKINS of Henry County to JOSIAH BRIANT for twenty pounds sells land on the Smith River containing 100 acres, it being the tract whereon ELKINS formerly lived, joins HALL'S. Signed: JAMES ELKINS. . .CATY ELKINS, the wife of JAMES relinquishes dower right. Proved 10 Sept 1787.

Pages 343-344: 12 May 1787. JAMES MC CRAW of the Parish of Antrim and County of Halifax to JESSE WITT of Henry County for the sum of one hundred fifty pounds sells 164 acres more or less on a branch of Horsepasture Creek, beginning at RANDOLPH & CO. line. Signed: JAMES MC CRAW. Wit: SAMUEL COLEMAN MORRIS, JOSEPH MORRIS, WILLIAM FRENCH, BENJAMIN KENNON.

Page 345: Power of Attorney. JAMES EAST of Henry County appoints JAMES EAST, SR. my lawful attorney to act to receive a certain sum of money due me the 1st day of March 1788 from JOHN WATSON and SAMUEL C. MORRIS as appears by bonds dated 30 Oct 1785. Signed: JAMES EAST. Wit: MARY EAST (X), SARAH BRADBERRY. Proved 10 Sept 1787.

Pages 346-347: 10 Sept 1787. BENJAMIN NEAL and his wife ELIZABETH of Patrick Parish County of Henry to PHILIP PENN for the sum of one hundred pounds sells land on both sides Grays Creek, it being the land and plantation whereon the said NEAL now lives, part of which was conveyed to NEAL by RICHARD DEACONS...part of a survey NEAL made...contains by estimate 568 acres. Signed: BENJAMIN NEAL, ELIZABETH NEAL. Proved 10 Sept 1787.

Pages 348-349: 1787. SAMPSON STEPHEN and his wife LEANNER of Henry County to THOMAS RICHARDSON of the same for the sum of fifty pounds sells 200 acres of land on Muster Branch of Leatherwood Crk joins: GEORGE RUNNOLDS, WILLIAM BARNARD. Signed: SAMPSON STEPHENS, LEANNER STEPHENS. Wit: ZACKARHIAH GROOM, ANNE GROOM, WILLIAM STEPHENS. Proved 14 Sept 1787.

Pages 349-350: 14 July 1783. THOMAS MATHEWS of Henrico County to JOHN HOLMES of Henry County for ninety pounds worth in land and thirteen pounds fifteen shillings...the land on the waters of Beaver Creek being 100 acres more or less joins ANTHONY BITTING, JAMES ANTHONY. Signed: THOMAS MATHEWS. Wit: JOHN COOPER, JAMES ANTHONY, JOSEPH ANTHONY. Proved 10 Sept 1787.

Pages 351-352: Dower Release. The Justices of Pittsylvania County, Virginia have examined SUSANNAH REYNOLDS, wife of GEORGE REYNOLDS, apart from her husband and she does relinquish her right of dower to a transaction of 600 acres of land to THOMAS RICHARDSON in Henry County, Va. Recorded 10 Sept 1787.

Page 353: 24 July 1787. Dower Release. The Justices of Franklin County, Virginia have examined ELIZABETH FUSON, wife of JOHN FUSON, apart from her husband and she does relinquish her dower right to a tract of 222 acres in Henry County, Va. conveyed to SAMUEL DUST. Recorded 10 Sept 1787.

Page 354: 10 Sept 1787. Dower Release. The Justices of Henry County, Virginia have examined

ELIZABETH YOUNG, wife of WILLIAM YOUNG, apart from her husband and she does freely relinquish her right of dower to a tract of 233 acres of land conveyed by her husband. Proved 24 Nov 1787.

Page 355: 8 Oct 1787. DUTTON LANE of Henry County to THOMAS JERVIS for the sum of fifteen pounds sells and conveys 243 acres of land on the waters of Horsepasture Creek...with lines of JAMES MAYS, COXE'S old line, CANNON'S line...agreeable to the patent granted DUTON LANE 11 April 1780. Signed: DUTTON LANE. Proved 8 Oct 1787.

Pages 356-357: 10 Feb 1787. LAMBOTH DOTSON, JR. and _____ to JOHN HUTCHINGS for the sum of fifty pounds sell land on the South Side of the South Fork of the Mayo River at the mouth of a branch below the plantation of FREDERICK HUTCHINGS on the other side, 50 acres. Signed: LAMBOTH DODSON, LAMBOTH (X) DODSON, JR., ELIZABETH DODSON. Wit: GEORGE TAYLOR, HENRY FEE, WILLIAM HAYS. Proved 8 Oct <u>1784</u>.

Pages 357-358: 8 Oct 1787. JONATHAN HANBY of Henry County to ARCHS. HUGHES of the same for the sum of fifty pounds sells 110 acres on the branches of the South Mayo River. Signed: JONATHAN HANBY. Proved 8 Oct 1787.

Pages 359-360: 12 Sept 1787. ALEXANDER JOYCE of Henry County to JOHN READ of the same for the sum of three hundred fifty pounds sells land on the north side of Marrowbone Creek, being 500 acres more or less. Signed: ALEXANDER JOYCE. Wit: GEORGE HAIRSTON, JOHN KING, MICH. (X) DILLINGHAM, DANIEL GOLDSBY BENJAMIN MOORE, THOMAS ADAMS, JR., THOMAS JAMISON.

Pages 360-361: 12 June 1787. GEORGE ALLEN of Henry County to AMES ROWARKE of the same for the sum of sixty pounds sells and conveys land on both sides of King Run...the South Fork of Ararat River being 126 acres more or less. Signed: GEORGE ALLEN, HANNAH H. ALLEN. Wit: JOHN CARTER, JOHN HANLEY, WILLIAM DENSON. Proved 8 Oct 1787.

Pages 362-363: 8 Oct 1787. JAMES EAST of the County of Henry to THOMAS JERVIS of the same for one hundred pounds sells land on both sides Horsepasture Creek being part of three surveys granted by patent to the said JAMES EAST in 1780...joins CANNON, 210 acres surveyed by JACOB COX, DUTTON LAIN'S line, 667 acres, DILLEN'S line, WATSON'S, it being the same more or less 375 acres. Signed: JAMES EAST. Recorded 10 Oct 1787.

Pages 364-365: 1 Oct 1784. JOHN JONES of Lincoln County, Kentucky to WILLIAM ISAM of Henry County, sells and conveys for the sum of one hundred ten pounds, 140 acres on the Smith River on Wiggins Creek. Signed: JOHN (X) JONES. Wit: ADAM LACKEY, SAMUEL ALLEN, THOMAS MARROW. Proved 12 Nov 1787.

Pages 365-366: 14 April 1787. PARISH SIMS of Henry County to JAMES SIMS of the same for the sum of five pounds sells and conveys 78 acres of land lying on the Middle fork of the South Mayo River. Signed: PARISH SIMMS. Wit: EDMD. TATUM, ELIPHAS SHELTON, JOHN (X) BARROTT. Proved 12 Nov 1787.

Pages 367-368: 22 June 1787. PATRICK HENRY and DORTHEA his wife of Prince Edward County to DAVID LANIER of Henry County for the sum of six hundred pounds sells all of that tract of land in Henry County on Smith River and Mulberry Creek containing 350 acres more or less being the same land that PATRICK HENRY purchased of MORDECAI HORD and on which WILLIAM HUTET now lives and known by ancient and established lines...joins JOHN FONTAINE and JOSEPH BOULDIN. Signed: PATRICK HENRY, DORTHEA HENRY. Wit: JOHN ALEXANDER, DANIEL RAMEY, JOHN SMITH. Proved 12 Nov 1787.

Pages 368-369: 11 Aug 1787. GEORGE WALTON of Prince Edward County as executor of ROBERT WALTON of Cumberland County, now deceased to WILLIAM FEE of Henry County. To comply with the will of the said ROBERT WALTON...did obtain patent for land on the South Fork of the Mayo River now in Henry County and whereas ROBERT WALTON son of the said ROBERT WALTON appears to have sold unto THOMAS FEE father of WILLIAM FEE 195 acres of land on the Mayo River at ten pounds a hundred, GEORGE WALTON hereby conveys same to WILLIAM FEE. Signed: GEORGE WALTON. Wit: MORRIS HUMPHREYS, FRED. FITZGERALD, HENRY (X) FEE. Proved 10 Dec 1787.

Page 370: 11 Aug 1787. Agreement. GEORGE WALTON of Prince Edward County to FREDERICK FULKERSON of Henry County. GEORGE WALTON being the executor of ROBERT WALTON, deceased to comply with certain contracts and to pay certain debts and legacys, whereas ROBERT WALTON, the younger son ROBERT WALTON of Cumberland County did convey unto FREDERICK FULKERSON part of the land on the Mayo River...said GEORGE WALTON relinquishes all right to the same. Signed: GEORGE WALTON. Proved 10 Dec 1787.

Page 371: 8 Oct 1787. MORRIS HUMPHREY and his wife SARAH to WILLIAM FEE of Henry County for the sum of twenty pounds sells and conveys 116 acres more or less on the waters of the North Mayo River, being part of 432 acre patent to JAMES SHARD and conveyed by deed to MORRIS HUMPHREY...lines: CRITZ old road and GEORGE TAYLOR. Signed: MORRIS HUMPHREY, SARAH HUMPHREY. Proved 10 Dec 1787.

Page 372: 31 Aug 1787. WILLIAM WILSON of Henry County to JAMES THOMPSON of the same for sixty pounds sells land on both sides of Spoon Creek being 411 acres joins PHILIP BUZZARD. Signed: WILLIAM WILSON. Wit: FRED. FITZGERALD, MICHAEL (X) PILGRIM, THOMAS FRASURE. Proved 10 Dec 1787.

Pages 373-374: 15 Aug 1787. MARTIN MILLER, attorney at law for JOHN FREDERICK MILLER of Halifax County to JOHN MARR of Henry County for the sum of one hundred pounds sells 305 acres of land on both sides of Stone's Creek. Signed: MARTIN (X) MILLER. Wit: GEORGE HAIRSTON, JOHN SALMON, JOHN DILLARD, JOHN WATSON. Proved 8 Oct 1787.

Page 375: 15 Aug 1787. MARTIN MILLER, attorney for JOHN FREDERICK MILLER of Halifax County & WILLIAM SHELTON heir at large of JAMES SHELTON late of Henry County to JOHN MARR of Henry County sell and convey for five hundred pounds land on the North Fork of the Mayo River, by estimate 810 acres more or less, including the plantation where JOHN MARR now lives. Signed: MARTIN (X) MILLER, WILLIAM SHELTON. Wit: GEORGE HAIRSTON, JOHN WATSON, JOHN SALMON, JOHN DILLARD. Proved 8 Oct 1787.

Page 376: 8 Jan 1787. JOHN GUSSETT of Henry County to THOMAS HOLLANDSWORTH, JR. of the same ...223 acres, it being half of tract granted JOHN GUSSETT the 29th of _____ 1784 on Blackberry Creek, joins WILLIAM WITT and is the dividing line between GUSSETT and HOLLANDSWORTH. Signed: JOHN (X) GUSSETT. Wit: WILLIAM WITT, JOHN WITT, JOHN (X) CALVIN.

Pages 377-378: 11 Feb 1788. JOHN PARR, SR. of Henry County to JOHN PETER CORNS of the same for the love and affection he bears toward his son-in-law...gives land on the east side of the Mayo River, being 70 and 3/4 acres. Signed: JOHN PARR, SR. Proved 11 Feb 1788.

Page 378: 1 Nov 1786. THOMAS MAN RANDOLPH of Goochland County to JOHN MATHEWS of Henry County for the sum of one hundred pounds sells land on the south side of Mayo River containing 200 acres and joins JAMES ROBERTS and ANTHONY SMITH. Signed: THOMAS M. RANDLOPH. Wit: GEORGE HAIRSTON, JOHN MARR, JOHN RENTFRO.

Pages 379: 3 Jan 1787. WILLIAM DANDRIDGE of Hanover County to GEORGE HAIRSTON of Henry County for five hundred pounds sells and conveys 530 acres more or less that WILLIAM DANDRIDGE purchased of JOSEPH SHORES PRICE on the north side of Marrowbone Creek. Signed: WILLIAM DANDRIDGE. Wit: JOHN MARR, JOHN RENTFRO, CONS. PERKINS. Proved 15 May 1787.

Pages 380-381: No date. HENRY LYNE is appointed sheriff and his securties are A. PENN, JAMES LYON, JAMES (X) TAYLOR, WILLIAM (X) SHELTON and THOMAS NUNN. Recorded 11 Feb 1788.

Page 381: No date. Bond of JAMES LYON as sheriff. Recorded 11 Feb 1788.

Pages 381-382: 11 June 1787. Dementions of the prison to be built in Henry County to be 20 feet long, 10 feet wide in the clear and 8 feet pitch in the clear, of sound oak timber logs hewed or sawed 12" sq two longs round above the upper floor, the upper and lower floor timbers of the same. Dementions of hewed or sawed timber 6 inches thick with a paratition to make the crimnals room 8 feet by 10 feet in the clear with sufficient partition door and lock, also double doors out and in the debeters room with a sufficient bolt secured by iron and sufficient lock to the out door. A window to each room sufficient secured by iron bars, light 2 inches square, the window to be 18 inches square. A stone or brick chimney in the debters room sufficiently secured where necessary with iron and timber. A good shingled roof nailed down laths. A sufficient pair of stocks, pillory and a gallow. Twenty pounds to be paid by the Sheriff out of the deposition in his hand to undertakes upon his giving bond and work to be finished by November Court next if finished sooner received an order by the Court will be made for the balance. We, the following agree to perform the building. Signed: WILLIAM SHARP, AB. PENN. Wit: JOHN DILLARD, JOHN MARR.

Page 383: 11 June 1787. Addition to Prison bond. We, WILLIAM SHARP and ABRAM PENN are bound unto the Justices of Henry County in the amount of four thousand pounds. The condition of the bond is to build the prison, stocks, pillory and a gallow on the premises of ABRAM PENN, near his mansion house on or before the 2nd Monday in November next coming. Signed: WILLIAM SHARP, ABRAM PENN. Wit: JOHN DILLARD, JOHN MARR. Recorded 11 Feb 1788.

Page 384: 6 Feb 1788. HENRY SUMPTER of Henry County to ABSOLUM ADAMS for the sum of one shilling six pence conveys 100 acres of land on Rock Run Creek, crosses DAVIS' branch joins JAMES BARKER. Signed: HENRY SUMPTER. Proved 10 March 1788.

Pages 385-386: 28 April 1785. WILLIAM EVANS of Washington County to ROBERT GRIMIT of Henry County for twenty pounds sell land on the Muddy Fork of Chestnut Creek being 349 acres...beginning on the north side of Chestnut Mountain. Signed: WILLIAM EVANS. Wit: JACOB STOVER, JOHN HOLLIDAY, JACOB STOVER. Proved 27 Oct 1785 and 12 Nov 1787.

Pages 386-387: 10 April 1788. ROBERT PERGEOY, SR. of Henry County to ROBERT PEREGOY, JR. of the same for seventy five pounds sells and conveys 100 acres more or less on the waters of Leatherwood Creek. Signed: ROBERT PEREGOY, SR. Proved 14 April 1788.

Page 387: 10 Feb 1788. ROBERT PERIGOY of Henry County to ROBERT WATSON of North Carolina living on the waters of Abbit Creek sells for ten pounds 50 acres more or less in Henry County, Va. on the Beaver Creek Waters, joins RICHARD PARSLEY. Signed: ROBERT (X) PEDIGO. Wit: none. Proved 14 April 1788.

Page 388: 10 April 1788. ROBERT PEREGOY of Henry County to JOSEPH PEREGOY of the same for one hundred five pounds sells 300 acres more or less on the waters of Beaver Creek. Signed: ROBERT (X) PEREGOY. Proved 14 April 1788.

Pages 388-389: 10 April 1788. ROBERT PEDEGOY of Henry County to ELIZABETH PEDEGOY for the sum of seventy five pounds sell 100 acres more or less on the waters of Leatherwood Creek...on the north fork above SAMUEL WATSON'S old place. Signed: ROBERT (X) PEDEGOY. Proved 14 April 1788.

Pages 389-390: 23 Jan 1788. Power of Attorney. ROBERT WATSON appoints his trusty friend ROBERT PEDIGO his attorney to sell for fifty pounds land on Beaver Creek that WATSON bought of RICHARD PARSLEY. Signed: RICHARD (X) WATSON. Wit: JOSEPH PEDEGO, JOHN PARKER. Recorded 14 April 1788.

Pages 390-391: 10 Sept 1787. WILLIAM EDWARDS of Henry County to CHARLES RAKES for the sum of sixty two pounds sells 200 acres of land in Henry and Franklin Counties, it being part of the land that the said EDWARDS now lives upon on Shooting Creek and branches of the Smith River...lines: top of the ridge that divides Shooting Creek and Turkey Cock Creek. Signed: WILLIAM EDWARDS. Wit: NATHAN AHLL, DAVID (X) COCKRAM, THOS. ROW. HALL. . .ANN EDWARDS, wife of WILLIAM relinquishes dower right. Proved 14 April 1788.

Page 391: No date. Deed of Trust. I, JOSEPH PHIFER of Henry County and justly indebted to HENRY LYNE in the amount of thirty pounds two shillins three pence sell to him land in Montgomery County being 320 acres on Mill Creek a branch of Meady Creek, 8 head of cattle, two black cows, 1 cow and yearling which JOHN REDD owes me, also two feather beds and furniture, 2 iron potts, 6 pewter plates, 1 dish, and 2 basons and all the rest of my household furniture, 1 bay mare, 8 hogs, 1 sow and 7 shoats. Signed: JOSEPH (X) PHIFER. Wit: JOHN (X) DILLINGHAM, MICHAEL (X) DILLINGHAM, JOSHUA (X) DILLINGHAM. Proved April 1788.

Page 393: 14 April 1788. THOMAS LOCKHART of Henry County to JESSE CORN of the same for thirty five pounds sells land on both sides of the South Fork of the Mayo River containing by estimate 180 acres on Russell's Creek. Signed: THOMAS LOCKHART. Proved April 1788.

Page 394: 10 Nov 1787. JOHN DAY of Henry County to JAMES HAILE of the same for thirty pounds sells 90 acres of land more or less on the North Fork of Spoon Creek beginning at DAY'S back line and joins MERRY ANDREW. Signed: JOHN (X) DAY. Wit: CHARLES BARKER, JOHN MEDLEY, WILLIAM KEETON, JOSEPH CUMMINGS.

Proved 14 April 1788.

Page 395: 12 April 1788. JONATHAN HANBY of Henry County to DAVID LAWSON of the same for the sum of five pounds sells and conveys land on the Big Dan River being 100 acres, part of a tract granted by patent to SAMUEL COX in 1782. Signed: JONATHAN HANBY. Wit: EDWARD TATUM, GEORGE ROGERS, GEORGE CARTER. Proved April Court 1788.

Page 396: No date. Power of Attorney. I, MILES JENNINGS of the State of Georgia appoint GEORGE TAYLOR my lawful attorney to transact all my business in Henry County. Signed: MILES JENNINGS. Wit: A. HUGHES, WILLIAM FRANCE, THOMAS WHITLOCK. Recorded 12 Jan 1787 or 9.

Pages 397-398: 27 July 1787. IGNATIOUS SIMMS and SABRA his wife of Henry County to RICHARD MITCHELL of the same for two hundred pounds sell 170 acres on the branches of Beaver Creek on a creek called Sims, joins THOMAS COOPER. Signed: IGNATIOUS SIMMS, SABRA SIMMS. Proved 14 Apr 1788.

Pages 398-399: 8 April 1788. SAMUEL CLARK of Henry County to DAVID CLARK of the same for ths sum of five hundred pounds sells 521 acres more or less on both sides of Spoon Creek joins WILLIAM POOR and MILLER'S lines. Signed: SAMUEL CLARK. Proved 14 April 1788.

Pages 399-400: 12 April 1788. JOHN PACE of Henry County to NEWSOM PACE of the same for sixty pounds sells 200 acres more or less on Smith River joins the lines of JOHN RICE. Signed: JOHN PACE. Proved 14 April 1788.

Page 401: 19 Nov 1787. HARRISON HOBARD of Henry County to HUMPHREY POSEY of the same for twenty pounds sells 40 acres, it being the plantation whereon JOSEPH BOLLING formerly lived on the south side of Smith River, beginning at the mouth of Bowen's Creek. Signed: HARRISON HOBARD. Wit: WILLIAM WITT, THOMAS POSEY, JOHN SMALLMAN. Proved 14 April 1788.

Page 402 --- same as deed on page 401.

Page 403: 12 Oct 1787. HENRY MAYSE of Henry County to JOHN SMITH of the same for the sum of five pounds sells 50 acres of land with the line of JOHN WITT as the old line up the ridge as the path goes, crossing the North Fork of Fall Creek. Signed: HENRY (X) MAYSE. Wit: DAVID (X) MAYSE, BEN. (X) MOORE, WILLIAM MOORE. Proved 14 April 1788.

Page 404: 25 Oct 1787. SHEROD MAYSE of Henry County to JOHN SMITH for the sum of forty pounds sell 75 acres joining ADONIJAH HARBOUR'S old line, up Fall Creek to JOHN WITT'S and JOHN JONNYKIN'S. Signed: SHEROD (X) MAYSE. Wit: BEN. (X) MOORE, DAVID (X) MAYSE, WILLIAM MOORE. Proved 14 April 1788.

Page 405: 12 Nov 1787. JAMES WILLIAMS of Henry County to WILLIAM BROWN of the same for a sum of money conveys 260 acres on Leatherwood Creek joining HAILE. Signed: JAMES WILLIAMS. Wit: ROBERT STOCKTON, SAMUEL JOHNSON, REUBEN NANCE. Proved 14 April 1788.

Page 406: 14 April 1788. JOSHUA DILLINGHAM of Henry County to JOHN CAHILL of the same for one hundred pounds sells 153 acres on Redy Creek. Signed: JOSHUA DILLINGHAM. Proved 14 April 1788.

Page 407: 17 Nov 1787. Deed of Trust. JOSIAS SHAW from JAMES WILSON. JAMES WILSON has layed himself liable to pay JOSIAS SHAW one hundred eighty pounds, the following in trust: One negro man FRANK, one bay horse called JALLAMACCUS, 1 bay horse called KING OF DIAMONDS, a crop of corn and tobacco, 1 feather bed and furniture, one walnut table, 1 cow and two yearlings, 8 hoggs, 2 sows, 14 shoats, 4 pewter plates, dish and basin, 2 plows, 2 grubing hoes, 2 hilling and 2 weeding hoes. Signed: JAMES WILSON. Wit: JOHN DILLARD, JOHN STAPLES. Recorded 18 Nov 1787. Add: I oblidge myself to send JAMES WILSON a sorrell mare called Poll Peachum or one hundred dollars by 17 Nov 1788. Recorded 14 April 1788.

Pages 408-409: 24 April 1788. Deed of Trust. SAMUEL WALKER is justly indebted to HENRY LYNE in the amount of seventy seven pounds 6 pence. Security: 2 negroes, DANIEL age 19 years and JUDA age 36 years, 1 wagon, 8 horses, that were left in the state of Georgia viz: 3 greys, 3 bays, 2 sorrell, one black left at CHARLES DUNCAN'S in Faquire City; 9 head cattle, 4 featherbeds and furniture, 3 iron pots, 1 dutch oven, 6 pewter basins, 3 dishes, 6 plates and all the rest of my estate. This due by the 1st day of April 1789 with interest or to be sold with 20 days notice. Signed: SAMUEL WALKER. Wit: JOSEPH STOVALL, GEORGE WALLER, JR. Recorded: No date.

Pages 409-410: 10 Nov 1787. GEORGE HAIRSTON of Henry County to JAMES BAKER of the same for two pounds sells 50 acres of land on Blackberry Creek beginning at JAMES BAKER'S south line and joins ALEXANDER HUNTER and THOMAS NUNN. Signed: GEORGE HAIRSTON. Proved 14 May 1788.

Pages 410-411: 12 May 1788. JOHN MARR of Henry County to BENJAMIN LANDRETH of the same for sixty pounds sells land on both sides Ararot Creek containing 200 acres, being part of his order of council claimed by Bill; this is the land whereon BENJAMIN LANDRETH now lives. Signed: JOHN MARR. Proved 14 May 1788.

Pages 411-412: 12 May 1788. HAMON CRITZ, SR. of Henry County to JACOB CRITZ of the same for one hundred pounds sells a parcel of land containing 425 acres that crosses Mill Creek. Signed: HAMON CRITZ, SR. Wit: JESSE ATKISSON, JOHN MILLER, WILLIAM CORNWELL. Proved 12 May 1788.

Page 413: No date. Bill of Sale. (Deed of Trust) JOHN COLLIER of Henry County to REUBEN TARRENT of the same sells one negro boy named BENJAMIN age 18 years for the sum of one thousand pounds of tobacco. Signed: JOHN (X) COLLIER. Wit: JOHN WELLS, JOHN MINN, ACHILLIS BALLINGER. . .If JOHN COLLIER do well and truly pay REUBEN TARRENT 1200# of Petersburg (tobacco) before the 25th December next then R. TARRENT will relinquish all claim to the said negro. Dated 5 April 1788. Recorded 12 May 1788.

Pages 414-415: 15 Feb 1788. ROBERT WARDEN of Henry County to JAMES INGRUM of the same, for forty pounds sells 180 acres of land on the branches of Goblingtown Creek and Smith River... lines: ANTHONY STREET and Falling Branch. Signed: ROBERT (X) WARDEN (WALDEN??). Wit: WILLIAM BRISTOW, NATHAN (X) WALDEN, BENJAMIN (X) WALDEN. Proved 14 April 1788.

Pages 415-416: 19 May 1788. TALMON HARBOUR of Halifax County to JOELL HARBOUR of Henry County for one hundred pounds conveys a parcel of land on the North side of Irvin River (Smith) and on both sides of Widgon Creek, being 229 acres. Signed: TALMON (X) HARBOUR. Wit: JOSEPH REYNOLDS, JOHN WITT, JOHN HENDERSON, ESAIAS HARBOUR. Proved 9 June 1788.

Pages 417-418: 19 May 1788. TALMON HARBOUR of Halifax County to ESIAS HARBOUR of Henry County for one hundred pounds sells land on the north side of Irvin River (Smith) containing 141 acres. Signed: TALMON (X) HARBOUR. Wit: JOSEPH REYNOLDS, JOHN WITT, JOHN HENDERSON, JOEL HARBOUR. Proved 9 June 1788.

Pages 418-419: 15 Nov 1787. JAMES WILLIAMS and WILLIAM BROWN of Henry County to FRANCIS NORTHCUT of Charlotte County for the sum of one hundred pounds sell and convey 150 acres on both sides of the west side of a fork on Leatherwood Creek ...being part of a tract formerly granted by patent to THOMAS BOLLING of Charlotte County; joins the lines of: ROBERT PEDIGO, JOHN HALEY and the WIDOW WILLIAMS. Signed: JAMES WILLIAMS, WILLIAM BROWN. Wit: JOHN ACUFF, SAMUEL JOHNSON, ROBERT STOCKTON, REUBEN NANCE, NATHAN NORTHCUT. Proved 9 June 1788.

Pages 420-421: 22 Feb 1788. Deed of Trust. SAMUEL TARRENT of Henry County is indebted to DAVID ANDERSON, Merchant of Dinwiddle County in the amount of six hundred thirty five pounds 14 shillings and 9 pence with legal interest from 15 July 1787 sell and secure with the following: 4 negroes, REUBEN 40, LUCY 23, GEORGE 6, ARMSTED 5, 6 horses, 6 cows, 4 featherbeds and furniture and a tract of land whereon I now live containing 317 acres. Due 1 May 1789 and with 10 days notice to be sold. Signed: SAMUEL TARRENT. Wit: HENRY LYNE, JOHN NICHOLS. Note: THOMAS DICKERSON, SR. was in partnership with me (SAMUEL TARRENT) but this shall not bar paying the above debt. Proved 9 June 1788.

Page 422-423: 9 June 1788. ISAAC MC DONALD of Henry County to JESSE REYNOLDS of the same for the sum of fifty pounds sell a parcel of land on the south fork of Nobuisness Fork of the Mayo River, being 200 acres more or less...being part of a patent of a greater quantity. Joins: JAMES TAYLOR and ROBERT HAMPTON. Signed: ISAAC MC DONALD. Proved 9 June 1788.

Pages 423-424: 7 Dec 1787. JOHN PRESTON of Henry County to MICHAEL LITRELL of the same for twenty pounds conveys land on a branch of Spoon Creek joining JACOB ADAMS and BARTON, containing 80 acres more or less. Signed: JOHN (X) PRESTON. Wit: WILLIAM ADAMS, JACOB ADAMS, NATHAN (X) LITRELL. Proved 9 June 1788.

Pages 424-425: 8 June 1788. JAMES ELKINS of Henry County to EZEKIEL MORRIS of the same for forty pounds sells tract of land containing 149 acres more or less joining GEORGE WALTON on Rockcastle Creek. Signed: JAMES ELKINS. . .CATY ELKINS, wife of JAMES relinquishes dower right. Proved 9 June 1788.

Pages 425-426: 25 March 1788. JOHN STOCKTON of Pittsylvania County to JAMES PIGG of Henry County for the sum of one hundred sixty pounds sells 130 acres on the north fork of the Mayo River. Signed: JOHN STOCKTON. Wit: JOHN RANDELLS, JOHN PULLIAM, JOHN SHARP, WILLIAM SHARP, JAMIMA SHARP. Proved 14 July 1788.

Page 426-427: 25 May 1788. CHARLES THOMAS of Henry County to JOHN LEE of the same for the sum of twenty pounds sells a parcel of land containing 394 acres on a branch of Joincrack Creek. Signed: CHARLES THOMAS. Wit: NATHAN HALL, THOS. ROW. HALL, JOHN BRAMMER, MOSES STANDLEY. Proved 14 July 1788.

Page 428-429: 11 May 1787. JOHN DANIEL and MARY DANIEL of Henry County to WILLIAM CARTER of the same for the sum of thirty pounds sell 300 acres, by survey 22 April 1780, being on both sides of the Big Dan River, joins NOWLIN and BELCHER. Signed: JOHN DANIEL, MARY (X) DANIEL. Wit: RALPH (X) SHELTON, DAVID ROWARK, GEORGE CARTER, JONATHAN HANBY. Proved 3 Oct 1787.

Page 430: No date. Bill of Sale. PHILLIP RYAN sells to MRS. MARY ROWLAND for the sum of one hundred pounds one negro woman PHILLIS and two children. Signed: PHIL RYAN. Wit: GEORGE (X) DYER, RACHEL (X) DYER. Proved 14 July 1788.

Pages 430-431: 14 July 1788. ALEXANDER JOYCE of Henry County to GEORGE HAIRSTON of the same for three hundred fifty pounds sells and conveys a tract of land on both sides of Marrowbone Creek joining the lines of: JOSIAS SHAW, GEORGE HAIRSTON, JAMES HICKS, BENJAMIN HICKS, DAVID LANIER, JAMES JOHNSON and JOSEPH CHANDLER to the Great Road containing by estimate 437 acres more or less. Signed: ALEXANDER JOYCE. Proved 14 July 1788.

Pages 432-433: 20 Dec 1787. ELIJAH DONATHAN and RACHEL DONATHAN to SAMUEL HOOKER all of Henry County, for the sum of one hundred pounds conveys land on RICHARD BARNET's Mill Creek, a south fork of the Little Dan River being 80 acres. Signed: ELIJAH (X) DONATHAN. Wit: JOHN MARR, CUTHBERT SHELTON, RALPH SHELTON. Proved 9 June 1788.

Pages 433-434: 20 Dec 1787. ELISHA IVEY and MARTHA his wife of Henry County to JOHN DUNCAN of the same for the sum of one hundred pounds in hard money sell land on both sides of the Little Dan River being 180 acres. Signed: ELISHA (X) IVIE, MARTHA (X) IVIE. Wit: RALPH (X) SHELTON, OBEDIAH HUDSON, SAMUEL (X) HOOKER. Proved 9 June 1788.

Pages 434-435: 14 July 1788. CHARLES THOMAS of Henry County to DAVID WILLIAMS of the same for the sum of thirty pounds sells sixty acres of land on Smith River joins SYLAS RATLIF. Signed: CHARLES THOMAS. Wit: EDWARD PEREGOY, NATHAN HALL, THOMAS ROW. HALL. Proved 14 July 1788.

Page 436: 11 July 1788. STEPHEN RENNO of Henry County to KINNEY MCKINNEY of the same for twenty pounds sells 50 acres more or less part of a tract granted ARCHABALD ROBERTSON, joins JOHN HARDMAN and JOHN SIMMONS. Signed: STEPHEN (X) RENNO. Wit: DANIEL SMITH, CALUP (X) SMITH, RUBIN (X) VOURN.

Page 437: 29 May 1787. Dower release. RUTH PENN, the wife of ABRAHAM PENN relinquishes dower right to land sold to GEORGE WALLER (290 acres). Recorded 14 July 1788.

Pages 438-439: 27 Oct 1785. MILES HICKS of Henry County to ALEXANDER JOYCE of the same for the sum of five hundred sixty pounds sells a tract of land on both sides of Marrowbone Creek joining the lines of JOSIAS SHAW, GEORGE HAIRSTON, JAMES HICKS, BENJAMIN HICKS, and DAVID LANIER, to intersect with the lines of land sold by HICKS to JAMES JOHNSTON and by JOHNSTON to JOSEPH CHANDLER and by CHANDLER to COL. GEORGE HAIRSTON, it being 437 acres more or less. Signed: MILES HICKS. Wit: DAVID LANIER, JAMES TAYLOR, THOMAS ADAMS, JR. Proved: North Carolina, Franklin County 30 May 1788 to be the act and deed of MILES HICKS. Proved and Recorded Henry Co., Va. 14 July 1788.

Pages 440-441: 20 April 1788. ZADOCK SMITH and his wife MARY of Henry County to ABRAHAM PENN of the same, for the sum of one hundred pounds sells land on the branches of the North Mayo River containing 130 acres more or less, beginning on the north side of the Creek on a branch of the said River near the path above PULLIAM'S new line...it being part of a tract granted SMITH by patent 14 March 1782, sold to WILLIAM SMITH, afterword purchased by ZADOCK SMITH, it being the land and plantation whereon WILLIAM SMITH now lives. Signed: ZADOCK SMITH, MARY SMITH. Wit: GEORGE PENN, LUCYNDA PENN, JAMES WALKER. Proved 14 July 1788.

Pages 431-442: 17 April 1788. Deed of Trust. EDWARD SMITH to ABRAHAM PENN for six thousand pounds inspected tobacco at Petersburg or Richmond, it being shipable and five shillings...land on both sides Turkey Cock Creek containing by deed 400 acres more or less, it being the plantation where EDWARD SMITH now lives also 1 horse, 6 head cattle, 3 feather beds and furniture, 1 negro boy MARTIN, all pewter and kitchen furniture. After 10 April 1789 the said ABRAHAM PENN may sell for the best price land and other items. Signed: EDWARD (X) SMITH. Wit: SAMUEL TARRENT, JAMES MORTON, GEORGE TUNSTALL. Proved 14 July 1788.

Page 443: 25 April 1780. THOMAS EARLS of Henry County to SAMUEL TARRANT of the same, for forty pounds sells 50 acres more or less bounded by WILLIAM TUNSTALL, part of the order of council of the said TARRENT lines, that he purchased from JAMES COX, JR. Signed: THOMAS (X) EARLS. Wit: DAVID DICKERSON, JOHN COLLIER, REUBEN TARRENT, JR. Proved 12 Nov 1787.

Pages 443-444: 18 June 1788. Deed of Trust. I, FRANCIS GILLEY, SENR. of Henry County and justly indebted to JOHN REDD in the amount of fifteen pounds 9 shilling and ten pence by account with interest. Secures same with a certain negro boy named ADAM. If not paid by the 1st Nov 1788, may sell the said ADAM for the best price. Signed: FRANCIS GILLEY, SENR. Wit: FRANCIS (X) GILLEY, JOHN WALLER. Recorded 15 Aug 1788.

Page 445: 15 Feb 1788. Inquisition at the house of JOHN WASH on the 15th of Feb 1788 on the body of a negro girl, the property of JOHN WASH, then and there lying dead. Upon the oaths of JOHN EAST, THOMAS R. G. ADAMS, THOMAS LEAK, EDWARD ADAMS, RUSSELL COX, JOELL PACE, ERASMUS ALLEY, THOMAS COOPER, JOHN RAY, THOMAS LETCHWORTH, RICHARD WILSON and THOMAS EAST, that on the 14th day of this month JOHN WOOD adjacant to the to the dwelling of JOHN WASH by the fall of a tree, unforseen to or through the means or design of any other person whatsoever the slave was then and there killed instantly.

Page 446: 22 Feb 1788. Bill of Sale. PETER RICKMAN of Henry County for the sum of twenty five pounds paid by HENRY LYNE sells to said LYNE the following: 1 gray horse 5 yrs old, 1 black horse 4 yrs old, 1 bay colt 2 yrs old, 2 cows and yearlings, 1 pott, 1 dish and 4 plates, 2 dutch blankets, 2 spinning wheels with cotton and flax and the rest of my goods. Signed: PETER RICKMAN. Wit: STEPHEN KING. Proved 15 Aug 1788.

Page 446: 15 March 1788. Bill of Sale. JOHN MINTER of Henry County to WILLIAM BRETHARD of the same sells and conveys a negro fellow BOB of yellow complexion about 25 yrs old for value received. Signed: JOHN MINTER. Wit: GRIFFIN (X) BURNETT, ARCHER (X) HATCHER. Proved 15 Aug 1788.

Page 447: No date. THOMAS CUMMINGS and JOHN HENDERSON are bound unto TALMON HARBOUR of Hallifax County in the sum of one hundred pounds to be paid by the 13th of Aug 1788. The condition of the above obligation is such that the said THOMAS CUMMINGS and JOHN HENDERSON shall keep and forever maintain the said TALMON HARBOUR and his heirs secure against all persons who shall hereafter make any lawful claim against the estate of WILLIAM BURNETT, deceased. Signed: THOMAS CUMMINGS, JOHN HENDERSON. Wit: JOHN WITT, GEORGE PENN. Proved 15 Aug 1788. . . .23 April 1772. Then received of TALMON HARBOUR sixteen pounds sixteen shillings 4 pence in full of the estate of WILLIAM BURNETT, deceased...I say received by me. Signed: SAMUEL ALLEN. Wit: ESAIAS HARBOUR. Recorded 15 Aug 1788.

Page 448: 11 Aug 1788. JOHN STAPLES, JOHN DILLARD justices shall pay and deliver unto JOSEPH ROBERTS orphan of JOSEPH ROBERTS, deceased all such estate is as now shall appear to be due the said orphan when he shall attain lawful age. Signed: JOHN STAPLES, JOHN DILLARD.

Pages 448-449: 14 May 1788. LEWIS DAVIS and JOHN COX ...LEWIS DAVIS is the administrator of the estate of ZACKERIAH MC GUIRE, deceased and shall make a true inventory of the estate. Signed: LEWIS DAVIS, JOHN COX.

Pages 450-451: 26 Sept 1787. WILLIAM LINCH of Henry

County to WILLIAM SPENCER of the same for the sum of twelve pounds sells land beginning on the main branch that runs through the land...a branch of the Mayo River at the mouth of a small branch running into the main branch with BAKER'S former line, DEAKINS line to LINCH'S west head line being 140 acres more or less. Signed: WILLIAM LYNCH, BECKY LYNCH. Wit: JOHN MARR, GEORGE PENN, JOHN (X) MC GEEHEE. Proved 14 Apr 1788.

Pages 452-453: 8 Sept 1788. GEORGE HAIRSTON and ELIZABETH his wife of Henry County to JOHN REDD of the same, for the sum of four hundred pounds conveys land on Ready Creek, being a branch of Smith River containing 570 acres, the land conveyed from PETER COPLAND to MICHAEL ROWLAND, bought by BRADLEY MEREDITH from COPLAND. Signed: GEORGE HAIRSTON, ELIZABETH HAIRSTON. Proved 8 Sept 1788.

Page 454: 1 Sept 1788. JOHN REDD of Henry County to GEORGE HAIRSTON of the same for three hundred fifty pounds sells a tract of land on Marrowbone Creek containing 300 acres. Signed: JOHN REDD. Proved 8 Sept 1788.

Page 455: 18 Apr 1788. BARTHOLOMEW FOLEY of Henry County to JOSEPH HANCOCK for the sum of ten shillings sells a tract of land containing 110 acres on a branch of Smith River called Foley's branch. Signed: BARTHOLOMEW FOLEY, BARBERY (X) FOLEY. Wit: CHARLES GOODMAN, SAMUEL NOE, THOMAS JAMISON. Proved 8 Sept 1788.

Page 456: 8 Sept 1788. JAMES MORRISON of Henry County to LEWIS HANCOCK of the same land on both sides of Sycamore Creek beginning at a dividing line agreed upon between JESSE CORN and JOHN PETER CORN containing 84 acres. Signed: JAMES MORRISON. Wit: DAVID HARBOUR, SR., MARTIN AMOS, WILLIAM AMOS. Proved 8 Sept 1788.

Pages 457-458: 8 Sept 1788. JAMES MORRISON of Henry County to JESSE CORN of the same, for twenty pounds sells land on both sides Sycamore Creek being 85 acres. Signed: JAMES MORRISON. Wit: DAVID HARBOUR, SR., MARTIN AMOS, WILLIAM AMOS. Proved 8 Sept 1788.

Page 459: 18 April 1788. BARTHOLOMEW FOLEY of Henry County to THOMAS TENISON of the same for seven pounds 10 shillings conveys 109 acres on a branch of Smith River. Signed: BARTHOLOMEW (X)FOLEY, BARBERY (X) FOLEY. Wit: CHARLES GOODMAN, SAMUEL NOE, JOSEPH HANCOCK. Proved 8 Sept 1788.

Page 460: 8 Sept 1788. GEORGE HAIRSTON and ELIZABETH his wife of Henry County to SAMUEL SHELTON of the same, for the sum of twenty five pounds sells 87 acres on the south side of the North Mayo River. Signed: GEORGE HAIRSTON, ELIZABETH HAIRSTON. Proved 8 Sept 1788.

Pages 461-462: 8 Sept 1788. GEORGE HAIRSTON and ELIZABETH his wife of Henry County to KINNEY MCKINNEY of the same sell and convey land on the south side of Smith River containing 50 acres with the lines beginning where MCKINNEY formerly lived, joins the land HAIRSTON bought of JOHN ROWLAND, crossing a path that goes from the Mill to COL. GEORGE WALLER'S still...Grassy Creek. Signed: GEORGE HAIRSTON, ELIZABETH HAIRSTON. Proved 8 Sept 1788. . . . ELIZABETH HAIRSTON, wife of GEORGE release dower right.

Pages 462-463: 8 Sept 1788. GEORGE HAIRSTON and ELIZABETH his wife of Henry County to JUNOR MEREDITH of the same, sell and convey for the sum of eighty pounds land on Reed Creek containing 225 acres. Signed: GEORGE HAIRSTON, ELIZABETH HAIRSTON. Proved 8 Sept 1788.

Page 463: 20 March 1788. Deed of Trust. DAVID LANIER of Henry County to JOHN ALEXANDER of the same. Security: 14 negros, PLOTH, CATE, PHILLIS, ARCHER, JEFF, BOB, FRAZER, JUDE, CHARLES, ISBILL, JANE, CHANEY, JOHN and ESTER, feather beds and furniture. The said DAVID LANIER shall pay unto PATRICK HENRY the above six hundred pounds which JOHN ALEXANDER is security for the said LANIER to PATRICK HENRY. Signed: DAVID LANIER. Wit: JOHN EAST, THOMAS EAST, JOHN SMITH, MORRIS WEBB, JOHN ROWLAND, JOHN MARTIN ALEXANDER. Recorded 13 Oct 1788.

Pages 465-466: 13 Oct 1788. JAMES LYON of Henry County to STEPHEN LYON of the same, for the sum of two hundred pounds sells and conveys a tract of land on Russell's Creek containing 200 acres and joins the lines of WILLIAM ROBERT HINTON. Signed: JAMES LYON. Proved 13 Oct 1788.

Pages 466-467: 10 Sept 1788. PALITIAH SHELTON of Henry County to STEPHEN LYON of the same for three hundred pounds sells land on Russell's Creek, being 204 acres more or less joins ROBERT WALTON and DAVID ROGERS and an additional 109 acres. Signed: PALITIAH SHELTON. Wit: JOSEPH CLOUD, ISAAC MC DONALD, HARVY FITZGERALD. . .ANNY SHELTON, the wife of PALITIAH relinquishes dower right. Proved 15 Oct 1788.

Pages 468-469: 10 April 1788. RALPH SHELTON and ELIZABETH his wife of Henry County to JACOB ADAMS, JR. sell and convey 251 acres of land on Mathews Creek for the sum of one hundred pounds. Signed: RALPH SHELTON. Wit: JOHN LOYD, ELIPHAZ SHELTON, RODE MOORE. Proved 15 Oct 1788.

Page 470: 10 April 1788. RALPH SHELTON and ELIZABETH his wife of Henry County to JACOB ADAMS, JR. of the same, for the sum of one hundred pounds sells land containing by survey dated 8 Nov 1788 145 acres on Mathews Creek beginning at the corner of RALPH and THOMAS SHELTON corner. Signed: RALPH SHELTON. Wit: JOHN LOYD, RODE MOORE, ELIPHAZ SHELTON. Proved 13 Oct 1788.

Pages 471-472: 31 Oct 1788. ESAIAS HARBOUR of Henry County to JAMES BARTLETT of the same for two hundred fifty pounds sells land on the north side of IRVIN River (Smith) and on both sides Widgen Creek containing 169 acres...lines: DARBY RYAN, near the meeting house, thence a straight line across to TALMON HARBOUR'S corner where ESAIAS HARBOUR and JOEL HARBOUR'S dividing line begins. Signed: ESAIAS HARBOUR. Wit: JOEL HARBOUR. Proved 11 Nov 1788. . . CATHERINE HARBOUR the wife of ESAIAS HARBOUR relinquishes her right of dower.

Pages 473-474: 10 Nov 1788. JOHN CONWAY of Henry County to PETER PERKINS of Rickinham County for the sum of eighty pounds sells land on the waters of Leatherwood Creek containing 175 acres... lines: PATRICK HENRY and REUBAN NANCE. Signed: JOHN CONNAWAY. Wit: TUNSTALL COX, SAMUEL COX, JOHN MINTER, JOHN COX. Proved 8 Dec 1788.

Pages 474-475: 23 Oct 1788. ESIAS HARBOUR of Henry County to JOEL HARBOUR of the same, for fifty five pounds sell land on the waters of Irvin (Smith) River and Widgeon Creek containing 100 acres more or less joins TALMON HARBOUR and DARBY RYAN. Signed: ESIAS HARBOUR. Wit: VALENTINE MAYO, NICHOLAS COGAR, JAMES BARTLET. . .CATHERINE HARBOUR, the wife of ESIAS relinquishes dower right. Proved 11 Nov 1788.

Page 476: 26 Sept 1788. FRANCES JOYCE, wife of ALEX-
ANDER JOYCE relinquishes her right of dower to deed made to GEORGE HAIRSTON for 437 acres.

Pages 477-478: 19 May 1788. JAMES MAY and ELIZABETH
his wife of Henry County to HENRY LYNE of the same, for the sum of one hundred twenty five pounds sells and conveys land on both sides of Horse-pasture Creek joins the land of RANDOLPH & COMPANY, it being the part of a tract surveyed by DUTTON LAYNE, contains 400 acres more or less. Signed: JAMES MAY, ELIZABETH (X) MAY. Wit: BRITT STOVALL, JOHN MAY, JOSEPH STOVALL, STEPHEN KING, JAMES WILSON. Proved 14 July 1788.

Pages 478-479: 4 Sept 1788. JOHN PRESTON of Henry
County to JOHN SIMMINS of the same for the sum of one hundred pounds sells a tract of land on a branch of the Mayo River called Roundabout, joins the lines of ADAMS and MICAEL LITRELL, contains 100 acres. Signed: JOHN (X) PRESTON. Wit: JACOB ADAMS, JR., JOHN FLETCHER, JACOB (X) ADAMS. Proved 13 Jan 1789.

Page 480: 2 Dec 1788. JOHN BARKER, SR. of Henry
County to ANDREW WOLVERTON of the same for the consideration of fifty pounds sells and conveys 100 acres of land on Spoon Creek. Signed: JOHN (X) BARKER, SR. Wit: SAMUEL STAPLES, JAMES (X) TAYLOR, WILLIAM (X) KEATON, JESSE REYNOLDS, JOSEPH STOVALL. Proved 12 Jan 1789.

Pages 481-482: 23 Feb 1789. PHILLIP BROSHEARS and
his wife ANN BROSHEARS of Henry County to WILLIAM HEWLETT of the same for the consideration of fifty pounds sells 50 acres more or less on the south side of Smith River. Signed: PHILLIP BROSHEARS. Proved 23 Feb 1789.

Pages 482-483: 25 Feb 1785. WILLIAM BAYS of the
County of Washington and state of Virginia to WILLIAM BRISTOW of Henry County for the sum of forty pounds sell land being 100 acres, joins JOHN DORRILS. Signed: WILLIAM (X) BAYSE. Wit: SAMUEL CRITCHFIELD, ROWLAND CHILES, TAFENIAH (X) TENASON. Proved 24 March 1785 & 23 Feb 1789.

Page 484: ___ Feb 1789. JAMES CROLEY (CROWLEY ?) of

Henry County to ADAM TURNER of the same for the consideration of forty pounds sells and conveys land on Smith River being 20 acres more or less. Signed: JAMES (X) CROLEY. Wit: FRANCIS TURNER, JAMES TURNER, RICHARD PILSON. Proved 23 Feb 1789.

Pages 485-486: 4 Sept 1788. JOHN PRESTON of the County of Henry to WILLIAM FINN of the same for the sum of one hundred pounds sells land on the branches of the Mayo River called Roundabout containing 250 acres more or less. Signed: JOHN (X) PRESTON. Wit: JOHN FLETCHER, JACOB (X) ADAMS, JACOB ADAMS, JR. Proved 23 Feb 1789.

Page 486: 23 Feb 1789. CARTER TARRENT, a Baptist member has been recommended by the Elders of the Church to be licensed to cillabrate the rights of matrimony within the pale of his Church. Signed: CARTER TARRENT, BARNA WELLS, JR., ROBERT STOCKTON. Proved 23 Feb 1789.

Pages 487-488-489: 10 Aug 1788. WILLIAM FINN of Henry County to FRANCIS HOLT of the same, for one hundred twenty pounds sells land on both sides of Spoon Creek joining SHELTON and PARR containing 292 acres. Signed: WILLIAM (X) PHINN. Wit: JOHN FLETCHER, JACOB ADAMS, WILLIAM ADAMS. Proved 23 Feb 1789.

Pages 489-490: 13 March 1789. GEORGE WALLER of the County of Henry to KINNEY MCKINSEY of the same, for the sum of seventy pounds sell all that plantation and tract of land purchased by GEORGE WALLER of ABRAHAM PENN, of WALTER KING located on Smith River. Signed: GEORGE WALLER. Proved 30 March 1789.

Pages 490-491: 30 March 1789. DEVARIX GILLIAM and EADY GILLIAM his wife of Henry County to JOSEPH STOVALL of the same for the consideration of two hundred pounds sells and conveys 336 acres on both sides of the North Mayo River on Racoon Branch. Signed: DEVERIX GILLIAM. Proved 30 March 1789.

Pages 492-493: 13 March 1789. DEVERIX GILLIAM of Henry County to HAMON CRITZ, SR. of the same for and in consideration of thirty pounds, conveys 100 acres it being part of a tract patented to DEVERIX GILLIAM for 202 acres; this transaction is for 100 acres more or less. The date of patent was 12 July 1780. Signed: DEVERIX GILLIAM. Proved 30 March 1789.

Pages 493-494: 7 Nov 1784. HENRY ARNOLD of Henry County to WILLIAM BRANNUM of the same for the sum of forty pounds sells land on Bull Mountain a fork of the Mayo River contains 227 acre tract. Signed: HENRY ARNOLD. Wit: WILLIAM CARTER, HALL HUDSON, ELIPHAZ SHELTON. Proved 28 April 1785 and 30 March 1789.

Pages 495-496: 11 March 1789. JOHN WARD of Campbell County to ROBERT HUGHES of Henry County for and in consideration of ninety pounds sells and conveys land on both sides of Buffalow Creek joins JOHN KENDRICK. Signed: JOHN WARD. Wit: BENJAMIN BUTTERWORTH, THOMAS MURRELL, MARTIN LAWRANCE. Proved 30 March 1789.

Page 497: 11 March 1789. JOHN WARD of Campbell County to NEWMAN HELTON of Henry County for the sum of one hundred pounds sells land on the head of head of the South Branch of the Middle fork of Jack's Creek, beginning at the top of Bluewridge being 278 acres. Signed: JOHN WARD. Wit: BENJAMIN BUTTERWORTH, THOMAS MURRELL, MARTIN LAURANCE. Proved 30 March 1789.

Pages 498-499: 11 March 1789. JOHN WARD, Gentleman of Campbell County to WILLIAM BRANHAM of Henry County for the sum of twenty five pounds sells a parcel of land containing 87 acres on the branches of Flat Creek of the Irvin (Smith) River. Signed: JOHN WARD. Wit: BENJAMIN BUTTERWORTH, THOMAS MURRELL, MARTIN LAURANCE. Proved 30 March 1789.

Page 500: 11 March 1789. JOHN WARD of Campbell County to BEVERIDGE HUGHES of Henry County for the sum of one hundred pounds sell land on both sides of Buffalow Creek being 89 acres. Signed: JOHN WARD. Wit: BENJAMIN BUTTERWORTH, THOMAS MURRELL, MARTIN LAURANCE. Proved 30 March 1789.

Page 501: 23 Feb 1789. MARTIN LAURANCE of Henry County to BENJAMIN BUTTERWORTH of the same for and in consideration of forty pounds sells land on both sides of Dols branch of the south side of Irvin (Smith) River, being 300 acres more or less. Signed: MARTIN LAURANCE. Proved 30 March 1789.

Pages 504-505: 1789. JOHN BOOTH of Henry County to JOHN BURCH, JR. of the same, for and in consideration of fifty pounds sells and conveys 206 acres on both sides of Meathouse Branch on Leatherwood Creek. Signed: JOHN BOOTH. Wit: ACHILLIS

BALLINGER, JOSEPH GRAVELY, GEORGE PHILLIPS. Proved 27 April 1789.

Page 506: 3 Oct 1788. JEREARD BURCH of Henry County to JACOB COULY of the same, for sixteen pounds ten shillings sells 50 acres of land. Signed: JERARD BURCH. Wit: ACHILLIS BALLINGER, JOSEPH GRAVELY, GEORGE PHILLIPS. Proved 27 April 1789.

Pages 507-508: 25 April 1789. JOHN ACUFF of Henry County to CARTER TARRANT of the same, for and in consideration of fifty five pounds sells a parcel of land on the branches of Leatherwood Creek, being 100 acres. Signed: JOHN ACUFF, JR. Proved 27 April 1789.

Pages 508-509: 18 April 1789. SAMUEL JOHNSON of Henry County to HENRY LAURANCE of the same for the sum of fifty pounds sells land on both sides of Turkey Cock Creek, tract being 100 acres, joins JOHN CUNNINGHAM and JOE LYALLS. Signed: SAMUEL JOHNSON, BETTEY JOHNSON. Wit: JAMES JOHNSON, ACHILLIS BALLENGER, WILLIAM CUNNINGHAM, WILLIAM LAURANCE. Proved 27 April 1789.

Pages 509-510: 27 Oct 1789. WILLIAM WHITSETT of Henry County to MARGARET BLAKEY, his daughter of the same county...conveys to MARGARET BLAKEY land on the Main Creek joining ANTHONY BITTING, JAMES ANTHONY, JOHN COOPER and crosses the Little Beaver Creek being 500 acres. Signed: WILLIAM WHITSETT. Proved 27 April 1789.

Pages 511-512: 20 April 1789. JOHN KELLY of Henry County to THOMAS CHEWNING of the same for the sum of twenty pounds sells and conveys a parcel of land on the north side of Smith River, beginning at the end (lower) of a tract that KELLY purchased of ABRA. WOMACK on the north side of Smith River on Turkey Cock Creek and with the line of SAMPSON MAXEY containing 70 acres. Signed: JOHN KELLY. Wit: JACOB (X) CATON, BENNETT KELLEY. Proved 27 April 1789.

Pages 513-514: 27 April 1789. WALTER KING COLE of Henry County to GEORGE HAIRSTON of the same for the sum of five hundred fifty pounds conveys all that mesuage, plantation and land on the south side of Smith River between twelve hundred to fifteen hundred acres; joins lines of ALEXANDER HUNTER, JAMES BARKER, HORD'S and is known as the Blackberry Tract. Signed: WA. KING COLE. Proved 27 April 1789.

Pages 514-515: 18 Jan 1786. WILLIAM HAMMIT of Henry County to GEORGE HAIRSTON of the same for sum of twenty five pounds sells land on the south side of the North Mayo River on Mill Creek, being 73 acres. Signed: WILLIAM HAMMIT. Wit: WILLIAM (X) WARD, JOHN (X) SULIVANT, ALLEN (X) BROCK. Proved 28 April 1787.

Pages 516-517: 27 April 1789. JOHN RANDALS of Henry County to THOMAS DODSON of the same, for twenty five pounds sells land being 103 acres more or less on Mayo River. Signed JOHN RANDALS. . . WENIFORD RANDALS, wife of JOHN release right of dower. Proved 27 April 1789.

Pages 518-519: 27 April 1789. JOHN RANDALS of Henry County to GEORGE DODSON of the same, for twenty five pounds sells 67 acres more or less bounded on the Ridge Path, Prater's fork of the Mayo River. Signed: JOHN RANDALS. Proved 27 April 1789.

Pages 519-520: 18 Dec 1788. REUBEN HILL of Hallifax County to GEORGE DODSON of Henry County for the sum of thirty pounds conveys 249 acres on both sides of a branch of Prater's fork of the Mayo River. Signed: REUBEN (X) HILL. Wit: CHARLES HOBBERT, JOHN RANDALS, ELIZABETH DODSON. Proved 27 April 1789.

Pages 521-522: 27 April 1789. PHILIP PENN of Henry County to GEORGE PENN of the same, for the love and regard for my son GEORGE PENN, give, grant and confirm and release a parcel of land on the head of Gray's Fork, by estimate 200 acres more or less, beginning with a line that DEACON'S formerly owned, line: BENJAMIN NEAL. Signed: PHILLIP PENN. Proved 27 April 1789.

Pages 522-523: 27 April 1789. JAMES PIGG of Henry County to WILLIAM WILLIS of the same, for the love and regard I have for my son-in-law, give, grant and confirm unto him 100 acres of land joins JAMES BARTLETT. Signed: JAMES (X) PIGG. Proved 27 April 1789.

Pages 523-524: 28 April 1789. JOHN MARR of Henry County to DAVID ROWARK of the same, for and in consideration of five hundred pounds sell and conveys land on each side of Arrat Creek containing 220 acres, it being part of his order of council, formerly claimed by BELL and the same is the land whereon DAVID ROWARK now lives. Signed: JOHN MARR.

Wit: EDWARD TATUM, JACOB CRITZ, JESSE ATKISSON. Proved 28 April 1789.

Pages 524-525: 28 April 1789. JOHN MARR of Henry County to WILLIAM GREEN of the same, for the sum of one hundred pounds sell land that was part of his order of council formerly claimed by BELL ...beginning at the top of Bell's Spur, containing 433 acres. Signed: JOHN MARR. Wit: EDWARD TATUM, JACOB CRITZ, JESSE ATKISSON. Proved 28 April 1789.

Page 526: 3 April 1789. WILLIAM BROWN of Henry County to JOSEPH MARTIN of the same, for and in consideration of twenty pounds sells and conveys land on the waters of Smith River beginning at RANDOLPH & COMPANY'S line to the mouth of Hammock Branch... lines by the plat from the surveyors offfice in Pittslyvania County, patent issued in June 1772, being 124 acres. Signed: WILLIAM BROWN. Wit: JOHN REDD, JOHN SALMON, WILL. STOKES, JAMES ANTHONY, JOSHUA DILLINGHAM. Proved 29 April 1789.

Pages 527-528: 27 April 1789. SAMUEL SHELTON of Henry County to SAMUEL STAPLES of the same for the consideration of one hundred fifty pounds sells 130 acres land beginning at a corner tree seperating the lands of JAMES SHELTON, deceased, WILLIAM SHELTON and JOHN DILLARD, on the north side of Horsepasture Creek...with JOHN STAPLES line, formerly JOSIAH SMITH. Signed: SAMUEL SHELTON. Proved 28 April 1789.

Pages 528-529: 18 Dec 1788. REUBEN HILL of Pittsylvania County to CHARLES HIBBERT of Henry County for the consideration of twenty pounds sells land on both sides Prator's Fork of the north fork of the Mayo River contains 404 acres by patent ...joins GEORGE DODSON. Signed: REUBEN (X) HILL. Wit: GEORGE DODSON, JOHN RANDALS, ELIZABETH DODSON. Proved 27 April 1789.

Page 530: 1789. JOHN BURCH, JR. of Henry County to GEORGE PHILLIPS of the same for and in consideration of ten pounds sells land by estimate 50 acres, known by the name of DICK THOMPSON'S Cabbin in the fork of the Meethouse Branch of Leatherwood Creek, bounded by old MR. BURCH'S pasture to the upper line of a certain survey for 206 acres sold by JOHN BOOTH to JOHN BURCH, JR. Signed: JOHN BURCH, JR. Wit: ACHILLIS BALLINGER, JOSEPH GRAVELY. Proved 27 April 1789.

A Pole kept for JOHN MARR at an Election held for Henry County, Virginia at the Courthouse on Monday, the 9th day of April 1787.

1. EDMUND PEGOE
2. THOMAS BOLLING
3. WILLIAM TOOMS
4. ANDREW RAY
5. JACOB KEATON
6. GEORGE BRITTON
7. JAMES MCBRIDE
8. THOMAS R.G.ADAMS (disd)
9. BENJAMIN NEAL
10. JAMES PIGG
11. JOHN CALLEY
12. JOHN DUNCAN
13. JAMES BOWLING (disd)
14. JESSE ELKINS
15. JOHN HOOKER
16. CHARLES FARRIS
17. CHARLES COX
18. JAMES EDWARDS
19. JOSEPH CHANDLER
20. JESSEE MURPHY
21. JOSEPH NUNN
22. BENJAMIN HUBBARD
23. JAMES TAYLOR
24. ZADOCK SMITH
25. THOMAS WILKINS
26. DANIEL NEWMAN
27. DAVID WATSON
28. JOHN GROGIN (disd)
29. WILLIAM STEVENS
30. JAMES EDWARDS
31. PRESTON KENDRICK
32. RICHARD MANNER
33. MATHEW RANEY
34. WILLIAM ROBERSON
35. DAVID MAYS
36. THOMAS LEAK (disd)
37. RUSSELL COX
38. MOSES REYNOLDS
39. DAVID JOHNSON (disd)
40. JOHN CAMERON
41. RICHARD WEALCH
42. JOHN SULIVENT (disd)
43. ISHAM EDWARDS
44. JOHN OLDHAM
45. GOODING MAYS
46. SHARED MAYS
47. JOHN DAVIS
48. JOSEPH GRAVELY
49. JOSEPH MORRIS
50. SAMUEL C. MORRIS (disd)
51. WASHINGTON LANIER
52. HENRY MAYS
53. THOMAS OAKLEY (disd)
54. JESSE CAMERON
55. DAVID CHADWELL
56. BENJAMIN BRISTO
57. ZACKERIAH SMITH
58. WILLIAM BRISTOE
59. JOHN NUCLDS
60. JOEL PACE (disd)
61. DANIEL SWILLIVANT
62. WILLIAM ADAMS
63. ERASMUS ALLEN (disd)
64. RICHARD PILSON
65. SAMUEL CROUCHER
66. THOMAS ADAMS
67. SAMUEL BUCKLEY
68. JOHN DAY
69. WILLIAM HAYES
70. JOHN PHILPOTT
71. JOHN KING
72. JESSE CORN
73. .... REUBIN
74. WILLIAM MOORE
75. JOSEPH BOLLING
76. GEORGE DODSON
78. JESSE REYNOLDS
79. JOHN HUDGINS
80. GEORGE EVINS
81. FRANCIS BARROTT
82. SHADRACK BARROTT
83. HAMON CRITZ, JR.
84. BARTLETT REYNOLDS
85. WILLIAM CLOUD
86. WILLIAM CARTER
87. JOHN NORTON
88. MILLER EASLY
89. PETER FRANCE
90. ISAAC ADAMS
91. NEHEMIAH PRATOR
92. JACOB CRITZ
93. JOHN PARR, SR.
94. DAVID WITT
95. WILLIAM TAYLOR
96. RICHARD WILSON
97. ABM. PAYNE (tenant)
98. JAMES HAILEY
99. BENJAMIN GARREOTT
100. LAMBORD DODSON
101. JOHN GRAVELY (tenant)
102. GEORGE TAYLOR
103. JOSEPH TAYLOR (tenant)
104. ANDREW WOLVERTON
105. WILLIAM BANKS
106. SAMUEL SHELTON
107. BENJAMIN KANNON
108. PHILLIP PENN
109. DANIEL GASLOBY
110. IGNATIOUS REDMAN
111. DRURY SALMON
112. WILLIAM SOWELL
113. ISAAC MC DONALD
114. GEORGE SANFORD (tenant)
115. ABRA. EADES
116. WILLIAM FORTNER
117. RALPH SHELTON
118. BRADLEY SMITH
119. OBADIAH HUDSON
120. WARSHAM EASLY
121. GEORGE CARTER
122. FREDERICK FULKERSON
123. GEORGE POOR, SR.
124. WILLIAM HUDSPETH
125. THOMAS STONE
126. DUTTON LAINE
127. THOMAS EDWARDS
128. MICHAEL DILLINGHAM
129. JOHN COOPER
130. WILLIAM SHARP
131. BENJAMIN HANCOCK
132. JACOB ADAMS, JR.
133. WILLIAM FRENCH, SR.
134. ALEXANDER JOYCE
135. JOHN HOLT
136. ABNER ACOLDS (ECHOLS)
137. JOHN FRANCE

138. WILLIAM ISHAM
139. HENRY KOGER
140. JOHN SPENCER
141. RICHARD ADAMS
142. WILLIAM SHELTON
143. AUGUSTINE BROWN
144. WILLIAM LYNCH
145. NICHOLAS AKIN
146. JOHN ACKOB JR. (ACUFF?)
147. JOHN SALMON
148. THOMAS LOCKHART
149. DEVERIX GILLIAM
150. JOHN RANDALS
151. MORDECIA HORD
152. FRANCIS GILLEY
153. JESSE ATKISSON
154. PETER BAYS
155. JACOB ADAMS, SR.
156. JOHN FERREL
157. THOMAS DODSON
158. ELISHA IVEY
159. JAMES MANKINS
160. RHODHAM MOORE
161. JOHN PARR, JR.
162. MORRIS HUMPHRIES
163. THOMAS SMITH
164. GEORGE RODGERS
165. MICHAEL BARKER
166. JOHN DANIEL
167. BARTLETT SMITH
168. WOODY BURGE
169. JOHN MATHEWS
170. JOHN MANNING
171. JAMES MAY
172. STEPHEN LYON
173. CHARLES RIGG
174. THOMAS HAMILTON
175. WILLIAM BRADBERRY
176. JOSEPH ANTHONY
177. ADAM STULTS
178. HARBERT SMITH
179. DAVID RODGERS
180. JAMES BARTLETT

181. JOHN PULLAM
182. CHARLES SIMMS (tenant)
183. CHARLES DODSON
184. JOHN MAY
185. HENRY SMITH
186. JOHN TAYLOR
187. BENJAMIN DILLEN
188. WILLIAM GRAY
189. ELIPHAZ SHELTON
190. JOHN BARROTT
191. ABSOLEM ADAMS
192. JOHN FLETCHER
193. WILLIAM MITCHELL
194. RHODHAM MOORE
195. WILLIAM COOKSEY (?)
196. WILLIAM GRIFFIN
197. RICHARD STOCKTON
198. HENRY FRANCE
199. NATHANEIL SCALES
200. JOSEPH SCALES
201. PETER LEAK
202. FRANCIS COX
203. NATHANIEL T. BASSETT
204. JOHN WASH (tenant)
205. ARCHL. HUGHES
206. SAMUEL TARRENT
207. WILLIAM JAMESON - sworn
208. EDWARD TATUM
209. QUILLES BLACK (tenant)
210. GEORGE HAIRSTON
211. DAVID LANIER
212. HENRY GUFFEY (disputed)
213. WILLIAM BARTEE
215. CHRISTOPHER PERKINS
216. SAMUEL WALKER
217. JAMES PITMAN (tenant)
218. WILLIAM CORNWELL
219. GREGORY DURHAM
220. JOHN CLARK
221. JAMES HALE
222. HEZEKIAH SHELTON
223. AUSTIN LAWLESS

A Copy.   Teste: J. WALLER for J. LYON

A poll taken of a section of Delegates at Henry County Courthouse the
9th of April 1787 for ABRAHAM PENN, Esq.

1. WILLIAM AMOS
2. BENJAMIN NEAL
3. JAMES PIGG
4. JOHN DUNKIN
5. JOHN HOOKER
6. JOSEPH NEWMAN
7. JAMES CROWLEY
8. LUKE FOLEY
9. EDWARD SMITH
10. HENRY JONES
11. WILLIAM WOODY
12. JAMES TAYLOR
13. ZADOCK SMITH
14. JOSEPH WALDEN
15. ROBERT WARDIN
16. ANDREW POLSON
17. JOHN BRAMMER (disputed)
18. DANIEL NEWMAN
19. JOSEPH HURT
20. CHARLES DAVIS
21. JAMES POTEAT

22. JOHN SHARP
23. RICHARD MANOR
24. JOHN NEVILLS
25. MOSES REYNOLDS
26. RICHARD BOATMAN (disputed)
27. WILLIAM BOLLING (disputed)
28. JOHN HOMES
29. JOHN GREGGS
30. BEVERAGE HUGHES
31. JOSEPH STREET
32. JOHN CAMERON
33. GEORGE DODSON
34. CHARLES BURNETT
35. SAMUEL PERRY
36. JAMES MORRISON
37. MARTIN LAWRANCE
38. JACOB FARRIS
39. JOHN HENDERSON
40. GEORGE MABRY
41. WILLIAM GARDNER
42. THOMAS MORROW

#	Name	#	Name
43.	JESSE CAMMERON	113.	RALPH SHELTON
44.	BARTLETT FOLEY	114.	OBEDIAH HUDSON
45.	JOSEPH TOWNLEY	115.	WARHAM EASLEY
46.	JAMES WILLIAMS	116.	GEORGE CARTER
47.	PETER TITTLE	117.	FREDK. FULKERSON
48.	ANTHONY TITTLE	118.	GEORGE POOR, JR.
49.	VALENTINE MAYO	119.	THOMAS HARBOUR
50.	WILLIAM ADAMS	120.	THOMAS STONE
51.	MATHEW SMALL	121.	JOHN BARKER
52.	JAMES ELKINS	122.	JOHN COOPER
53.	SAMUEL CRUTCHER	123.	JAMES MURPHY
54.	JAMES DENNY	124.	WILLIAM SHARP
55.	ELISHA VINSON (disputed)	125.	BENJAMIN HANCOCK
56.	JAMES INGRUM	126.	JACOB ADAMS, JR.
57.	JOHN INGRUM	127.	JAMES SHARP
58.	SAMUEL JOHNSON	128.	FRANCIS TURNER
59.	JOHN DAY	129.	JOHN FRANCE
60.	WILLIAM WITT	130.	CHARLES FOSTER
61.	GEORGE WALLER	131.	WILLIAM ISON
62.	JOHN HAYLEY (HAILEY ?)	132.	HENRY KOGER
63.	DANIEL SMITH	133.	CHARLES BARNARD
64.	ROBERT WARDEN	134.	JOHN SPENCER
65.	JOSEPH BOLLING	135.	RICHARD ADAMS
66.	PHILLIP ANGLIN	136.	WILLIAM SHELTON
67.	GEORGE DODSON	137.	WILLIAM LYNCH
68.	JESSE REYNOLDS	138.	WILLIAM TURNER
69.	JOHN HUTCHENS	139.	THOMAS LOCKHART
70.	MICHAEL WATSON	140.	DEVERIX GILLIAM
71.	REUBIN NANCE	141.	JOSEPH BROADY
72.	THOMAS GARNOR	142.	JOHN RANDALS
73.	JOHN JAMASON	143.	JAMES ANTHONY
74.	THOMAS RICHARDSON	144.	JAMES MORTON
75.	JOHN MORRIS	145.	SAMUEL ALLEN
76.	FRANCIS BARROTT	146.	PETER BAYS
77.	SHADRACK BARROTT	147.	JOHN MINTER
78.	HAMON CRITZ	148.	REUBIN HILL
79.	BARTLETT REYNOLDS	149.	JACOB ADAMS
80.	WILLIAM CLOUD	150.	JOHN FERRELL
81.	WILLIAM CARTER	151.	JOHN GUSSETT
82.	JOHN NORTON	152.	ISAAC HARBOUR
83.	MILLER EASLEY	153.	SAMUEL PACKWOOD
84.	PETER FRANCE	154.	JOHN KOGER
85.	NEHEMIAH PRATOR	155.	THOMAS DODSON
86.	JACOB ADAMS	156.	JAMES MANKINS
87.	JACOB CRITZ	157.	JOHN PARR, JR.
88.	JOHN PARR, SR.	158.	THOMAS SMITH
89.	WILLIAM TARYLOR	159.	GEORGE RODGERS
90.	CAIN ACUFF	160.	MICHAEL BARKER
91.	BENJAMIN GARRETT	161.	BARTLETT SMITH
92.	NICHOLAS KOGER	162.	WILLIAM BREATHEART
93.	GEORGE TAYLOR	163.	JOHN WELLS
94.	JOSEPH TAYLOR	164.	WILLIAM ACUFF
95.	MARKHAM LOVELL	165.	THOMAS STOVALL
96.	THOMAS NUNN	166.	JOHN MATHEWS
97.	ANDREW WOLVERTON	167.	JOHN DILLARD
98.	EUSEBOUS STONE	168.	JAMES EAST (sworn)
99.	MOSES HARBOUR	169.	AUGUSTINE THOMAS
100.	WILLIAM BANKS	170.	THOMAS HOLLAND
101.	PHILLIP PENN	171.	WILLIAM GRAVES
102.	IGNATIOUS REDMAN	172.	HERBAT SMITH
103.	DRURY SALMON	173.	JAMES BARTLETT
104.	WILLIAM SOWELL	174.	CHARLES DODSON
105.	GEORGE REAVES	175.	HENRY DILLEN
106.	ALEXANDER HUNTER	176.	HENRY SMITH
107.	SPENCER JAMES	177.	JOHN TAYLOR
108.	JOHN STOKES	178.	HENRY CLARK
109.	WALLER DENT	179.	JOHN WATSON
110.	JOHN BOLLING (disputed)	180.	HENRY HARRIS
111.	HENRY SUMPTER	181.	ELIPHAZ SHELTON
112.	ABRAHAM EADS	182.	JOHN BARRIOTT

183. ABSOLEM ADAMS
184. JOHN FLETCHER
185. RHODA MOORE
186. WILLIAM COOKSEY
187. WILLIAM GRIFFIN
188. RICHARD STOCKTON
189. HENRY FRANCE
190. NATHAN HALL
191. IGNATIOUS SIMS
192. NATHANIEL SCALES
193. WILLIAM FAGAN
194. JOHN WASH (disputed)
195. ARCHELOUS HUGHES
196. SAMUEL TARRANTS
197. WILLIAM JAMARSON
198. ACQUILLA BLAKLEY
199. DAVID ROWARD (disputed)
200. JOHN LACKEY
201. EDWARD TATUM
202. WILLIAM DODSON
203. JOHN MARR
204. GEORGE HAIRSTON
205. ROWLAND CHILES
206. HENRY GUFFE (disputed)
207. HENRY BARKSDALE
208. CHARLES HIBBERT (disputed)
209. STEPHEN KING (disputed)
210. WILLIAM BARTEE (disputed)
211. CHRIST. PERKINS
212. JOHN BRAMMER
213. JOHN STAPLES
214. SAMUEL CRITCHFIELD (disputed)
215. WILLIAM CROMWELL
216. JOHN CLARK
217. JOHN REDD
218. JAMES HAILE
219. HEZEKIAH SHELTON
220. AUGUSTINE LAWLESS

A Copy.   Teste: SAMUEL STAPLES, Clerk

A Poll taken on the election of Delegates held at Henry County Courthouse on the 9th April 1787 for THOMAS COOPER, Esquire.

1. EDWARD PEDEGO
2. WILLIAM AMOS
3. ROBERT PEDEGO
4. WILLIAM TOOMS
5. GEORGE BRITTIAN
6. JAMES BOLDIN (disputed)
7. JAMES EDWARDS
8. STEPHEN RENNO
9. RICHARD MITCHELL
10. JAMES CONLEY
11. BENJAMIN HUBBARD
12. LUKE FOLEY
13. EDWARD SMITH
14. HENRY JONES
15. SAMUEL MOBLEY
16. JOSEPH WALDEN
17. JEREMIAH TURNER
18. JOHN BRAMMER (disputed)
19. JOSEPH HURT
20. THOMAS WILKINS
21. CHARLES DAVIS
22. DAVID WATSON
23. JOHN GROGGING (GROGAN ?)(disp)
24. JOSEPH PEDEGO
25. WILLIAM STEPHENS
26. JAMES EDWARDS
27. MATHEW RANEY
28. WILLIAM ROBERSON
29. RICHARD BOATMAN (disputed)
30. WILLIAM BOLLING (disputed)
31. DAVID JOHNSON (disputed)
32. JOHN HOMES
33. JOHN GRIGGS
34. BEVERAGE HUGHES
35. JOSHUA DILLINGHAM
36. JOHN BIRD
37. CHARLES BURNETT
38. RICHARD WEALCH
39. WILLIAM RICE
40. JOHN OLDHAM
41. JAMES MORRISON
42. MARTIN LAWRANCE
43. JACOB FARRIS
44. RICHARD CORNWELL
45. JOHN MITCHELL
46. NEHEMIAH NORTON
47. GEORGE MABERRY
48. JOHN ACUFF
49. JOHN DAVIS
50. JOSEPH GRAVELY
51. JOSEPH MORRIS
52. SAMUEL C. MORRIS (disputed)
53. WILLIAM GARDNER
54. THOMAS MORROW
55. HENRY MAYS
56. WILLIAM GARDNER (disputed)
57. BARTLETT FOLEY
58. JOSEPH TOWNWELL
59. JAMES WILLIAMS
60. JOHN RICHARDSON
61. JOHN BRAMMER
62. JOHN CONNAWAY
63. VALENTINE MAYO
64. JAMES MC WILLIAMS
65. JOHN PACE
66. JAMES RAY
67. JAMES OAKES
68. RICHARD PILSON
69. JAMES MASTERS (disputed)
70. JAMES DENNY
71. JAMES MEREDITH
72. CALEB SMITH (disputed)
73. WILLIAM HEARD
74. DAVID WILLIS
75. ELISHA VINSON (disputed)
76. BENJAMIN POSEY
77. JOHN INGRUM
78. JOSEPH GOODWIN
79. SAMUEL JOHNSON
80. WILLIAM WITT
81. ABRA. ROWDIN
82. WILLIAM ADAMS
83. JOHN PHILPOTT
84. DANIEL RAMEY
85. GEORGE WALLER
86. JOHN HALEY
87. JESSE CORN
88. DANIEL SMITH

89. JOHN REDD
90. LARKIN TURNER
91. WILLIAM HEARD, SR.
92. HENRY BAUGHN
93. MICHAEL WATSON
94. REUBEN NANCE
95. THOMAS GARNER
96. JOHN JAMERSON
97. JOHN STANDLEY
98. THOMAS RICHARDSON
99. JOHN MORRIS
100. JOHN RENNOE
101. DAVID WITT
102. JOHN WEAVER
103. KAN (CAIN) ACUFF
104. JAMES HAILEY
105. JOHN GRASBY (disputed)
106. NICHOLAS COGAR
107. MARKHAM LOVELL
108. SAMUEL SHELTON
109. BENJAMIN KANNON
110. STARKE BROWN
111. FRANCIS GRIMES
112. ROBERT FRAZER
113. GEORGE REAVES
114. MOSES WALDEN
115. JOHN MASTERS
116. JOSEPH KING
117. JOHN STOKES
118. WALTER DENT
119. JOHN BOLLING (disputed)
120. GEORGE SANFORD (disputed)
121. HENRY SUMPTER
122. JOHN JAMERSON
123. JOSEPH HANDY
124. WILLIAM FALKNER
125. WILLIAM HARRIS
126. BRADLEY SMITH
127. THOMAS HARBOUR
128. DUTTON LANE
129. THOMAS EDWARDS
130. JAMES MURPHEY
131. JAMES SHARD (sworn)
132. JOHN STAMPS
133. FRANCIS TURNER
134. ABNER ECHOLDS
135. CHARLES FOSTER
136. CHARLES BARNOT
137. NICHOLAS AKIN
138. JOHN ACUFF
139. JOHN SALMON
140. WILLIAM TURNER
141. JOSEPH BRADLEY
142. JAMES ANTHONY
143. MORDECAI HORD
144. JAMES MORTON
145. JESSE ATKINS
146. SAMUEL ALLEN
147. DANIEL MC KINSEY (disputed)
148. KINNEY MC KINSEY
149. JOHN MINTER
150. JOHN GUSSETT
151. ISEAU HARBOUR
152. SAMUEL PACKWOOD

153. JOHN KOGER
154. PHILIP RYAN
155. ELISHA IVEY
156. JOHN PYRTLE
157. MORRIS HUMPHRIES
158. JOEL HARBOUR
159. WILLIAM MULLINS
160. JESSE WITT
161. WILLIAM BRETHEART
162. AMBROSE JONES
163. JOHN WELLS
165. WILLIAM ACUFF
166. JAMES TAYLOR
167. THOMAS STOVALL
168. WOODY BURGE
169. WILLIAM BROWN
170. THOMAS JAMISON
171. JOHN DILLARD
172. JAMES EAST (sworn)
173. JAMES MAY
174. AUGUSTINE THOMAS
175. CHARLES RIGGS
176. THOMAS HAMALTON
177. THOMAS HOLLAND
178. JOHN PELFER
179. JOSEPH ANTHONY
180. WILLIAM GRAVES
181. ADAM STULTS
182. THOMAS FLOWERS
183. DAVID RODGERS
184. UMPHREY POSEY
185. HUGH MC WILLIAMS
186. DAVID MORRAK
187. JOHN BARKSDALE
188. HENRY DILLEN, SR.
189. WILLIAM PERKINS
190. JOHN MAY
191. BENJAMIN DILLIN
192. WILLIAM GRAY
193. HENRY CLARK
194. JOHN WATSON
195. HENRY HARRIS
196. DAVID HARBOUR
197. NATHAN HALL
198. IGNATIOUS SIMS
199. THIS..NUCOM.... (disputed)
200. JOSEPH SCALES
201. WILLIAM TENCH
202. NATHANIEL BASSETT
203. JAMES SANFORD (disputed)
204. JOHN LACKEY
205. ELIAS BRIANT (disputed)
206. ROWLAND CHILES
207. ARIS VAUGHAN
208. THOMAS CRAGG
209. HENRY BARKSDALE
210. CHARLES HEBBERT (disputed)
211. STEPHEN KING (disputed)
212. RICHARD PARSLEY
213. JOHN BRAMMER
214. JULIUS SCRUGGS
215. JAMES PITMAN
216. SAMUEL CRUTCHFIELD (disputed
217. GREGORY DURHAM

Taken by SAMUEL READ. A Copy. Teste: J. WALLER for JAMES LYON.

Page 531: 25 April 1789. JOHN BURGESS, SENR. of Henry County to DAVID BURGESS and JOHN BURGESS, JR. of the same for the sum of one hundred pounds conveys 300 acres of land on the south side of Smith River...said tract formerly belonging to JACOB STARLING and conveyed to DANIEL RAMEY...Note: this deed is signed by DANIEL RAMEY. Signed: DANIEL RAMEY. Wit: PHIL. RYAN, JOSEPH BOULDIN, DAVID WITT. Proved in Henry Co., Va. 27 April 1789 by oath of DANIEL RAMEY.

Pages 531-532: 18 April 1789. SAMUEL JOHNSON of Henry County to WILLIAM LAURANCE of the same for the sum of fifty pounds sells land by estimate 100 acres more or less on both sides of Turkey Cock Creek joins JOE LYALL'S old order line. Signed: SAMUEL JOHNSON, BETTEY JOHNSON. Wit: ACHILLIS BALLINGER, WILLIAM CUNNINGHAM, JAMES JOHNSON, HENRY LAURENCE. Proved 27 April 1789.

Pages 533-534: 19 Sept 1788. Deed of Trust. ROBERT LORTON is indebted to GEORGE HAIRSTON in the consideration of the sum of five pounds and secures this with: one negro man, 1 black horse, all my stock and hogs, all household furniture, all crops. Note due 19 Sept 1789 after which date these goods may be sold. Signed: ROBERT LORTON. Wit: ROBERT ANDERSON, ALEXANDER JOYCE. Proved 11 Nov 1788.

****
DEED BOOK 4
****

Pages 1-2: 19 Sept 1788. ROBERT LORTON to GEORGE HAIRSTON, said LORTON indebted to HAIRSTON in the amount of sixty five pounds, he secures said debt with the following: one negro girl, 1 black horse, all his stock, cattle, household and kitchen furniture and all of his crop of corn. Signed: ROBERT LORTON. Wit: ROBERT ANDERSON, ALEXANDER JOYCE. Proved at a Court held for Henry County 11 Nov 1788.

Pages 3-4: 19 Nov 1788. SAMUEL S. ROBERTS of the county of Henry to JOSEPH AMBROSE of the same, for the sum of twenty pounds conveys 140 acres on the head of Home Creek being part of the land granted SAMUEL ROBERTS by patent at Richmond 2 Aug 1787. Signed: SAMUEL S. ROBERTS, SALLEY ROBERTS. Wit: MATHEW RAINEY, JOHN (X) STEPHENS, MOSES (X) WILSON. Proved 27 April and 25 May 1789.

Pages 5-6: 19 Nov 1788. SAMUEL ROBERTS of Henry County to MOSES WILSON of the same for the sum of thirty five pounds sells and conveys a parcel of land containing 160 acres on Home Creek, adjoining the lines of JOHN STEPHENS, ROBERT WEST and LOMAX & CO. Signed: SAMUEL S. ROBERTS, SALLEY (X) ROBERTS. Wit: JOHN (X) STEPHENS, MATHEW RAINEY, JOSEPH (X) AMBROSE. Proved 25 May 1789.

Pages 7-8: 8 June 1789. JOHN WARD of Campbell County, Va. to JAMES COX of Henry Co., Va. for the sum of one hundred pounds sells a tract of land containing 200 acres on both sides of Smith River and Running (Runnet) Bag Creek. Signed: JOHN WARD. Wit: EDMOND SWEENY, JOHN JAMES, JAMES (X) INGRUM, EZEKILL TALBOTT. Proved 29 June 1789.

Pages 9-10: 25 Feb 1789. THOMAS SMITH and SALLY SMITH his wife of Henry County to WILLIAM BANKS of the same for and in consideration of one hundred pounds sells and conveys 300 acres of land on Mill Creek and Rackoon Branch, joins Chiles old line (now Farris'). Signed: THOMAS SMITH. Wit: GEORGE HAIRSTON, A. HUGHES, THOMAS STOVALL. Proved 29 June 1789.

Pages 11-12: 19 Nov 1788. SAMUEL ROBERTS of Henry County to JOHN STEPHENS, both of Henry County, for and in consideration of the sum of twenty pounds sell a parcel of land on Home Creek being 100 acres more or less. Signed: SAMUEL ROBERTS, SALLEY ROBERTS. Wit: MATHEW RAINEY, MOSES (X) WILSON, JOSEPH (X) AMBROSE. Proved 27 April 1789.

Pages 12-13: 10 Feb 1789. SUSANAH CAMERON of Henry County to JOHN STAPLES of the same for and in consideration of one black mare, valued at thirty pounds, sell and conveys one-third part of a tract of land on Horsepasture Creek where she now lives. This one-third part being her dower of the 400 acre that that he deceased husband JOSEPH CAMMERON died seized and possessed of. Her son JESSE CAMMERON sold the other part to said JOHN STAPALES. Signed: SUSANNAH CAMERON. Wit: GEORGE FULCHER, JOHN NORTON, JOSEPH CAMERON. Proved 25 May 1789.

Pages 14-15: 5 March 1787. JOSEPH SOWELL and MARY his wife of Henry County and HAMON CRITZ to JOHN MARR for and in consideration of two hundred fifty eight pounds, sells and conveys three tracts of land containing 318 acres more or less. Land on Stones Creek, tract (1) 212 acres on both sides of the Creek with the plantation and mill where LOWELL now lives, it being part of a larger tract formerly the property of JOHN WILDRICK BENDER, deceased and willed by him to his daughter MARY SOWELL wife of JOSEPH SOWELL (2) 56 acres surveyed by JOSEPH SOWELL and joins the above tract and JAMES BREWER (3) 50 acres purchased by SOWELL of HAMON CRITZ though never received in fee simple. Signed: JOSEPH SOWELL, MARY (X) SOWELL, HAMON CRITZ. Wit: ABRM. PENN, ROBERT HUDSPETH, JOHN DILLARD. Proved 8 Oct 1787.

Page 20: 29 Jan 1789. EDWARD SMITH and JOSEPH MORTON of Pittsylvania County, Va. to ACHILLIS BALLENGER of Henry County for the sum of one hundred seventy pounds for a tract of land on both sides of Turkey Cock Creek by estimate being 425 acres. Signed: EDWARD SMITH, JOSEPH MORTON. Wit: SAMUEL JOHNSON, ANDREW FORD, JOHN OLIVER, ELIJAH SMITH.

Pages 21-22: 31 Aug 1789. EZEKEL MORRIS of Henry County to BENJAMIN KINSEY of the same for the sum of four pounds sells land on the north fork of Rock Castle Creek being 20 acres. Signed: BENJA. KINSEY. No witness. Received of BENJAMIN KINSEY the sum of four pounds, signed BENJA. KINSEY.

Pages 23-24: 31 Aug 1789. BENJAMIN KINSEY,JR. of Henry County to GEORGE MABRY, JR. of the same for the consideration of one hundred pounds sells land on both sides of Rock Castle Creek, beginning on the north fork of Rock Castle Creek to the top of the Ridge being 150 acres. Signed: BENJAMIN (X) KINSEY. No witness. Proved 31 Aug 1789.

Pages 24-26: 17 Aug 1789. MILES JENNINGS of Wilks County, Georgia to BALLENGER WADE of Henry County, Virginia in consideration of two negro boys, sell and convey 2 tracts of land on the south side of the Mayo River, adjoining GEORGE TAYLOR, BRADLEY SMITH and JESSE ATKISSON. Containing 215 acres (1) by survey dated 3 April 1749 being 80 acres (2) conveyed by deed from GEORGE TAYLOR for 135 acres. Signed: MILES JENNINGS. Wit: GEORGE TAYLOR, JOSIAH TAYLOR, SAMUEL C. MORRIS, JOHN DILLARD, JAMES TAYLOR, JR.

Pages 26-28: 17 Aug 1789. MILES JENNINGS of Wilkes County, Georgia to JOHN DILLARD of Henry County, Virginia for the consideration of two negroes, by his attorney GEORGE TAYLOR, sells and conveys 3 tracts of land being on both sides of the North Fork

of the Mayo River joins JESSE ATKINS, JOHN EASLEY and
WILLIAM HAIZE a total acreage of 1,112 acres...(1)
185 acres patented 12 May 1759 (2) 474 acres patented
1 March 1781 (3) 453 acres patent 1 March 1781...joins
DANIEL GOLDSBY and LAMBRETH DODSON. Signed: MILES
JINNINGS. Wit: BALLENGER WADE, GEORGE TAYLOR, SAMUEL
C. MORRIS, JOSIAH TAYLOR, JAMES TAYLOR, JR.

Pages 29-30: 4 Nov 1788. PHILIP RYAN and his wife
OBEDIANCE RYAN of Henry County to GEORGE
HAIRSTON of the same for debt of two hundred pounds
gives Deed of Trust...land on the north side of Smith
River containing by patent 150 acres, it being the
land that was conveyed by the executors of MERRY WEBB,
deceased. Signed: PHIL. RYAN, OBEDIANCE RYAN. Wit:
JOSEPH GOODWIN, JOHN PACE, HENRY BUTLER. Memo: Should
PHILIP RYAN pay his debt of two hundred pounds by the
25th December 1789 this deed to be of no effect.

Pages 31-32: 1789. JOHN KOGAR and ELIZABETH KOGER,
his wife of Henry County, Patrick Parish
to GEORGE PENN, JR. for the consideration of four
hundred pounds sell and conveys a tract of land on
the branches of the Mayo River containing 386 acres
adjoining JORDON'S line. Signed: JOHN (X) KOGAR. No
witness.

Pages 32-33: 20 Jan 1789. ISAAC CLOUD of Surry
County, North Carolina to ISAAC PENNING-
TON of Henry County, Virginia for the sum of thirty
pounds sells and conveys unto PENNINGTON 167 acres of
land in Henry County on Elk Creek adjoining the lines
of: MARR, HANBY. Signed: ISAAC CLOUD. Wit: JOSEPH
FRANUS, ANTHONY STREET, RICHARD (X) DAVISON, SAMUEL
KING. Proved 31 Aug 1789.

Pages 33-34: 31 Aug 1789. JOHN MARR and his wife
SUSANAH MARR of Henry County to WARHAM
EASLEY for the sum of sixty pounds sell and convey
land on the Little Dan River, being part of an order
called Bell's Order...crosses the Sandy Creek and
contains 115 acres. Signed: JOHN MARR. Wit: none.

Page 35: 31 Aug 1789. Bill of Sale. We are hereunto
moving and more especially for the love and
goodwill we have to our lawful sister MARY REYNOLDS
and her lawful heirs for ever give right, title to
a certain negro boy named DANIEL who was the property
of our brother DAVID REYNOLDS, deceased. To her to
possess upon her arrival of age 18 years or her mar-
riage, whichever may happen first. Signed: MOSES

REYNOLDS, JESSE REYNOLDS, ARCHALUS REYNOLDS, BARTUS REYNOLDS, REUBEN REYNOLDS, MILLENTON REYNOLDS. Wit: none.

Page 36: 31 Aug 1789. In the Presence of the Court. Bond of HENRY LYNE to serve as Sheriff of Henry County. Signed: JOHN PULLIAM, JAMES TAYLOR, JAMES LYON, W. KING COLE, JOHN SALMON, BALLENGER WADE, THOMAS NUNN, GEORGE HAIRSTON and BALD. ROWLAND.

Pages 37-39: 1 June 1789. Deed of Trust from DAVID LANIER and MARY LANIER his wife of Henry County to JOHN OSBORNE of Petersburg Town...Said LANIER being indebted unto JAMES CAMPBELL and LUKE WHEELER, partners in Trade, in the amount of four hundred twenty four pounds and eighteen shillings nine pence. LANIER places secures with: all those tracts in Henry County being land he purchased of PATRICK HENRY and GEORGE LUMPKIN, one tract he now resides on of 350 acres on the Smith River and Mulberry Creek joins lands of JOHN FONTAINE and JOSEPH BOULDING, the latter on Marrowbone Creek containing 272 acres. After 1 May 1789 land to be sold if payment has not been made. Signed: DAVID LANIER, MARY LANIER, JOHN OSBORNE. Wit: JOHN ROWLAND, THOMAS EAST, BENJAMIN LANIER. Proved 28 Sept 1789.

Pages 39-40: 2 May 1789. Deed of Trust from DAVID LANIER of Henry County to JOHN ALEXANDER and ROBERT WILLIAMS of Pittsylvania County. Said LANIER indebted four hundred twenty five pounds secures with land on Smith River, 350 acres purchased of PATRICK HENRY also one negro boy named PETER, one wagon, 8 head horses, 30 head cattle...on condition that the said LANIER pay a certain debt due FREELAND & LENOX in the amount of three hundred pounds also another due DAVID ROSS on a Judgement Bond given unto JOHN REDD in behalf of the said ROSS. Signed: DAVID LANIER. Wit: BENJAMIN LANIER, THOMAS EAST. Proved 28 Sept 1789.

Pages 42-42: 23 Sept 1789. THOMAS JAMISON of Franklin County to JOHN JAMISON of Henry County for one hundred pounds sells and conveys a tract of land containing 350 acres adjoining HARRIS' line (on an unnamed creek). Signed: THOMAS JAMISON, HANNAH (X) JAMISON. Wit: JOHN NORRIS, HENRY HARRIS, THOMAS JAMISON, JR.

Pages 42-43: 28 Sept 1789. JOSEPH KING of Henry County to MICHAEL MC DANIEL of the same

for five pounds sells land on the Little fork of
Reedy Creek being 101 acres more or less...part of a
150 acre tract granted KING 1 Feb 1781 at Richmond.
Signed: JOSEPH KING. Proved 28 Sept 1789.

Pages 45-46: 23 June 1788. GEORGE SUMPTER of Henry
County, Patrick Parish to JOSEPH DILLION
of the same for a certain sum conveys and sells 277
acres land on the head of Horsepasture Creek adjoining
JOHN WATSON and the Waggon Road. Signed: GEORGE SUMP-
TER, ELIZABETH SUMPTER. Wit: SAMUEL CRITCHFIELD,
LARKING TURNER, DAVID (X) CHADWELL.

Pages 46-47: 5 Aug 1789. SAMUEL CLACK to JOHN DILLARD
and DAVID CLACK, trustees for MARY FRANCE,
wife of HOMON FRANCE and others...for natural love and
affection and fifty pounds said SAMUEL CLACK gives
and sells unto JOHN DILLARD and DAVID CLACK a negro
wench named SALL and her child JUSY...for the use of
MARY FRANCE during her natural life and then to her
children. Signed: SAMUEL CLACK.

Pages 48-49: 8 April 1787. GEORGE WATKINS of Surry
County, North Carolina to WARSHAM EASLEY
of Henry County for the sum of fifteen hundred pounds
sell and conveys land on the west side of the Little
Dan River and on both sides of Johnsons Creek (no
quantity given). Signed: GEORGE (X) WATKINS. Wit:
JABUS FISHER, WILLIAM SCAIFE, SR., WILLIAM SCAIFE, JR.
Proved 20 Nov 1789.

Pages 49-50: 20 Nov 1789. Bill of Sale, PHILIP RYAN
being indebted to MARY ROWLAND, son
JOSEPH RYAN and JOHN RYAN his younger son in the
amount of one hundred two pounds sells and conveys to
them three negros, JACOB, HAMPTON and BLACKSMITH, 3
feather beds and furniture, all his stock of cattle
and hoggs. Signed: PHILIP RYAN. Wit: JOHN SALMON,
THADDEOUS SALMON. Proved 30 Nov 1789.

Pages 50-51: 28 Nov 1789. NICHOLAS COGAR (KOGAR) to
ADAM TURNER both of Henry County, for the
sum of sixty pounds KOGER sells land on Smith River,
with lines of THOMAS HUFF and opposite THOMAS HAR-
BOUR'S corner on Smith River and crosses Buffalow
Creek containing 250 acres. Signed: NICHOLAS KOGER.

Pages 53-54: 6 Oct 1789. JOHN PARR, SR. of Henry
County to ARTHUR PARR of the same, for
love and affection he bears his son, grants him two
parcels of land on the Mayo River...on the south side

212 acres and the other tract 148 acres. Signed: JOHN PARR. Wit: none. Proved 30 Nov 1789.

Page 55: 27 Oct 1789. JOHN FOSSIE to JOHN REDD both of Henry County. JOHN FOSSIE sells to said REDD one negro WILL 16 years of age in consideration of thirty seven pounds, 1 shilling, 8 pence. Signed: JOHN FOSSIE. Wit: WILLIAM STOKES, FRANCIS COX. . . Memo: If JOHN FOSSIE will pay the sum above JOHN REDD will return the said negro by the 25th of November next.

Page 56: 28 May 1789. SAMUEL JORDON of Buckingham County for the love and affection he bears unto his daughter CAROLINE MATILDA ROSE and her husband HUGH ROSE all said JORDON'S right to a tract of land he possesses in Henry County on Grassy Creek, acreage 2400 acres...Provided that the money arising from the sales be vested in lands in Amherst. Signed: SAMUEL JORDON. Wit: JOHN LINDSLEY, THOMAS JARVIS, JOHN NICHOLAS, ROBERT NICHOLAS. Proved 25 Jan 1790.

Pages 56-57: 28 Dec 1789. JAMES LYON of Henry County to MILLER WOODSON EASLEY of the same for and in consideration of the love for his daughter MARY EASLEY wife of M. W. EASLEY, he gives and conveys land on both sides of the Mayo River containing 167 acres. Signed: JAMES LYON. Proved 25 Jan 1790.

Page 58: 20 Jan 1790. FREDERICK FULKERSON of Henry County to MANNING HILL of the same, for and in consideration of fifty pounds sells land on the South Mayo River containing 156 acres. Signed: FREDERICK FULKERSON. Proved 25 Jan 1790.

Pages 59-60: 25 Jan 1790. JOHN COGAR of Henry County to WILLIAM SOWELL of the same for and in consideration of fifty pounds sells and conveys 33 acres of land on the waters of Cogers Creek...by patent 1 Sept 1780. Signed: JOHN (X) KOGER, ELIZABETH KOGER. Proved Jan 1790.

Pages 60-61: 21 Jan 1790. GEORGE BLAKEY of Henry County to MARKHAM LOVEL of the same, for one hundred pounds sells a parcel of land on the Little Beaver Creek containing 300 acres more or less joins HOLMS corner and JAMES ANTHONY. Signed: GEORGE BLAKEY. Wit: JOSEPH ANTHONY, JAMES ANTHONY, WILLIAM WHITSILT.

Pages 62-63: 24 Sept 1784. STEPHEN HARD of Henry

County to WILLIAM AUSTIN late of the county aforesaid for the sum of forty pounds sells land on Poplar Camp Creek containing 100 acres more or less. Signed: STEPHEN HEARD. Wit: JAMES MASON, JOHN HEARD, STEPHEN (X) HEARD, JR. Proved 24 March 1785 and 25 Jan 1790.

Page 64-65: 20 Feb 1790. JOSHUA HUDSON of Henry County to ROBERT HALL and GOLDEN DAVIDSON of the same, for and in consideration of the sum of ten pounds sells and conveys land, by survey, dated 10 March 1786 to be 82 acres on the branches of the Mayo River and Russells Creek. Signed: JOSHUA HUDSON. Wit: none. Proved 25 Feb 1790.

Pages 65-66: 21 Aug 1789. Deed of Trust between ACHILLIS BALLENGER and CALLAND & SMITH, Merchants. Said BALLENGER is indebted in the amount of seventy five pounds and conveys a parcel of land being 325 acres more or less, it being the balance of 425 acres which he purchased of JOSEPH MORTON as will appear by a deed from JOSEPH MORTON and EDWARD SMITH and recorded in Henry County. To include the plantation and all land that lies on the north side of Wells' Road and one negro wench named LIZA. Signed: ACHILLIS BALLENGER. Wit: LA. TOMPKINS, JR., SAMUEL JOHNSTON, JAMES ISHAM.

Pages 67-68: 2 Aug 1788. JOHN NORTON of Henry County to GARROT WILLIAMS of the same for the consideration of forty five pounds sells a tract of land on Jennings Creek containing 250 acres adjoining the lines of JOHN NICOLS, JOHN MARR, EDMOND WINSTON. Signed: JOHN NORTON. Wit: DANIEL TAYLOR, THOMAS STOVALL, GEORGE PENN. Proved 2 Aug 1788.

Pages 69-70: 22 Feb 1790. JOHN KOGER of Henry County to WILLIAM CARTER of the same, for and in consideration of fifteen pounds sells a 260 acre tract of land on the north side of the South Fork of Goblintown Creek, joins ADAMS and CALLAWAY. Signed: JOHN (X) KOGER.

Pages 69-70: 7 Sept 1790. WILLIAM TANZEY of Henry County, North Carolina (??) to BENNETT POSEY of Henry County, Virginia for the sum of sixteen pounds sells 350 acres, by patent 9 Feb 1781, being on the South Fork of Bowens Creek. Signed: WILLIAM TANZEY. Wit: CHARLES HIBBERT, RICHARD BAKER, ISAAC HOLLINSWORTH.

Pages 72-74: 25 March 1790. ALEXANDER HUNTER of Patrick Parish, Henry County, Planter, for the love, good will and affection he bears toward his loving daughter RUTH HORD grants, gives and conveys a parcel of land containing 400 acres and being on the branches of Horsepasture Creek adjoining GREGORY DURAM, JESSE WITT, JOSEPH MORRIS. RUTH HORD is the wife of JOHN HORD. Signed: ALEXANDER HUNTER. Proved 29 March 1798.

Pages 74-75: 26 March 1790. JAMES TAYLOR of Henry County to WILLIAM DEAL of the same for fifteen pounds conveys land on Spoon Creek adjoining the plantations of WILLIAM DEAL and JOHN MEDLEY, being 75 acres. Signed: JAMES TAYLOR.

Pages 75-76: 26 Mar 1790. WILLIAM WITT of Henry County to JOHN CAVORN of the same, for the consideration of Twelve pounds sells and conveys 50 acres land on the waters of Blackberry Creek. Signed: WILLIAM WITT. Wit: HENRY LYNE, JOHN PYRTLE, THOMAS CUNNINGHAM. Proved 29 Mar 1790.

Pages 76-77: 29 Mar 1790. JAMES POTEET of Henry County to JAMES NOWLING of the same, for and in consideration of the sum of one hundred pounds conveys a tract of 250 acres being on the White Oak Creek. Signed: JAMES POTEET. Wit: none.

Pages 78-79: 23 Feb 1790. CHARLES HIBBERT and LYDIA HIBBERT his wife of Henry County to JOHN DUNCAN of the same for twenty pounds sells a tract of land on both sides Praythor's Fork of the North Fork of the North Mayo River being 404 acres and joins RICKMAN'S. Signed: CHARLES HIBBERT, LYDIA (X) HIBBERT.

Pages 79-80: 29 Mar 1790. JOHN DUNCAN and his wife JANE DUNCAN of Henry County to SAMUEL VESS of the same sells for the consideration of ten pounds 200 acres of land on both sides of Prathors Fork of the North Mayo River. Signed: JOHN DUNCAN.

Page 81: 22 Jan 1790. HENRY SUMPTER of Henry County to ISHAM CRADOCK of the same, for the sum of twenty pounds conveys 300 acres of land on Rock Run Creek and the plantation whereon the said CRADOCK now lives...joins ABSOLUM ADAMS, JOHN GOING. Signed: HENRY SUMPTER. Wit: GEORGE PENN, BENJAMIN COOPER, HENRY LYNE.

Page 82: 26 March 1790. ANTHONY TITTLE of Henry

County to DAVID TITTLE of the same for the sum of twenty pounds sells and conveys a tract of land containing 201 acres by patent on the Goblingtown Creek. Signed: ANTHONY TITTLE.

Page 83: 23 Nov 1789. THOMAS MAN RANDOLPH of Goochland County to JOHN STAPLES of Henry County for the consideration of one hundred twenty five pounds sells and conveys a tract of land on both sides of the north fork of the Mayo River containing 130 acres more or less. It being part of a tract sold by THOMAS M. RANDOLPH to JOSEPH ROBERTS, deceased and sold by JOHN ROBERTS, son of JOSEPH ROBERTS, to JOHN STAPLES it being that part of the said tract that was left JOHN ROBERTS by his deceased father. Signed: THOMAS MANN RANDOLPH. Wit: ABRAM PENN, GEORGE PENN, THOMAS COOPER.

Pages 84-85: 2 Mar 1790. PETER LEAK of Henry County to WILLIAM MOORE of the same, for and in consideration of one hundred ninety pounds sells a tract of land on the waters of Marrowbone Creek containing 240 acres. Signed: PETER LEAK. Wit: none.

Pages 85-86: 9 Apr 1790. HENRY SUMPTER of Henry County to THOMAS BOLLING of the same, for the sum of twenty five pounds conveys a tract of land on Rock Run Creek of the Smith River containing 100 acres. Signed: HENRY SUMPTER. Wit: JAMES BAKER, CHARLES SMITH, SAMUEL CRITCHFIELD, GEORGE REIORS (?). Proved 28 Apr 1790.

Page 87: 28 April 1790. Bond of WILLIAM TUNSTALL to service as Sheriff of Henry County with GEORGE HAIRSTON and ARCH. HUGHES as his securities for the said bond. Proved 28 April 1790.

Page 88: 24 Apr 1790. CHARLES BERNARD of Henry County to WILLIAM JAMES MAYO of the same for the consideration of fifty pounds sells and conveys a tract of land on Sycamore Creek containing 130 acres, joins land of WILLIAM HANCOCK and JOHN LEVISTONES. Signed: CHARLES BERNARD. Wit: JESSE CORN, WILLIAM HANCOCK, SAMUEL LAYNE.

Pages 89-90: 20 April 1790. SAMUEL HILTON of Henry County to WILLIAM BURNET of the same, for and in consideration of the sum of fifty pounds sells a 364 acre tract of land on Jacks Creek. Signed SAMUEL HILTON. Wit: WILLIAM GARDNER, JOSEPH HURTT, MOSES HURTT.

Pages 90-91: 20 April 1790. WILLIAM GRAVES and MARY GRAVES to THOMAS GRAVES all of Henry County for consideration received, convey a tract of land on the south side of Smith River with the old order line of WILLIAM GRAVES containing 100 acres and said land now in the possession of COL. GEORGE HAIRSTON. Signed: WILLIAM GRAVES, MARY GRAVES. Wit: WILLIAM MARTIN, DANIEL HAMMOCK, POLLY GRAVES, JR.

Pages 92-93: 26 Apr 1790. JACOB CAYTON (CATON) of Henry County to WILLIAM CATON of the same for a consideration conveys land on the branches of Drag Creek containing 100 acres on Morgan's Road, joins WILLIAM COX. Signed: JACOB (X) CAYTON. Wit: WILLIAM MOORE, JACOB (X) DILLENDER, JAMES (X) EDWARDS.

Pages 94-95: 26 Apr 1790. JOSEPH MORRIS and SAMUEL C. MORRIS to JONADAB WADE all of Henry County, for the consideration of one hundred twenty five pounds sells a tract of 150 acres on the waters of Little Horsepasture Creek...joins: PETER LEAK, ALEXANDER HUNTER and JAMES OFFICER. Signed: JOSEPH MORRIS, MARY MORRIS, SAMUEL C. MORRIS. Wit: PETER LEAK, BENJAMIN KANNON. Proved 26 Apr 1790.

Pages 95-97: 26 Apr 1790. JOSEPH MORRIS of Henry County to PETER LEAK of the same, for the consideration of one hundred twenty five pounds sells a tract of land containing 154 acres on Horsepasture Creek...joins JONADAB WADE, ALEXANDER HUNTER, WILLIAM SHELTON and JOHN DILLARD. Signed: JOSEPH MORRIS, MARY MORRIS. Wit: JONDAB WADE, BENJAMIN KANNON. Proved 26 Apr 1790.

Pages 97-98: 6 Nov 1789. LEWIS HANCOCK of Henry County to JOHN HANCOCK of the same, for the consideration of one hundred fifty pounds sells a tract of land on both sides of Sycamore Creek containing 300 acres and joins THOMAS MORRISON. Signed: LEWIS HANCOCK. Wit: WILLIAM AMOS, BENJAMIN HANCOCK, MAJOR HANCOCK. Proved Apr Court 1790.

Pages 99-100: 20 Apr 1790. RICHARD MITCHELL and his wife ELIZABETH MITCHELL of Henry County to JOHN MANNEN of the same, for and in consideration of one hundred thirty pounds sells and conveys a tract of land on Beaver Creek containing 277 acres also on a branch called Simms Creek with the lines of THOMAS COOPER and ROBERT STOCKTON. Signed: RICHARD MITCHELL, ELIZABETH MITCHELL. Wit: MARTIN BUNCH, DAVID BUNCH, CHARLES BURNETT. Proved 26 Apr 1790

Pages 100-101: 26 Apr 1790. GEORGE WALLER and ANN WALLER his wife of Henry County to JOHN WALLER of the same convey in fee simple a part of a tract of land on Smith River that GEORGE WALLER purchased of ABRAM PENN this portion of said tract containing 100 acres. Signed: GEORGE WALLER, ANN WALLER. Wit: SAMUEL SHUMATE, HENRY JONES.

Pages 101-102: 18 Apr 1790. JOHN PARR of Henry County to GEORGE CORN of the same, for and in consideration of fifty pounds sells and conveys a tract of land on Meadowry Creek containing 100 acres...as mentioned in the Patent. Signed: JOHN PARR. Proved 26 Apr 1790.

Pages 103-104: 22 Feb 1790. FRANCIS COX of Henry County to THOMAS RICHARDSON of the same, for the consideration of fifty pounds conveys a tract of land on a branch of Leatherwood Creek called the Fishing Fork...on both sides thereof... lines: NICHOLAS AKIN. According to a patent issued to PETER PERKINS. Signed: FRANCIS COX, MARY (X) COX. Wit: JOHN WINN, JOHN OLDHAM, ELLIOTT (X) WOODS, THOMAS RICHARDSON. Proved 26 Apr 1790.

Pages 104-105: 1 Apr 1790. JOHN PELFREE of Henry County to WILLIAM PELFREE of the same, for the love and affection he bears his son WILLIAM PELFREE does grant and convey land on the north side of Smith River containing 38 acres. Signed: JOHN PELFREE. Wit: HENRY LYNE, JAMES BAKER, JOHN (X) PELFREE, JR. Proved 26 Apr 1790.

Pages 105-106: 12 Apr 1790. JAMES LYON of Henry County to HUMBERSTON LYON of the same, for love and affection and goodwill towards his son HUMBERSTON LYON does grant 222 acres by survey on Russells Creek. Signed: JAMES LYON.

Page 107: 12 Apr 1790. HUMPHREY POSEY of Henry County to THOMAS POSEY of the same, for the love and affection he bears his son does convey the land that came to me from HARISON HOBART, it being 80 acres on both sides of Smith River...lines...where JOSEPH BOLLING formerly lived...surveyed by DAVID HAILY...goes to the mouth of Bowens Creek. Signed: HUMPHREY POSEY. Wit: HENRY LYNE, GEORGE WALLER, JR.

Pages 108-109: 27 Feb 1788. JAMES MEREDITH of Henry County to JOHN ROWLAND of the same, for the consideration of one hundred eighty pounds sells and conveys a tract of land on the south side of Smith River containing 200 acres more or less with the lines of JOHN ALEXANDER, BRICE MARTIN, WALTER K. COLE, REUBEN PAYNE and SAMUEL BUCKLES. Signed: JAMES (X) MEREDITH. Wit: MARTIN BUNCH, DAVID BUNCH. Proved April Court 1790.

Pages 109-110: 23 April 1790. MATHEW RAINEY of Henry County to JOHN HAMMOND of the same, for and in consideration of seventy five pounds conveys 225 acres joins with FRED RICKEL'S field so called Meeting House Fork of Cascade Creek to a sour wood in meeting house branch. Signed: MATHEW RAINEY, JUDITH RAINEY. Wit: NAT. (X) DURHAM, WILLIAM (X) STEPHENS, WILLIAM C. R. HAMMOND. Proved 26 Apr 1790.

Pages 111-112: 24 Apr 1790. ANDREW REA of Henry County to EDWARD DANIEL of the same, for the consideration of one hundred pounds sells and conveys a tract of land containing 211 acres on Marrowbone Creek and joins: GEORGE HAIRSTON, THOMAS JAMISON, GOODWIN MAYSE, DAVID MAYSE. Signed: ANDREW REA. Wit: EDWARD ADAMS, JESSE MURPHY, GOODWIN MAYSE. Proved 26 Apr 1790.

Page 113: 8 July 1790. JOHN DAVIS of the District of 96 state of South Carolina to JAMES MEREDITH of Henry County for the consideration of fifty pounds conveys a tract of 269 acres by survey, in Henry County on Beaver Creeks waters. Signed: JOHN DAVIS. Wit: WILLIAM RYAN, DAVID WILLIS, SAMUEL BIRD, JOHN (X) BIRD.

Pages 114-115: 26 April 1790. SAMUEL VESS of Henry County to PETER VESS of the same, for the consideration of ten pounds sells and conveys 100 acres land, it being part of a larger survey on Prathors fork of the north fork of the North Mayo River. Signed: SAMUEL VESS, CATHERINE VESS.

Page 115: 27 Apr 1790. ELIZABETH SHELTON does hereby discharge and acquit WILLIAM JOYCE as her attorney from all further proceedings. Signed: ELIZABETH (X) SHELTON.

Pages 116-117: 26 Apr 1790. JOHN PYRTLE, SR. of Henry County to JOHN PYRTLE, JR. of the same, does convey a tract of land containing 250 acres on the waters of Reedy Creek. Signed: JOHN PYRTLE, SENR.

Pages 117-118: 27 Apr 1790. ABRAHAM PENN, WILLIAM WHITSITT and ELENOR WHITSITT his wife of Henry County to BENJAMIN JONES of Prince William County for the sum of two hundred twenty five pounds sells and conveys a tract of land on both sides of Little Beaver Creek also on Red Bank Creek containing by estimate 550 acres, with the lines of: GEORGE BLAKEY, WILLIAM BRETHART, ROBERT STOCKTON, THOMAS COOPER and JAMES ANTHONY. Signed: ABRAHAM PENN, WILLIAM WHITSITT, ELENOR WHITSITT. Proved 27 Apr 1790.

Pages 119-120: 26 April 1790. MUNFORD SMITH of Henry County to JAMES LANDERS of the same, for fifty pounds sells 70 acres of land on both sides of Burds Run, a south fork of Ararott River. Signed: MUNFORD SMITH. Wit: SAMUEL STAPLES, JAMES PIGG, DAVID CLARK, RICHARD STOCKTON, DEVERIX GILLIAM.

Pages 120-121: 21 Apr 1790. JACOB MC CRAW of Surry County, North Carolina to WILLIAM HIGGINBOTTOM of Henry County for the sum of fifty pounds sells land on Lovings Creek near Wards Gap being 111 acres. Signed: JACOB MCCRAW. Wit: JAMES ARMSTRONG, JAMES LOYD, PAUL MCMILLION. Proved 27 Apr 1790.

Page 122: 14 Dec 1789. Deed of Trust from JOHN HAILEY of Henry County to CALLAND & SMITH, Merchants of Pittsylvania County...said HAILEY indebted in the amount of twenty seven pounds, 8 shilling, 3 pence, secures said debt with: 6 head cattle, 5 head sheep and a sorrel mare. Signed: JOHN HAILEY. Wit: SAMUEL TOMPKINS, JR., JOHN TOMPKINS. Proved 27 Apr 1790.

Page 123: 15 Apr 1790. RICHARD CORNWELL and his wife PEGGY CORNWELL of Henry County to JAMES MASTIN for and in a valuable consideration do hereby convey 75 acres of land on Rugg Creek, it being part of a survey of 132 acres. Signed: RICHARD CORNWELL. Wit: JOSEPH MARTIN, WILLIAM MARTIN, SUSANAH MARTIN. Proved 26 Apr 1790.

Page 124: 6 Feb 1790. Wilkes County, Georgia - MILES JENNINGS of said county and state did convey unto BALLENGER WADE a tract of land in Henry County, 215 acres...the wife of said MILES JENNINGS does hereby relinquish her right of dower to this transaction. SUSANNAH JENNINGS, wife of MILES JENNINGS.

Page 125: 16 Nov 1790. Wilkes County, Georgia - MILES

JENNINGS did convey unto JOHN DILLARD 1,112 acres of land in Henry County...SUSANAH JENNINGS wife of MILES JENNINGS hereby relinquishes her right of dower.

Page 126: 25 April 1792. NANCY THOMAS of Wilkes County, Georgia, the mother of MILES JENNINGS, does relinquish her right of dower in the transaction whereby her son did convey unto JOHN DILLARD 1,112 acres of land on both sides of Mayo River in Henry County.

Pages 126-127. Bill of Sale. THOMAS DICKERSON, SENR. to CHARLES DICKERSON for two hundred fifty pounds sells the following negros: 1 fellow named MOSES, one negro wench called ESTHER, one wench called BARBARY, one boy GILBERT, one wench SARAH, PHEBE and child LATT, one dark bay horse called SOPHIA and one dark bay stallion. Signed: THOMAS DICKERSON, SENR. Wit: DAVID DICKERSON, NELSON DICKERSON, GEORGE TUNSTALL. Proved 31 May 1790.

Pages 127-128: 24 July 1790. MICHAEL DILLINGHAM of Henry County to ARISTIPHUS BAUGHAN of the same for sixty pounds sells and conveys land on Reedy Creek adjoining his own land and WILLIAM HORD. By estimate, 190 acres. Signed: MICHAEL (X) DILLINGHAM. Proved 25 July 1790.

Pages 129-131: 21 June 1790. ELIZABETH ANTHONY, MARK ANTHONY and BOWLING ANTHONY of Wilks County, Georgia to ZACKERIAH PHILPOTT of Henry County for and in consideration of two hundred fifty pounds sells and conveys land on Beaver Creek by estimate 370 acres, joins AMBROSE JONES. Signed: ELIZABETH ANTHONY, MARK ANTHONY, BOWLING ANTHONY. Wit: THOMAS COOPER, JOHN BARKSDIL, THOMAS STOVALL, JOHN WHEAT. Proved 26 July 1790.

Pages 131-133: 14 Mar 1787. BENJAMIN HUBBARD of Henry County to JAMES OAKES of the same for and in consideration of thirty five pounds paid by JAMES ROBERTS of Henry County conveys 124 acres (said land was granted to THOMAS GRISHAM by patent at Williamsburg and recorded in Pittsylvania County) ...located on the south side of Smith River. Signed: BENJAMIN HUBBARD. Wit: GABRIEL ROBERTS, WILLIAM RICE, MARY RICE. Proved 26 July 1790.

Page 133: 27 July 1790. ELISHA WALLIN (WALDEN??) of Hawkins County, North Carolina hereby appoints his beloved friend STEPHEN LYON his attorney to recover by law a certain negro man slave by the name of JACK who was plundered from JOHN ROBERTS in the time of the last war by DANIEL CARLIN. Signed: ELISHA (X) WALLIN.

Pages 133-134: 30 Aug 1790. JOHN STAPLES of Henry County to ARCH. HUGHES of the same, for and in consideration of twenty five pounds conveys a parcel of land containing 80 acres by survey dated 19 May 1786 on the north side of the Mayo River. Signed: JOHN STAPLES. Proved 30 Aug 1790.

Page 135: 11 Aug 1790. JOHN WARD of Campbell County, Virginia to THOMAS JURDON of Henry County for the sum of two hundred pounds sells a tract of land containing by survey dated 2 Sept 1788, 230 acres being on Widgen Creek on the south side. Signed: JOHN WARD. Wit: GEORGE MABRY, DAVID CALDWELL. Proved 13 Aug 1790.

Pages 136-137: 22 May 1789. WILLIAM FORTNER of Henry County to JONAH FORTNER of the same, for fifty pounds sells land on the south side of Fall Creek containing 50 acres. Signed: WILLIAM (X) FORTNER. Wit: EDWARD TATUM, WILLIAM (X) HENSLEE, JOHN (X) FORTNER.

Pages 137-138: 23 Sept 1790. THOMAS CUMMINS of Montgomery County, Virginia to JOHN HENDERSON of Henry County for the sum of one hundred fifty pounds sells and conveys a tract of land by estimate to be 213 acres on both sides of Goblingtown Creek. Signed: THOMAS CUMMINS, SUSANAH (X) CUMMINS.

Pages 139-140: 24 Aug 1789. WILLIAM FORTNER of Henry County to JOHN FORTNER of the same, for the consideration of five pounds sells and conveys a tract of land being 50 acres more or less, it being part of a tract granted WILLIAM FORTNER by patent 15 April 1784. Signed: WILLIAM (X) FORTNER. Wit: EDWARD TATUM, JONAS (X) FORTNER, WILLIAM (X) HENSLEY.

Page 140: 19 Sept 1788. RICHARD REYNOLDS of Madison County, (Madison County, Virginia was not formed until 1792...in 1786 Madison County, Virginia was to later become a part of Kentucky)...appoints his beloved friend WILLIAM PERKINS, JR. to receive money due him and to pay all his just debts. Signed: RICHARD (X) REYNOLDS. Wit: ESAIAS HARBOUR, NICHOLAS KOGAR, JOEL HARBOUR, W. PERKINS, JR., DAVID PERKINS, WILLIAM SMITH.

Pages 141-142: 23 Sept 1790. ELEANOR WHITSITT, wife of WILLIAM WHITSITT relinquishes her right of dower to a deed executed to BENJAMIN JONES for 550 acres. Proved 25 Sept 1790.

Page 142: 23 Sept 1790. MARGARET BLAKEY wife of GEORGE BLAKEY relinquishes her right to dower in a deed executed to MARKHAM LOVELL for 300 acres.

Pages 143-144: 10 May 1790. HENRY VAUGHAN and FANNY VAUGHAN of Henry County to JOHN BURCHETT of the same for the sum of one hundred pounds sells land on Little Reedy Creek, being 100 acres more or less. Signed: HENRY (X) VAUGHAN. Wit: WILLIAM HEARD, WILLIAM WELLS, WILLIAM WARREN.

Pages 144-145: 25 Oct 1790. Bond of GEORGE HAIRSTON who is to be the Collector of the Taxes his securities being: ROBERT HAIRSTON, THOMAS JAMISON, JOHN REDD, JAMES ARMSTRONG, A. HUGHES, JOHN FONTAINE, JOHN MARR. Proved 25 Oct 1790.

Pages 146-147: 15 May 1790. GEORGE ADAMS of Pittsylvania County to JOHN OAKES of Henry County for the consideration of thirty pounds sells and conveys 100 acres lying on the north side of Smith River. Signed: GEORGE ADAMS. Wit: WILLIAM OAKES, BENJAMIN (X) SMITH, MARY MORGAN, JOHN (X) MORGAN, WILLIAM (X) WILSON. Proved 31 May 1790 & 26 Oct 1790.

Pages 147-148: 24 Apr 1790. CHARLES BARNARD of Henry County to SAMUEL LAYNE of the same, for fifty pounds sells a parcel of land containing 100 acres on the waters of Sycamore Creek. Signed: CHARLES BARNARD. Wit: WILLIAM J. MAYO, JESSE CORN, WILLIAM HANCOCK. Proved 29 Nov 1790.

Pages 149-150: 25 Sept 1788. RALPH SHELTON of Henry County to ELIZABETH TERRY of the same, for the consideration of two hundred pounds sells and conveys all that land with orchards, houses, etc on the east side of the Big Dan River containing 78 acres. Signed: RALPH SHELTON (X). Wit: ROBERT HUDSPETH, WILLIAM WILLIAMS, JOHN HOOKER.

Pages 150-151: 24 Apr 1790. CHARLES BARNARD of Henry County to WILLIAM HANCOCK of the same for the consideration of thirty five pounds sells 130 acres on the waters of Sycamore Creek. Signed:

CHARLES BARNARD. Wit: WILLIAM J. MAYO, JESSE CORN, MAJOR HANCOCK.

Page 152: 1790. WILLIAM THOMPSON of Henry County appoints JOHN CHEADLE of Prince Edward County to recover or receive of and from ROBERT EASTES and ELISHA EASTES executors of ELISHA EASTES, deceased of Lunenburg County all that part of the estate ELISHA EASTES, deceased which may fall to the share of my wife MARY THOMPSON. Also the sum due me from WILLIAM READER and the sum due me from MELICENT EASTES. Signed: WILLIAM THOMPSON, MARY (X) THOMPSON. Wit: THOMAS NUNN, NEWSOM PACE.

Page 153. I, ELIZABETH SHELTON of Henry County am hereunto moving and do appoint my friend EZEKIEL SHELTON my attorney to recover or received from ELIPHAZ SHELTON, JOHN NITE and THOMAS DUDLEY of rye in said county for the sum of five hundred pounds. Signed: ELIZABETH SHELTON. Wit: THOMAS BARTON, PETER ADAMS, JOHN LIMING.

Page 154: 20 Nov 1790. JOHN DILLARD of Henry County to WILLIAM HAYSE of the same for ten pounds sells and conveys 115 acres of land in the fork of the two Mayo Rivers...joins DANIEL GOOLDSBAYS on the north fork of Mayo River and said HAYSE and LAMBURT DODSON. Signed: JOHN DILLARD.

Pages 155-156: 29 Nov 1790. BRADLEY SMITH of Henry County to BALLENGER WADE of the same for forty pounds sells a tract of land on the branches of the Mayo River containing by patent 244 acres more or less...lines of: GEORGE TAYLOR, HENRY FEE and JESSE ATKINSON. Signed: BRADLEY (X) SMITH.

Pages 156-157: 29 Nov 1790. DANIEL GOLDSBAY of Henry County to ANDREW REA of the same, for fifty five pounds sells land on both sides of the Mayo River being land whereon the said DANIEL GOLDSBAY now lives, containing 120 acres more or less joins ANGLIN (formerly HARBOUR). Signed: DANIEL GOLDSBAY. Proved 29 Nov 1790.

Pages 158-159: 21 Oct 1790. NEHEMIAH PRATOR and BARTLETT REYNOLDS of Henry County and of Montgomery County to JOHN WATSON of Henry County for the sum of thirty pounds sell a 175 acre tract that was granted to NEHEMIAH PRATOR by patent dated 14 Feb 1784 and also part of another tract containing 10 acre by patent to the said REYNOLDS, all of which land being on the south prong of Kogers Creek adjoining said WATSON'S land he purchased of MARVEL NASH. Signed NEHEMIAH PRATOR (X), BARTLETT (X) REYNOLDS. Wit: JAMES PIGG, JOHN (X) CRUM, JOHN (X) DUNKAN.

Pages 159-161: 5 Aug 1790. JOHN WARD and his wife of Campbell County to WILLIAM MCALEXANDER of Henry County and JOHN MCALEXANDER of Amherst County for the sum of four hundred pounds sell and convey a tract of land containing 470 acres being part of a survey...the balance belonging to THOMAS JORDON, said land on the Little Widgen Creek, a branch of Smith River. The said land divided between WILLIAM and JOHN MCALEXANDER by dividing to WILLIAM a south west course laying next to his own land and divided by Little Widgen Creek. Payment acknowledged this date. Signed: JOHN WARD. Wit: ALEXANDER MCALEXANDER, JENNY (X) MCALEXANDER, GEORGE MABRY. Proved 27 Dec 1790.

Pages 161-163: 5 Aug 1790. JOHN WARD of Campbell County to WILLIAM MCALEXANDER of Henry County and JOHN MCALEXANDER of Amherst County for the sum of twenty pounds sells 128 acres by survey dated 2 Dec 1768 lying and being in Henry County, formerly Pittsylvania County on the draughts of Rockcastle Creek. Signed: JOHN WARD. Wit: ALEXANDER MCALEXANDER, JENNY (X) MCALEXANDER, GEORGE MABRY. Proved 17 Dec 1790.

Pages 162-163: 5 Aug 1790. JOHN WARD of Campbell County to WILLIAM MCALEXANDER of Henry County and JOHN MCALEXANDER of Amherst County for the sum of twenty pounds sells 250 acres of land by survey dated 20 Nov 1768 being in Henry County on the waters of Giles Creek beginning at the top of the mountain and joins KENDRICKS. Signed: JOHN WARD. Wit: ALEXANDER MCALEXANDER, JENNY (X) MCALEXANSER, GEORGE MABRY. Proved 27 Dec 1790.

Page 164: 3 Dec 1790. JOSEPH ALLET of Henry County does make over all his wordly estate to his beloved son GEORGE ALLET, first a gracious gift of one horse and two cows, one yearling, four head of hoggs and likeways all my household goods and furniture, all his working tools and shops. Likewise, to his beloved son ELIASE ALLET he makes a gracious gift of one sorrel mare, one heffer and three head of hoggs. He does hereby make over all of his wordly goods to his two sons. Signed: JOSEPH ALLET. Wit: DANIEL CAMELL, JOHN (X) TUGGLE, OBEDIAH (X) DICKERSON.

Pages 164-165: 31 July 1789. JOHN MARR of Henry County to SAMUEL CANNON of the same, for the consideration of sixty pounds sells a certain tract of land containing 200 acres on Kings Run near the old ford. Signed: JOHN MARR. Wit: RODE MOORE, DAVID ROWARK, HUGH LARIMORE.

Pages 166-167: 30 Aug 1790. STEPHEN LYON of Henry County to ROBERT WILSON of Campbell County...said LYON indebted to WILSON in the amount of six hundred nine pounds, fifteen shillings seven pence to be paid on or before 1 Jan 1791, being anxious to discharge said debt hereby assigns, sells one tract of land on the north fork of Russells Creek by estimate 290 acres, also one tract on Snow Creek in the state of North Carolina in Stokes County purchased of WILLIAM HICKMAN containing 360 acres more or less, also the following negros: JACK, SHADOCK, ISACK, ELIZABETH, CORMWAL, ANDERSON, HARRY and ISACK. Signed: STEPHEN LYON. Wit: ____ FONTAINE, SAMUEL STAPLES, ABRM. PENN.

Pages 167-168: 2 Dec 1788. JOHN BAKER, SENR. of Henry County to ABRAHAM PENN of the same for the sum of thirty pounds sells land being 81 acres more or less on the waters of Spoon Creek, it being the land and plantation where my family now lives. Signed: JOHN (X) BAKER, REBECCAH BAKER, his wife. Wit: SAMUEL STAPLES, THOMAS STOVALL, B. W. PHILPOTT. Proved 31 Aug 1789 and 27 Jan 1791.

Pages 168-170: 5 Oct 1787. WILLIAM LYNCH and BECKY LYNCH his wife of Henry County to ABRAHAM PENN all of Patrick Parish, for the sum of forty pounds sells and conveys a parcel of land by estimate to be 155 acres joins JOHN SPENCER'S field. Signed: WILLIAM LYNCH, BECKY LYNCH. Wit: JOHN MARR, GEORGE PENN, JOHN (X) MAGEHEE.

Pages 170-171: 20 Nov 1790. PHILLIP ANGLIN of Henry County to ANDREW REA of the same, for the consideration of seventy pounds sells a parcel of land containing 80 acres on the north side of the North Mayo River. Signed: PHILLIP (X) ANGLIN. Wit: JESSE ATKINSON, ZACKERIAH KING, MORRIS HUMPHREYS. Proved 20 Nov 1790.

Page 172: 25 Feb 1789. THOMAS SMITH and SARAH his wife of Henry County to DEVERIX GILLIAM of the same for ten pounds conveys 50 acres of land on the south side of the North Mayo River with CHILES old line (now FARRIS), Rackoon Branch, it being a parcel of land said SMITH exchanged with GILLIAM. Payment received this date. Signed: THOMAS SMITH. Wit: A. HUGHES, THOMAS STOVALL, BRETT STOVALL.

Page 173: 4 Dec 1790. THOMAS COOPER conveyed unto GEORGE HAIRSTON a tract of land containing 521 acres and now his wife SARAH COOPER does hereby relinquish her right of dower. Proved: 31 Jan 1791.

Pages 175-176: 4 Dec 1790. Dower release of SARAH COOPER wife of THOMAS COOPER to a deed he issued GEORGE HAIRSTON. Proved 31 Jan 1791.

Page 177: 16 Oct 1790. Prince Edward County, Virginia. PATRICK HENRY conveyed unto DAVID LANIER a tract of 350 acres being in Henry County and his wife DOROTHY HENRY does hereby relinquish her right of dower. Proved 31 Jan 1791.

Page 178: 11 March 1789. THOMAS SMITH did convey unto WILLIAM BANKS a tract of 300 acres... his wife SALLY SMITH relinquishes her dower right. Proved 31 Jan 1791.

Pages 179-180: 12 Oct 1789. ROBERT MEAD, attorney for WILLIAM MEAD of Bedford County sells unto CHARLES THOMAS of Henry County for sixty four pounds 19 shillings 4 pence 742 acres on Poplar Camp Creek which joins his own land. Signed: ROBERT MEAD. Wit: JAMES NOWLIN, THOMAS ROW HALL, SPENCER JAMES.

Pages 180-181: 2 July 1790. STEPHEN LYON of Henry County to JAMES CAMPBELL and LUKE WHEELER of Petersburg, Merchants, indebted to the same in the amount of three hundred and two pounds secures said debt with the several tracts of land in Henry County whereon the said LYON now resides containing by estimate 1200 acres which was purchased by LYON from his father and a certain PALITIAH SHELTON. The above sum due by the first of January next plus a further sum of one hundred fifty pounds due before 1 January 1792. Signed: STEPHEN LYON. Wit: WILLIAM FRENCH, JAMES GALLAWAY, ROBERT GALLAWAY, METITIZAH SPRAGINS. Proved 2 Mar 1791.

Pages 182-183: 24 Feb 1791. ALEXANDER HUNTER of Henry County to JAMES BAKER of the same sells and conveys for the sum of seven pounds ten shillings a tract of land containing 100 acres on the branches of Blackberry Creek...on the north side up the branch of the south fork of the branch to HUNTER'S old line to JOHN GOINGS. Signed: ALEXANDER HUNTER. Wit: none. Proved 28 Feb 1791.

Pages 183-184: 16 Aug 1790. STEPHEN LYON of Henry County to WILLIAM FRANCE of the same for the sum of two hundred pounds to which payment I do bind myself...Condition of the said obligation that STEPHEN LYON hath this day promised to deliver unto WILLIAM FRANCE two negro boys 10 years old which are to be healthy, likely and clear from infirmities. To be delivered on or before the 15th day. In case of failure then STEPHEN LYON obligates himself to deliver a negro man named ABRAHAM, a blacksmith by trade. Signed: STEPHEN LYON. Wit: LEA. HUGHES, A. HUGHES. Proved 28 Feb 1791.

Pages 184-185: March 1791. DANIEL SMITH of Henry County to CHARLES SMITH of the same for the sum of five pounds sells and conveys a parcel of land containing 50 acres on Butterontown Creek, with the lines of GEORGE REAVES. Signed: DANIEL SMITH. Wit: none.

Pages 185-186: 28 Mar 1791. JOHN STAPLES of Henry County to JOHN SMITH of the same for the sum of sixty pounds sells land on the branches of the Mayo River being more or less 140 acres, it being part of a tract that JOHN STAPLES purchased of JOSIAH SMITH and joins the lines of ANTHONY SMITH. Signed: JOHN STAPLES. Wit: none. Proved 28 Mar 1791.

Page 187: 1791. JOSEPH HANCOCK of Henry County to WILLIAM FUSON of the same for the sum of fifty pounds sells a parcel of land situated and lying on the waters of Smith River, containing 109 acres, joins JOHN WARD. Signed: JOSEPH (X) HANCOCK. Wit: NATHAN HALL, JOEL HUBBARD, CHARLES FOSTER.

Pages 188-189: 30 Sept 1790. DAVID CHADWELL of Henry County to STANWIX HORD and JOHN HORD of the same county for the sum of sixty pounds sells and conveys 380 acres of land on the south side of Smith River, it being land granted CHADWELL by patent dated 16 Nov 1780. Signed: DAVID (X) CHADWELL, ELIZ- ABETH (X) CHADWELL. Wit: JAMES BAKER, WILLIAM BRIS- TOW, WILLIAM (X) FRASHER.

Pages 189-190: 30 Sept 1790. DAVID CHADWELL of Henry County to STANWIX HORD and JOHN HORD of the same county for the sum of sixty pounds convey a tract of land by estimate 200 acres on the north side of Smith River. Signed: DAVID (X) CHADWELL, ELIZABETH (X) CHADWELL. Wit: JAMES BAKER, SAMUEL CRITCHFIELD, THOMAS POSEY, WILLIAM (X) FRASHER, ALEXANDER FRASHER.

Page 191: Sept 1790. DAVID CHADWELL of Henry County to STANWIX HORD and JOHN HORD of the same county for the sum of sixty pounds conveys a parcel of land containing 40 acres on the branches of the south side of Smith River. Signed: DAVID (X) CHADWELL. Wit: JAMES BAKER, THOMAS POSEY, SAMUEL CRITCHFIELD, WILLIAM (X) FRASHER, ALEXANDER FRASHER.

Pages 192-193: 28 Mar 1791. WILLIAM REED and his wife to GEORGE HAIRSTON all of Henry County for the sum of eighty pounds sells a parcel of land containing by survey 270 acres dated 18 Nov 1780 located on the Blackberry Creek on both sides. Signed: WILLIAM REED. Wit: GEORGE PENN, WILLIAM MOORE, JAMES WALKER. Proved 28 Mar 1791.

Pages 193-194: 28 Mar 1791. WILLIAM REED and his wife of Henry County to GEORGE HAIRSTON of the same for the sum of one hundred pounds sells and convey a tract of land being on both sides of Blackberry Creek and Bowens Creek, including a small survey that has been patented many years, which patent got burnt, a total of 259 acres and dated 18 Nov 1780. Signed: WILLIAM REED. Wit: GEORGE PENN, WILLIAM MOORE, JAMES WALKER. Proved 28 Mar 1791.

Pages 195-196: 25 Mar 1791. BENJAMIN KENNON of Henry County to JAMES COOK of the same, for the sum of one hundred pounds sell and convey land on the south side of Horsepasture Creek with the lines of THOMAS JARVIS containing 117 acres and one other tract and part of another both patented to JAMES EAST dated 10 Apr 1781 the other 1 June 1782 located on Camp Branch with the lines of WILLIAM WOOLARD. KENNON purchased the said land from JAMES EAST 8 Mar 1783. Total acres 310 more or less. Signed: BENJAMIN KENNON. Proved 28 April 1791. . . .Memo: It appears an error of 17 acres date: 23 Apr 1791.

Pages 197-198: 19 Mar 1791. JOHN SMALLMAN and JOSEPH WALDEN of Henry County to JOHN ADAMS of the same for the sum of sixty pounds sell and convey a tract of land (dividend) on Goblintown Creek by estimate 269 acres. Signed: JOHN SMALLMAN, JOSEPH

WALDEN, RACHEL WALDEN. Wit: BENJAMIN WALDEN, JOSEPH WALDEN, JOSEPH STREET, JAMES COX, WILLIAM BRISTOW. Proved 28 Mar 1791.

Pages 199-200: 25 Apr 1791. JAMES INGRAM of Henry County to SAMUEL PERRY of the same for the sum of twenty pounds sells a parcel of land containing 75 acres more or less adjoining JOSEPH STREET. Signed: JAMES (X) INGRAM. Wit: JAMES PERRY, WILLIAM BRISTOW, JOSEPH STREET. Proved 28 Apr 1791.

Pages 200-201: 26 Apr 1791. JOHN MARR and his wife SUSANNAH MARR of Henry County to JOHN REA of the same for the sum of fifty four pounds sell and convey land on Sandy Creek, a branch of the Little Dan River, it being part of the Order formerly called BELL'S ORDER containing 160 acres more or less. Signed: JOHN MARR. Wit: none. Proved 28 Apr 1791.

Pages 201-202: 25 Apr 1791. JOHN SMITH of Henry County to JOHN WRIGHT of the same for the sum of twenty pounds sells a parcel of land on the waters of the north fork of the Mayo River containing by estimate 51 acres more or less, being part of a tract JOHN STAPLES sold SMITH and joins lines of ANTHONY SMITH. Signed: JOHN SMITH. Wit: none.

Page 203: 20 Nov 1790. JOHN RENNO of Henry County to JOHN WEAVER of the same for the sum of twenty pounds sells land on a branch of IRVIN (SMITH) River containing 237 acres on Grassy Creek joining JOHN WINNINGHAM and STEPHEN RENNO. Signed: JOHN (X) RENNO. Wit: DANIEL TAYLOR, WASHINGTON LANIER, EDWARD ADAMS. Proved 25 Apr 1791.

Pages 204-205: 25 Apr 1791. JOHN STAPLES of Henry County to JAMES INNIS of the same for the sum of seventy five pounds sells land on the south side of the North Mayo River by estimate 100 acres beginning at the mouth of Mill Creek of the Mayo River. Signed: JOHN STAPLES. Wit: none. Proved 25 Apr 1791.

Pages 205-206: 17 Feb 1789. AMBROSE JONES of Henry County to WILLIAM JONES of the same for the sum of fifty pounds sells land on Beaver Creek with the lines of WILLIAM JONES being 120 acres. Signed: AMBROSE JONES. Wit: THOMAS COOPER, JOHN STOKES, JAMES ANTHONY. Proved 25 Apr 1791.

Pages 207-208: 8 Jan 1791. ROBERT PERRYMAN of Franklin County to RICHARD STONE of Henry County for the sum of sixty pounds sells and conveys a tract of land containing 226 acres by estimate on both sides of Mill Creek, this being the same land on which the said STONE now lives. Signed: ROBERT PERRYMAN, ANNA (X) PERRYMAN. Wit: JOSIAH TURNER, SAMUEL PACKWOOD, MICAJAH (X) STONE.

Pages 208-209: 28 Mar 1791. SAMUEL VESS of Henry County to PETER VESS of the same county for the sum of five pounds sells and conveys a part of a larger quantity of land on both sides of Praters Fork of the North Mayo River containing 50 acres more or less. Signed: SAMUEL (X) VESS. Wit: none.

Pages 209-210: 15 Feb 1790. ANDREW REA of Henry County to WILLIAM COX of the same, for and in consideration of the sum of forty pounds sells a parcel of land on Stewart's Creek containing 100 acres more or less joins lines of JACOB KEATON, EDWARD COCKRAN, JOHN COX and the Dutchmans Branch. Signed: ANDREW REA. Wit: THOMAS STOVALL, CHARLES COX, JOHN COX. Proved 15 Feb 1790.

Page 211: 25 Apr 1791. JOHN GROGAN of Henry County to JAMES CLAYBROOK of the same for and in consideration of the sum of fifty pounds sells and conveys a parcel of land containing 50 acres on Stewarts Creek and the Smith River. Signed: JOHN GROGAN.

Pages 212-213: 20 Apr 1791. JOHN BRAMMER, SR. of Henry County to EDMUND BRAMMER of the same for the sum of ten pounds sells and conveys a parcel of land containing 50 acres...from chestnut to oak trees. Signed: JOHN (X) BRAMMER, SR.

Pages 213-214: 23 Apr 1791. JAMES POTEET, SR. of Henry County to JOHN POTEET of the same for the sum of twenty pounds conveys land on the south fork of Goblintown Creek containing 100 acres more or less...joins a wagon ford and lines of WILLIAM GARDNER. Signed: JAMES POTEET, SR. Wit: WILLIAM B. PRICE, JAMES POTEET, JOHN HENDERSON.

Pages 215-216: 23 Apr 1791. JOHN HENDERSON of Henry County to JAMES POTEET, JR. of the same for the sum of fifty pounds sells land on the south fork of Goblintown Creek being by estimate 250 acres. Signed: JOHN HENDERSON. Wit: WILLIAM GARDNER, WILLIAM B. PRICE, JOHN POTEET, JAMES POTEET.

Pages 216-217: 18 Mar 1791. JEREMIAH CLONCH of Montgomery County to JAMES INGRAM of Henry County for the sum of twenty pounds conveys land on the waters of Smith River containing...not given... Signed: JEREMIAH (X) CLONCH. Wit: CHARLES FOSTER, WILLIAM FEWSON, WILLIAM B. PRICE, QUIL. BLAKLEY. Proved 25 Apr 1791.

Pages 218-219: 19 Mar 1791. WILLIAM PRICE of Henry County to BERNARD MOORE PRICE of the same for the sum of fifty pounds conveys a parcel of land on the waters of Puppy Creek containing 150 acres adjoining the lines of NOE and CALLAWAY. Signed; WILLIAM PRICE. Wit: JOHN LEACKEY, SAFFANA TENNESON, WILLIAM B. PRICE. Proved 25 Apr 1791.

Pages 219-220: 19 Apr 1791. JAMES ELKINS of Henry County to WILLIAM HARRIS of the same for and in consideration of the sum of twenty five pounds sells and conveys a tract of land containing 100 acres and joins the lines of BRIENTS. Signed: JAMES (X) ELKINS.

Pages 220-221: 1 Feb 1791. WILLIAM ADAMS and SARAH ADAMS his wife of Henry County to WILLIAM B. PRICE of the same, for and in consideration of the sum of fifteen pounds sell and convey land on Puppy Creek, being part of the tract WILLIAM PRICE bought of WILLIAM ADAMS by estimate 200 acres. Signed: WILLIAM ADAMS. Wit: BARNET (X) PRICE, LUCY (X) PRICE, SALLEY (X) PRICE.

Pages 221-222: 16 Oct 1790. PETER TITTLE and PATTY TITTLE his wife of Henry County to GEORGE TITTLE of the same for the sum of one hundred pounds sell a parcel of land on the waters of Goblintown Creek containing 59 acres. Signed: PETER (X) TITTLE, PATTY (X) TITTLE. Wit: DAVID TITTLE, THOMAS (X) MC CLANE, PATTY (X) RICHARDS.

Pages 223-224: 25 Apr 1791. STEPHEN SENTER of Henry County to CHARLES BURRES of the same for the sum of fifty pounds sell and convey a tract of land, it being the upper end of the tract that said SENTER now lives on, on both sides of Pauls Creek. Signed: STEPHEN SENTER. Proved 25 Apr 1791.

Pages 224-225: 25 Apr 1791. JAMES CHARLES of Henry County to TANDY SENTER of the same for the sum of twenty pounds sells 50 acres of land being the upper end of the tract that the said CHARLES now liveth on situated on a branch of Pauls Creek. Signed: JAMES CHARLES. Proved 25 Apr 1791.

Pages 225-226: 25 Apr 1791. DAVID ROGERS of Henry County to CLEM ROGERS of the same for the sum of ten pounds sells 154 acres by survey dated 16 Mar 1768 on the north fork of Russels Creek, joining GEORGE CARTER. Signed: DAVID ROGERS. Wit: EDWARD TATUM, HOLDEN MEGEE, HUMBERSTONE LYON. Proved 25 Apr 1791.

Pages 226-227: 27 Nov 1790. JOHN MCGOWAN of Henry County to JAMES DICKERSON of Surry County, North Carolina for the sum of three hundred twenty four pounds sells a parcel of land containing 182 acres on both sides of Johnsons Creek. Signed: JOHN MC GOWAN. Wit: JAMES ARMSTRONG, WILLIAM HUDSPETH, ROBERT HUDSPETH, THOMAS HUDSPETH. Proved 25 Apr 1791.

Pages 228-229: 25 Apr 1791. WILLIAM WANN of Henry County to JOSEPH BOYD of the same for the sum of one hundred pounds sells a parcel of land on the north fork of Johnsons Creek containing 114 acres. Signed: WILLIAM (X) WANN. Wit: JOHN MC GOWN, JAMES BOYD, JOHN BOYD. Proved 25 Apr 1791.

Pages 229-230: 1 Dec 1790. JOHN DAY of Kentucky Country to JACOB ADAMS, JR. of Henry County for the sum of fifty pounds sells and conveys a parcel of land on the north fork of Spoon Creek, it being the land and plantation where he lately lived and since rented to JAMES HALE by estimate 140 acres. This being part of a 458 acre land grant by patent to JOHN BARKER dated 1 June 1782 and conveyed to the said JOHN DAY. Signed: JOHN DAY. Wit: JAMES (X) HAIL, WILLIAM (X) MANNEN, JOHN MELY. Proved 25 Apr 1791.

Pages 231-232: 29 Sept 1790. JOHN RICHARDSON of the state of Georgia to WASHINGTON LANIER of Henry County for the sum of fifteen pounds sells and conveys a parcel of land, it being part of a tract RICHARDSON formerly lived on on the headwaters of Marrowbone Creek...36 acres. Signed: JOHN (X) RICHARDSON. Wit: THOMAS VERNON, GREGORY DURHAM, JAMES WILSON. Proved 25 Apr 1791.

Pages 232-233: 25 Apr 1791. ABRAHAM PENN of Henry County to ANDREW HERON of the same, for and in consideration of forty pounds sells 260 acres more or less on Koger Creek joining THOMAS STOCKTON...it being the land now in possession of the said ANDREW HERON. Signed: ABRAHAM PENN. Wit: SAMUEL STAPLES, JOHN NEWMAN, JOHN BRAMMER. Proved 25 Apr 1791.

Pages 233-234: 25 Apr 1791. STANWIX HORD, WILLIAM HORD and JOHN HORD of Henry County to LEWIS FRANKLIN of the same, for a valuable consideration sell and convey 50 acres of land on the south side of Smith River. Signed: STANWIX HORD, JOHN HORD, WILLIAM HORD. Proved Apr Court 1791.

Page 235: 25 Apr 1791. JOSEPH BOYD of Henry County to JOHN BOYD of the same, for and in consideration of fifty pounds sells and conveys a parcel of land containing 59 acres on the north fork of Johnsons Creek. Signed: JOSEPH (X) BOYD. Proved 15 Apr 1791.

Pages 236-237: 6 Dec 1790. ROBERT HUGHES of Henry County to MARTIN AMOS of the same, for the sum of sixty pounds sells land on both sides of Buffalow Creek with lines of JOHN KINDRICK and a small branch of the Smith River containing 240 acres. Possession taken this day. Signed: ROBERT HUGHES. Wit: JOHN HENDERSON, ELISHA HARBOUR, MOSES (X) HARBOUR. Proved 25 Apr 1791.

Page 238: 22 Apr 1791. GEORGE CARTER of Henry County to HOLDEN MEGEE of the same for the sum of twenty pounds sells land on the north fork of the Mayo River containing 53 acres as by patent may appear. Signed: GEORGE CARTER. Wit: SAMUEL STAPLES, DANIEL NEWMAN, WILLIAM CARTER. Proved 25 Apr 1791.

Pages 239-240: 5 Apr 1791. JACOB ADAMS, JR. of Henry County to EDWARD O'NEAL of the same for sixty pounds sells land on both sides of the north fork of Spoon Creek, it being the land and plantation ADAMS purchased of JOHN DAY containing by estimate 140 acres, it being part of a 458 acre tract granted JOHN BARKER 1 June 1782. Signed: JACOB ADAMS, JR. Proved 25 Apr 1791.

Page 240-241: 25 Apr 1791. SAMUEL VESS of Henry County to EDWARD DANIEL of the same, for the sum of ten pounds conveys a certain parcel of land (it being part of a larger survey) located on the branches of Praters fork of the North Mayo River being 100 acres, joins JOHN RANDEL and GEORGE DODSON, SR. Signed: SAMUEL VESS, CATHERINE VESS, his wife. Proved 25 Apr 1791.

Pages 241-243: 3 Jan 1789. WILLIAM ARNOLD of Henry County to SAMUEL CORN of the same, for sixty pounds sells 200 acres land on Russels Creek with the lines of JAMES MANKINS and WILLIAM SMITH... it being part of the WILLIAM SMITH tract of 353 acres on the South Mayo River. Signed: WILLIAM (X) ARNOLD. Wit: STEPHEN LYON, PETER (X) CORN, GEORGE (X) CORN, WILLIAM (X) JONES, CHARLES (X) ROSS, HARVEY FITZ-GERALD. Proved 25 Apr 1791. . .Memo: possession was given 3 Jan 1791.

Pages 243-244: 3 Mar 1791. SAMSON MAXEY of Henry County to JOSEPH GOODWIN of the same, for the sum of thirty five pounds sells land on the north side of Smith River and Rock House Branch with the lines of JOHN KELLY and WILLIAM RICE containing 150 acres. Signed: SAMSON (X) MAXEY. Wit: GEORGE WALLER, JOSEPH MARTIN, DAVID LANIER, JAMES ARMSTRONG, JAMES ANTHONY. Proved 25 Apr 1791. . .SUSAN MAXEY, wife of SAMSON MAXEY releases right of dower.

Pages 244-245: 30 Sept 1790. DAVID CHADWELL of Henry County to STANWIX HORD and JOHN HORD of the same for sixty pounds sells land by estimate 110 acres surveyed...on the south side of Smith River. Signed: DAVID (X) CHADWELL, ELIZABETH (X) CHADWELL. Wit: JAMES BAKER, WILLIAM BRISTOW, WILLIAM (X) FRASHER, SAMUEL CRITCHFIELD, THOMAS POSEY, ALEXANDER FRASHER. Proved 25 Apr 1791.

Pages 246-247: 30 Sept 1790. DAVID CHADWELL of Henry County to STANWIX HORD and JOHN HORD for the sum of sixty pounds sells 340 acres by survey dated 10 Oct 1786 on the north side of Smith River crosses Payne's Branch and Rowland's Branch. Signed: DAVID (X) CHADWELL, ELIZABETH (X) CHADWELL. Wit: same as above. Proved 25 Apr 1791.

Pages 247-248: 30 Sept 1790. BENJAMIN POSEY of Henry County to STANWIX HORD and JOHN HORD of the same for the sum of forty pounds sell 106 acres by survey dated 13 Dec 1773, 62 acres part thereof surveyed by CHRISTOPHER BOLLING (since sold to BENJAMIN POSEY) on both sides of Smith River, with lines of WILLIAM COX and ADAMS. Signed: BENJAMIN POSEY, SUSANAH POSEY. Wit: same as above. Proved 25 Apr 1791.

Page 249: 25 Apr 1791. JOSEPH GOODWIN of Henry County to WILLIAM QUARLES of the same for twenty pounds sells 39 acres...trees, stumps, etc are lines given. Signed: JOSEPH GOODWIN. No witness. Proved 25 Apr 1791.

Pages 249-251: 16 Apr 1791. ISHAM EDWARDS of Franklin County to JAMES CLAYBROOK of Henry County for the sum of thirty pounds sells land on the Draughts of Toeclout Creek joining WILLIAM JAMISON containing 154 acres. Signed: ISHAM EDWARDS. Proved 25 Apr 1791.

Pages 251-252: 25 Apr 1791. JAMES SHELTON and his wife of Henry County to HEZEKIAH SHELTON of the same for the sum of thirteen pounds sells a parcel of land on both sides of the Mayo River, beginning on the south side at a ford called the Laurel containing 209 acres. Signed: JAMES (X) SHELTON. Proved 25 Apr 1791.

Pages 252-254: 17 Nov 1787. DOROTHY MINISS of Henry County to HENRY GROGAN of Rockingham County, North Carolina for the sum of one hundred pounds sells land on the Draughts of Toeclout Creek containing 157 acres joining WILLIAM EDWARDS. Signed: DOROTHY MINISS. Wit: ISHAM EDWARDS, JAMES EDWARDS, LETTY EDWARDS. Proved 25 Apr 1791.

Pages 254-256: 15 Oct 1790. JOHN DAWSON (for himself) and said JOHN DAWSON as attorney for JOHN DAWSON GRYMES and the said JOHN DAWSON in virtue of a deed from THOMAS DAWSON dated 2 July 1785 of the one part to JOHN MARR of the second part for the sum of five shillings and for in consideration of a promise and agreement of JOHN HORD estimate the land to be worth...JOHN DAWSON is moving...There is 2,816 acres of land in Lunenburg now Henry County on both sides of the Arrart River beginning where the said country lines begins...Clarks Creek, Cloud's Run, Bowmans Creek, Johnsons Creek, Beaver Pond Creek. Signed: JOHN DAWSON. Wit: NICHOLAS SCALES, BUCKNER JONES, JAMES PRYOR. Proved 25 Apr 1791.

Pages 257-258: 15 Apr 1791. MARY OLDHAM of Henry County to THOMAS OLDHAM of the same, for the sum of sixty pounds conveys and sells land on the south side of Little Sycamore Creek joining RICHARD KIRBY'S line and a corner of THOMAS MORROW containing 158 acres. Signed: MARY (X) OLDHAM. Wit: WILLIAM AMOS, MOSES HARBOUR, ELISHA HARBOUR. . . Possession taken the 15th Apr 1791.

Pages 259-160: 10 Jan 1790. BENJAMIN BRISTOW of Henry County to WILLIAM ADAMS of the same for the sum of forty pounds sells and conveys 52 acres on the Goblintown Creek with GRAY'S line. Signed: BENJAMIN BRISTOW. Wit: JOHN HENDERSON, JOHN ADAMS, HENRY SUMPTER. Proved 25 Apr 1791. Possession given 10 Jan 1790.

Pages 261-262: 21 Mar 1791. JOHN BURCH of Henry County to JOHN GRAVELY of the same, for and in consideration of fifty pounds sells and conveys land on the branches of Leatherwood Creek and Meat House Branch containing by estimate 200 acres with the order lines of LOMAX & COMPANY and TWITTYS order line and the lines of JOHN BURCH, SR. Signed: JOHN BURCH, SUSAN BURCH. Wit: RANDOLPH DILLON, JOHN NICHOLAS, SAMUEL ELLIOTT. Proved 25 Apr 1791.

Page 263: 23 Apr 1791. BUTLER STONE STREET of Pittsylvania County to THOMAS STEWART of Henry County for the sum of forty three pounds sells land being 133 acres, by survey 19 Apr 1768 on both sides of Leatherwood Creek with lines of MERRY WEBB. Signed BUTLER STONE STREET. Wit: DAVID WEATHERFORD, JAMES WILSON, DUDLEY (X) STEPHENS.

Pages 264-265: 7 Mar 1791. NEHEMIAH NORTON of Henry County to DAVID WEATHERFORD of Pittsylvania County in consideration of fifty pounds sells and conveys part of a tract bought of PATRICK HENRY that formerly belonged to WATERS DUNN located on the waters of Leatherwood Creek being 140 acres, beginning where the line crosses the creek below the Mill excluding all the east side of the creek with 200 acres of the west side excluded also the Mill. Signed: NEHEMIAH NORTON. Wit: THOMAS PARRY, ANDERSON (X) MC GUIRE, JOHN (X) WILSON. Proved 26 Apr 1791.

Pages 265-267: 7 Mar 1791. GEORGE ADAMS of Pittsylvania County to DAVID WEATHERFORD of the same for the sum of fifty pounds sells 260 acres by survey dated 15 Feb 1784 on both sides Leatherwood Creek with the lines of DUNN, LOMAX & COMPANY and RANDOLPH & COMPANY. Signed: GEORGE ADAMS. Wit: THOMAS PARRY, ANDERSON MCGUIRE (X), JOHN (X) WILSON.

Proved 26 Apr 1791.

Pages 267-268: 25 Apr 1791. JOHN MARR of Henry County to WILLIAM GRIFFIN of the same, for and in consideration of twenty five hundred pounds sells and conveys land on Arrarat River, 444 acres it being part of his Order of Council, formerly claimed by DAWSON, the same is the land on which WILLIAM GRIFFIN now lives, joins WILLIAM HUDSPETH. Signed: JOHN MARR. Wit: ROBERT HUDSPETH, THOMAS HUDSPETH, WILLIAM HUDSPETH. Proved 27 Apr 1791.

Pages 268-269: 25 Apr 1791. CHARLES FARRIS, JR. of Henry County to CHARLES FARRIS, SR. of the same for the sum of twenty pounds sells land on both sides of Little Marrowbone Creek joins JOHN PACE, W. KING COLE and JOHN REA contains 25 acres. Signed: CHARLES (X) FARRIS, JR. Proved 27 Apr 1791.

Pages 269-270: 25 Apr 1791. BENJAMIN KENNON of Henry County to WILLIAM WOOLLARD of the same for the sum of fifty pounds sells land on the head branch of Bull Run...it was JAMES EAST'S patent for 287 acres, now laid off for 200 acres more or less with A. PENN'S line. Signed: BENJAMIN KENNON. Proved 25 Apr 1791.

Pages 270-271: 28 May 1791. WILLIAM ADAMS and his wife SARAH ADAMS of Henry County to CHARLES FOSTER of the same county, for and in consideration of sixty pounds sells and conveys 330 acres of land beginning at a big branch that empties into ABNER ECHOLS Mill Pond, crosses Goblintown Creek and joins lines of SAMUEL NOWLIN. Signed: WILLIAM ADAMS. Wit: ZAPHENIAH TENISON, GIDION NOE, ANTHONY TITTLE. Proved 30 May 1791.

Pages 271-273: 28 May 1791. WILLIAM ADAMS and his wife SARAH ADAMS of Henry County to ZEPHINIAH TENISON of the same, for and in consideration of the sum of twenty pounds sells and conveys land on Goblintown Creek being 300 acres...THOMAS HUTCHENS line to the main county road that leads to DANIEL ROSS'. Signed: WILLIAM ADAMS. Wit: same as above excluding TENISON and adding CHARLES FOSTER. Proved 30 May 1791.

Pages 273-274: 29 May 1791. JOSEPH WALDEN of Henry County to MARTIN MARTIN of the same, for the sum of fifty pounds sells 50 acres on the Goblintown Creek with Streets Branch. Signed: JOSEPH

WALDEN. Proved 30 May 1791.

Pages 274-275: 30 May 1791. Bond of WILLIAM TUNSTALL to be Sheriff of Henry County with GEORGE HAIRSTON his bondsman.

Pages 275-276: 18 Oct 1790. THOMAS EDWARDS, SR. of Henry County to CALEB MAY of the same, for the sum of fifty pounds sells land on which the said CALEB MAY now lives, by estimate 275 acres joins DANIEL WILSON. Signed: THOMAS EDWARDS, SR. Wit: GEORGE BRITTAIN, DAVID HILER, HENRY LANSFORD, JOHN EDWARDS, BENJAMIN LOYD. Proved 25 Apr 1791 & 27 June 1791.

Pages 276-277: 12 Sept 1790. CHARLES COPLAND executor of PETER COPLAND, deceased of the city of Richmond to JOHN BIRD of Henry County for the sum of ten pounds one shilling to him paid or to be paid by a certain RICHARD COPLAND sells and conveys 256 acres which said tract granted to PETER COPLAND by patent 1 Oct 1784 and is part of the land divided by the said PETER COPLAND by his last will and testament and to be sold for the payment of debts. Signed: CHARLES COPLAND, executor of PETER COPLAND. Wit: RICHARD STOCKTON, THOMAS BOWLIN, JOHN RANDELS, ALEXANDER (X) MC CULLOCK. Proved Apr Ct 1791.

Pages 277-278: 27 June 1791. JOHN PACE and his wife ELIZABETH PACE of Henry County to DAVID QUARLES of the same for two hundred ten pounds sell a tract of land on the south side of Smith River being 142 acres with the lines of JOHN RICE and NEWSOM PACE. Signed: JOHN PACE. Proved 25 July 1791.

Pages 278-279: 27 June 1791. To the Justices of Henry County...the bond of GEORGE HAIRSTON and JAMES ANTHONY each of them or either shall at anytime when requested by the Justices convey by good and lawful deed unto them 50 acres adjacent to the Court House of Henry County in such manner and form as shall best suit for erecting of a Town when a law shall be past for that purpose. Signed: GEORGE HARISTON, JAMES ANTHONY. . . .Memo: That the true intent and meaning of the Bonds as relates JAMES ANTHONY is only to convey such part of the 50 acres that shall include the spring most convenient to the Courthouse which spring is now made use of. Also one dire part of the within 50 acres whereon the said GEORGE HAIRSTON has erected his buildings to be for his own use.

Page 279: March 1791. ROBERT LORTON and DAVID LANIER of Henry County are bound unto JOHN FONTAINE in the sum of one hundred pounds...Whereas an order of the County Court made for the repairing of the Ford at Leatherwood Creek. Wit: JOSEPH MARTIN.

Pages 280-281: 25 July 1791. WILLIAM MILLS of Henry County to ARCHELAUS HUGHES of the same for the sum of seventy five pounds sells and conveys a tract of land containing 1,000 acres more or less on Crooked Creek with the lines of Fontaine and Walton...crosses five branches and with pointers in the Country Line. Signed: WILLIAM MILLS. Wit: JOHN CHILDRESS, LEA. HUGHES, HENRY FRANCE. Proved 25 July 1791.

Pages 281-282: 25 July 1791. JOHN OLDHAM and his wife ELIZABETH OLDHAM of Henry County to DAVID LANIER for the consideration of fifty pounds sells and conveys 97 acres joins LOMAX lines and was granted to the said OLDHAM by patent 10 Aug 1783. Signed: JOHN OLDHAM, ELIZABETH OLDHAM. Proved 25 July 1791.

Pages 282-283: 8 June 1791. JOHN MARR of Henry County to JOHN EARLEY of Franklin County for the sum of eight hundred pounds sells and conveys a parcel of land containing 650 acres on the north fork of the Mayo River and on both sides of Horsepasture Creek joins the lines of PHILIP PENN. Signed: JOHN MARR. Proved 25 July 1791.

Pages 284-285: 8 June 1791. JOHN LINDSAY of Wilks County, Georgia to JOHN MARR of Henry County for the sum of eight hundred pounds sells and conveys a tract of land containing 650 acres on the north fork of the Mayo River and on both sides of Horsepasture Creek joins lines of PHILIP PENN. Signed:: JOHN LINDSAY. Wit: CALEB MAY, CHARLES GILLIAM, POLLEY SCALES, JAMES (X) DIKES. Proved 25 July 1791.

Page 286: 24 June 1791. JOHN MCWILLIAMS of Franklin County, Virginia to JOSHUA DILLINGHAM of Henry County for the sum of forty pounds sells 100 acres more or less on Reedy Creek joining WILLIAM HEARD. Signed: JOHN MC WILLIAMS. Proved 25 July 1791.

Pages 287-288: 3 Jan 1791. JOHN BIRD of Franklin County, Virginia to JOHN NORRIS of Henry County sells for the consideration of forty pounds a tract of land by estimate 356 acres more or less with water courses unnamed. Signed: JOHN BIRD. Proved 25 July 1791.

Pages 288-289: 12 Apr 1791. BARNA WELLS of Henry County sells to DAVID JOHNSON of the same one negro girl named DINAH for the sum of twenty pounds. Be it remembered if the said WELLS pays JOHNSON the sum of twenty pounds before the 25th Dec next ensuing the said negro shall be returned and this bill of sale void. Signed: BARNA WELLS, DAVID JOHNSON. Wit: RUBEN NANCE, JOSEPH GRAVELY, JOHN (X) GRIGGS. Proved 25 July 1791.

Page 289: 20 July 1791. Power of Attorney. We, STANWIX HORD and JOHN HORD of Henry County, Virginia do appoint WILLIAM HORD our true and lawful attorney to convey in fee simple unto DAVID CHADWELL one certain tract of land in the County of Russell in Powell's Valley. It being the land divided unto us by the last will and testament of MORDECAI HORD, deceased. Signed: STANWIX HORD, JOHN HORD. Wit: JOHN COX, TUNSTALL COX, JOHN SALMON. Proved 26 July 1791.

Page 290: 4 Dec 1790. Bill of Sale. THOMAS CUNNINGHAM of Henry County sells unto JOHN P. PYRTLE of the same one black mare 4 years old next spring. Signed: THOMAS CUNNINGHAM. Wit: JOHN WALLER. Proved July Court, 1791.

Pages 290-291: 16 Aug 1791. THOMAS BOLLING of Henry County to JOSEPH CORN of the same for the sum of thirty pounds sells and conveys a tract of land containing 100 acres more or less on Rock Run Creek. Signed: THOMAS (X) BOLLING. Wit: TUNSTALL COX, HENRY LYNE, JAMES OFFICER. Proved 29 Aug 1791.

Pages 291-292: 10 Dec 1790. RUSSELL COX of Henry County to FRANCIS GILLEY, JR. of the same for the sum of thirty pounds sells and conveys a tract of land on both sides of the Bold Branch of Leatherwood Creek, the said FRANCIS GILLEY'S part is 300 acres more or less and joins the land of COL. PATRICK HENRY. Signed: RUSSELL COX, FRANKY (X) COX. Wit: JAMES WILSON, AARON (X) WILSON, WILLIAM (X) MAQUIRE. Proved 29 Aug 1791.

Pages 292-293: 28 Feb 1791. JAMES MEREDITH of Henry County to DAVID BUNCH of the same, for the sum of six pounds sells land on the branches of Leatherwood Creek being 68 acres with the lines of WILLIAM BROWN, NATHAN JONES and MARTIN BUNCH. Signed:

JAMES (X) MEREDITH. Wit: MARTIN BUNCH, WILLIAM BROWN, JOHN CONNAWAY.

Page 294: 4 Mar 1791. JAMES MEREDITH of Henry County to MARTIN BUNCH of the same, sells and conveys a tract of lane on the branches of Leatherwood Creek containing 68 acres more or less and joins the lines of DAVID BUNCH and Beaver Creek. Signed: JAMES (X) MEREDITH. Wit: JOHN CONNAWAY, WILLIAM BROWN, DAVID BUNCH. Proved 19 Aug 1791.

Pages 295-296: 22 Mar 1791. JAMES HICKS of Brunswick County, Virginia to JOHN NANCE of Henry County for the sum of one hundred pounds sells and conveys land on the waters of Leatherwood Creek by estimate 350 acres more or less with the lines of JAMES HICKS, CHARLES BURNETT, ROBERT STOCKTON, DANIEL JACKSON, CAIN ACUFF, JOHN HAILEY, and to the said HICKS' sons line again. Signed: JAMES HICKS, SENR. Wit: RICHARD STOCKTON, JOHN MINTER, JOHN HALEY. Proved 26 Sept 1791.

Pages 296-297: 26 Sept 1791. GEORGE HAIRSTON and JAMES ANTHONY of Henry County to the Acting Justices of Henry County, for and in consideration of the benefit of the tythable persons in Henry County liable to a County levy, conveyed to the said Justices and their successors 49 acres of land, part of a 50 acre tract layed off by the Surveyor of Henry County adjacent to the Courthouse. Reserving to GEORGE HAIRSTON the other one acre in the plot. The 49 acres to be sold out in one and one-half acre lots and the money derived to defray the cost of public buildings that may from time to time be necessary for the use of the County. Signed: GEORGE HAIRSTON, JAMES ANTHONY. . . Memo: That the Courthouse is to be fixed on the piece of land to the east of the within GEORGE HAIRSTON buildings now fixed on his said acre, on or near the place which had formerly been agreed on by the Justices of Henry County. Dated: 26 July 1791. Wit: JOHN SALMON, EL. HUNTER, A. HUGHES, JOSEPH MARTIN, THOMAS STOVALL.

Pages 298: 9 July 1791. Assignment: To STANWIX HORD the land I (WILLIAM HORD) am intitled to by the last will and testament of MORDECAI HORD, deceased which lies below the mouth of a branch commonly called the Lowground Branch then running to the Great Fall. Signed: WILLIAM HORD. Wit: STEPHEN KING, JOHN P. PYRTLE. Proved 26 Sept 1791. . .I agree that the said WILLIAM HORD shall fully possess the within mentioned land until the 25 Dec 1792. Signed: STANWIX HORD. Proved 26 Sept 1791.

Page 299: 9 July 1791. Assignment: STANWIX HORD and JUSTIANIA HORD his wife to WILLIAM HORD, without recourse assign my lands on the Western Waters by which I am entitled from the last will and testament of my father MORDECAI HORD, deceased. Signed: STANWIX HORD, JUSTIANIA HORD. Proved 26 Sept 1791.

Pages 299-300: 31 Oct 1790. WILLIAM JONES of Henry County to GEORGE HAIRSTON of the same for the sum of sixty pounds sells and conveys land on the branches of Beaver Creek joining AMBROSE JONES and containing 120 acres. Signed: WILLIAM JONES.

Page 301: 31 Oct 1791. JAMES ANTHONY of Henry County to GEORGE HAIRSTON of the same for the sum of one hundred fifty pounds sells and conveys land on both sides of Beaver Creek by estimate 200 acres more or less joins Cooper's Creek and JOHN STOKES. Signed: JAMES ANTHONY.

Pages 302-303: 31 Oct 1791. STARK BROWN to JOSEPH MARTIN all of Henry County, for the sum of fifty pounds sells and conveys land on the Smith River on the north side, by estimate 50 acres ...below the field fence formerly occupied by CHRISTOPHER BOLLING, SENR. across to the low grounds to GEORGE HAIRSTON'S line on the hill side...to a line on the river bank opposite a small island. Signed: STARK BROWN, TABITHIA (X) BROWN.

Pages 303-304: 27 Nov 1789. THOMAS WILKINS of Henry County to NICHOLAS AKIN of the same, for the consideration of fifty pounds sells 50 acres land on a branch of Leatherwood Creek, joins LOMAX order line and JESSE DELOZEARS to JOHN COLLINS. Signed: THOMAS (X) WILKINS, ELIZABETH (X) WILKINS. Wit: REUBEN NANCE, FLEMING THOMASON, JOHN DAVIS. Proved Oct Court 1791.

Pages 304-305: 26 Jan 1791. Power of Attorney. ELIJAH BAKER of North Hampton County, Virginia appoints RICHARD STOCKTON and JAMES ANTHONY of Henry County, Virginia and JOSEPH BLAKEY and RICHARD LOCKHART of Wilkes County, and Green County, Georgia attorneys to ask, sue and recover of JOSEPH FOREGUSON and RICHARD COPLAND both of Georgia one fourth of eleven negros. That is the 7 held by

JOSEPH FARGUESON to wit: a woman JUDITH, her children and grandchildren. Also in the hands of RICHARD COPLAND 5 negros HANAH, WILL, JACOB and a girl child. These (1/4th) descended to me from ELIZABETH COPLAND, deceased who was the legal heir of PATIENCE FERGUSON, deceased in the state of Georgia as will more fully appear by the last will and testament of GEORGE REIVES of Spotsylvania County, Virginia, deceased. Signed: ELIJAH BAKER. Wit: JOHN (X) HAILEY, ROBERT STOCKTON, ROBERT STOCKTON, JR. Proved 25 Oct 1791.

Pages 305-306: 9 July 1791. Agreement between WILLIAM HORD and JOHN HORD. WILLIAM HORD has agreed to exchange part of his land whereon he now lives, which lays above the Lowground Branch. WILLIAM HORD oblidges himself to make title to the said land to JOHN HORD in consideration that JOHN HORD release his right to lands on the Western Waters left him by his father MORDECAI HORD'S last will and testament, also 1/3 part of 250 pounds which he is entitled to by the death of my brother MORDECAI HORD. Also all my part of the debts of GL. SUMPTERS, JOSEPH MARTIN, RICHARD DAVIS and BALDWIN ROWLAND and any other debts under five pounds due to our fathers estate. The said JOHN HORD assigns with recourse to the said WILLIAM HORD. Signed: WILLIAM HORD, JOHN HORD, RUTH HORD, wife of JOHN HORD. Wit: JOHN SUMPTER, STEPHEN KING, JOHN P. PYRTLE. Proved 1 Nov 1791. . .Memo: We hereby agree that WILLIAM HORD is to fully possess the within mentioned land until 15 Jan 1792.

Pages 307-308: 13 Oct 1791. THOMAS COOPER of Henry County to GEORGE HAIRSTON of the same for the sum of eight hundred pounds sells and conveys a tract of land on both sides of Beaver Creek being 521 acres, begins on the south side of Pounding Mill Creek in ROBERT STOCKTON'S line...to the main creek below the Mill...crosses Beaver Creel. Signed: THOMAS COOPER. Wit: JOHN REDD, MICHAEL DILLINGHAM, JOHN NORTON, DANIEL (X) BURCHET. Proved 28 Nov 1791.

Pages 309-310: 15 Oct 1791. THOMAS COOPER of Henry County to GEORGE HAIRSTON of the same for the consideration of three hundred twenty five pounds sells land on both sides of Beaver Creek joins lines of Lomax Order Line, AMBROSE JONES and ROBERT STOCKTON, containing 521 acres. Signed: THOMAS COOPER. Wit: JOHN REDD, MICHAEL DILLINGHAM, JOHN NORTON, DANIEL (X) BURCHET. Proved 28 Nov 1791.

Pages 310-312: 15 Oct 1791. THOMAS COOPER of Henry

County to GEORGE HAIRSTON of the same, for the sum of one hundred pounds sells land on both sides Beaver Creek containing 159 acres. Signed: THOMAS COOPER. Wit: same as above deed. Proved 28 Nov 1791.

Pages 312-315: 3 Oct 1791. JAMES ANTHONY of Henry County to WILLIAM HORD of the same, for and in consideration of fifty pounds sells and conveys a tract of land on Little Beaver Creek containing 590 acres beginning on the Main Road with the lines of GEORGE HAIRSTON, crosses said Road to a corner of a lot JAMES ANTHONY conveyed to Henry County. Signed: JAMES ANTHONY. Wit: THOMAS STOVALL, JOHN REDD, GEORGE PENN, J. W. HUNTER. Proved 28 Nov 1791. MEMO: WILLIAM HORD is to give any timber of the within tract of land as shall be sufficient to improve one (1) acre of land whereon ROBERT WILLIAMSON'S Store now stands to HENRY KOGER. Also, my pine timbers JOSEPH ANTHONY may want for his own use westwardly of an old path that makes from where BENJAMIN POSEY now lives... in the road making from the mouth of Beaver Creek to Henry Courthouse. Wit: JOHN REDD, LEA. HUGHES, GEORGE PENN, J.W. HUNTER. Dated 3 Nov 1791.

Pages 315-316: 28 Nov 1791. CHARLES GILLEY of Henry County, son and heir of FRANCIS GILLEY, deceased to WILLIAM MITCHELL of Patrick County, Virginia. FRANCIS GILLEY in his lifetime sold GEORGE HAIRSTON land on the south side of Smith River and said HAIRSTON sold the land to WILLIAM MITCHELL. FRANCIS GILLEY died without conveying a deed to either HAIRSTON or MITCHELL and therefore CHARLES GILLEY being the eldest son and in consideration of two hundred pounds paid by the said WILLIAM MITCHELL conveys this 250 acre tract which is located on the south side of Smith River and begins at the mouth of Turkey Cock Creek. Said land was formerly the property of MERRY WEBB and by his survey 250 acres. Signed: CHARLES GILLEY. Proved 28 Nov 1791. . .ELIZABETH GILLEY, wife of CHARLES GILLEY release her right of dower.

Page 317: 28 Oct 1791. WILLIAM HORD of Henry County to HENRY COGER (KOGER) of Patrick County for the sum of twenty shillings sells and conveys one (1) acre of land in Henry County near the Courthouse, beginning on the south side of the Road and includes the house where Mr. WILLIAMSON now keeps a Store. Signed: WILLIAM HORD. Wit: JOHN REDD, THOMAS STOVALL, J. W. HUNTER, GEORGE PENN. . .MEMO: HENRY COGER (KOGER) is to give ROBERT WILLIAMSON peaceful possession of half of the one acre until such time as the said

WILLIAMSON shall be paid for his improvements on the said one half acre, to be compensated by Nov 1791.

Pages 318-319: 28 Nov 1791. Bond of GEORGE WALLER to be Sheriff of Henry County, his securities being: HENRY LYNE, JOHN ALEXANDER, DANIEL RAMEY and HENRY JONES. Proved 28 Nov 1791.

Pages 320-321: 15 Aug 1789. CHARLES FARRIS, SENR. of Henry County to CHARLES FARRIS, JR. of the same for the sum of ninety pounds sells land whereon the said CHARLES FARRIS, SENR now lives, located on a branch of Big Marrowbone Creek contains 100 acres more or less and joins land of W. K. COLE, SANFORD RAMEY and JOHN PACE. Signed: CHARLES (X) FARRIS, SENR., EDY (X) FARRIS. Wit: W. KING COLE, JOHN PACE, SANFORD RAMEY. Proved Nov Court 1791

Pages 322-323: 7 Dec 1791. GEORGE WALTON of Prince Edward County, Virginia Partner and Executor of ROBERT WALTON deceased of Cumberland County, Virginia of the one part and WILLIAM FEE of Henry County son and heir of THOMAS FEE, deceased of the other part. GEORGE WALTON for a certain consideration, an agreement entered into by said ROBERT WALTON and THOMAS FEE the 29 Mar 1749 also for a sum of four pounds with interest from 5 Nov 1751 which the said GEORGE WALTON doth hereby acknowledge, grant and sell to WILLIAM FEE a parcel of land containing 35 acres on then north side of the south fork of the Mayo River, being the land on which the said FEE now lives. Signed: GEORGE WALTON. Wit: THOMAS (X) PHILLIPS, JOHN NORTON, HENRY FEE, ALEXANDER MOORE, JAMES TAYLOR.

Pages 323-325: 23 Dec 1791. THOMAS COOPER of Green County, Georgia to GEORGE HAIRSTON of Henry County, Virginia for the sum of twenty five pounds sells land on both sides of Beaver Creek containing 420 acres. Signed: THOMAS COOPER. Wit: REUBEN PAYNE, JOHN EAST, EDWARD ADAMS, THOMAS STOVALL. Proved 18 Dec 1791...payment received.

Pages 326-327: 22 Mar 1785. BENJAMIN BRISTOW of Henry County to WILLIAM BRISTOW of the same for the sum of forty pounds sells and conveys land on the north side of Goblintown Creek being 52 acres. Signed: BENJAMIN BRISTOW. Wit: JAMES BOWLES, WILLIAM ADAMS, JOHN ADAMS. Proved Dec Court 1791.

Pages 327-328: 6 Dec 1791. Power of Attorney. BRICE MARTIN, SENR. appoints JOSEPH MARTIN to sell or dispose of his lands in Russell County in Powells Valley. And further empowers JOSEPH MARTIN to transact all his business in Henry County in his absence and to pay out of the said sale a Judgement with Costs obtained against him by JOHN WALLEN of Carolina County, Virginia. Signed: BRICE MARTIN. Wit: JOHN SALMON, THADEUS SALMON, JOHN COX, TUNSTALL COX.

Page 329: 29 Feb 1792. Power of Attorney. HENRY LYNE appoints EDMUND LYNE of Bourbon County on the Western Waters to execute a deed to RICHARD REYNOLDS for land in the County of ____ by estimate 500 acres after deducting the quantity the said EDMUND LYNE agreed to for locating or the whole if the said REYNOLDS will convey the part as per agreement made to the Locater. Signed: HENRY LYNE.

Pages 330-331: 28 Apr 1792. JOHN MITCHELL of Pittsylvania County to JOSEPH JONES of Henry County for the sum of five pounds sells and conveys land on the branches of Rocky Branch of the Sandy River and on the north side of the Great Road containing 33 acres, formerly the property of SAMUEL MOSLEY. Signed: JOHN MITCHELL, ELIZABETH (X) MITCHELL. Wit: FRANCIS COX, JOHN CREASEY, WILLIAM CRAIN. Proved 30 Apr 1792.

Pages 331-333: 28 Apr 1792. JOHN MITCHELL of Pittsylvania County to WILLIAM CRINE (CRANE??) of Henry County for the sum of thirty pounds sells land on the Rocky Branch of Sandy River formerly the property of SAMUEL MOSLEY containing 349 acres, being part of JOHN MITCHELL'S 379 acre survey. Signed: JOHN MITCHELL. Wit: FRANCIS COX, JOHN CREASEY, JOSEPH JONES. Proved 30 Apr 1792.

Pages 333-334: 30 Apr 1792. SAMUEL BUCKLEY of Henry County and his wife to GEORGE HAIRSTON of the same for the sum of fifty pounds sells a tract of land containing 400 acres and joins lines of CONWAY and MEREDITH. Signed: SAMUEL BUCKLEY. Proved 30 Apr 1792.

Pages 335-336: 30 Apr 1792. BENJAMIN DILLION, SENR. of Henry County to AUGUSTINE LAWLESS of the same for the sum of thirty pounds sells a tract of land containing by estimate 315 acres more or less on the branches of Jordon's Creek beginning at HENRY DILLION'S. Signed: BENJAMIN DILLION, SENR. Proved 30 Apr 1792.

Page 336: 10 Nov 1788. WILLIAM PARKS and MARY PARKS his wife of Rockingham County, North Carolina to WILLIAM ROBERTS of Henry County, for the consideration of one hundred pounds sells land on both sides of Smith River at the mouth of Leatherwood Creek being 100 acres and formerly the property of THOMAS WILSON. Signed: WILLIAM PARKS, MARY (X) PARKS. Wit: WILLIAM ST. COX, FRANCIS GILLEY, THOMAS STEWART. Proved 30 Apr 1792.

Pages 337-338: 26 Mar 1792. JOHN REDD and JOHN JAMISON of Henry County to JOHN NORRIS of the same for the sum of thirty pounds sell and convey a tract of 60 acres on a large branch of Reedy Creek. Signed: JOHN REDD, JOHN JAMISON. Proved 30 Apr 1792. MEMO: JOHN REDD is only liable to JOHN NORRIS for 4 to 5 acres lying on the upper end of the tract.

Pages 338-340: 17 Apr 1784. JOHN MORTON, SENR. of Pittsylvania County to JOHN BOOTH of Henry County for the consideration of one thousand six hundred pounds sells and conveys a tract of land containing 854 acres on both sides of a branch of the Sandy River and joins ROBERTS. Signed: JOHN MORTON. Wit: JOHN WELLS, BARNABA WELLS, JR., MATHEW WELLS, THOMAS DICKERSON, JR. Proved 22 Apr 1784 and 30 Apr 1792.

Pages 340-341: 30 Apr 1792. GEORGE DYER of Henry County to THOMAS CHANDLER of Franklin County, Virginia for the sum of fifty pounds sells a parcel of land on the branches of the Muster Branch of Leatherwood Creek containing by survey 200 acres with lines of GEORGE REYNOLDS and WILLIAM BARNARD. Signed: GEORGE (X) DYER. Proved 30 Apr 1792.

Pages 341-342: 30 Apr 1792. ABRAHAM PENN of Patrick County, Virginia to STEPHEN CARTER of Henry County for the sum of thirty pounds sells a tract of land on Beaver Creek being 450 acres. Signed: ABRAHAM PENN. Wit: JOHN SALMAN, BENJAMIN LANIER, ROBERT STOCKTON, JR. Proved 30 Apr 1792.

Page 343: 15 Feb 1792. ANDREW REA of Henry County to JOHN COX of the same, for and in consideration of forty pounds sells land, 163 acres, it being part of a tract on Stewarts Creek that ANDREW REA purchased of EDMUND EDWARDS joins JACOB KEATON, EDWARD COCKRAM, WILLIAM COX and Dutchman's Creek. Signed: ANDREW REA. Wit: THOMAS STOVALL.

Pages 344-345: 29 Apr 1792. WILLIAM HUNTER of Franklin County, Virginia to THOMAS WHITE RUBLE of Henry County for the sum of thirty pounds sells and conveys a parcel of land containing 100 acres more or less on both sides of Town Creek...being part of a survey dated at Williamburg 20 Oct 1779... joins DANIEL SMITH and SHADRACK TURNER. Signed: WILLIAM HUNTER. Wit: WILLIAM TURNER, JEREMIAH TURNER, SAMUEL PACKWOOD. Proved 30 Apr 1792.

Pages 345-346: 13 Apr 1792. JOHN HAILEY of Henry County to BARNETT HAILEY of the same, for the consideration of twenty five pounds sells land on Leatherwood Creek joining EDMOND TOOMBS and WILLIAM TOMBS, being 100 acres. Signed: JOHN HALEY Proved 30 Apr 1792.

Pages 346-347: 28 Apr 1792. JACOB CAYTON of Henry County to JOHN HARRIS of the same, for the sum of six pounds sells 50 acres of land, one line being the Cuntry line. Signed: JACOB (X) CAYTON, PEGGY (X) CAYTON. Wit: CORNELIUS (X) CAYTON. Proved 30 Apr 1792.

Pages 347-348: 2 Oct 1786. DANIEL MC BRIDE and SARAH MC BRIDE his wife to WILLIAM TOMBES all of Henry County, for the sum of sixteen pounds sells a tract of land containing 150 acres on the branches of Leatherwood Creek. Signed: DANIEL MC-BRIDE, SARAH MC BRIDE. Wit: JOHN MINTER, JOHN HALEY, JOHN CONNAWAY. Proved 9 Apr 1787 & Apr Court 1792.

Pages 348-349: 16 Dec 1789. DANIEL MC BRIDE and SARAH MC BRIDE his wife of Henry County to WILLIAM TOOMS of the same county for the sum of thirty five pounds sells 136 acres of land on the waters of Leatherwood Creek. Signed: DANIEL MC BRIDE, SARAH MC BRIDE. Wit: JOHN COLLIER, DANIEL CARLAN, WILLIAM BECKNELL. Proved 26 Apr 1790 & Apr Court 1792.

Pages 350-351: 28 May 1792. JAMES LYON Sheriff of Henry County to GEORGE REAVES...JAMES LYON as Sheriff and acting on behalf of the Commonwealth of Virginia and the consideration of six pounds conveys to REAVES a tract of land, part of a tract the property of WILLIAM COOTS, deceased located on both sides of Buttrum Town Creek containing 60 acres. Sold to satisfy Revenue Tax. Signed: JAMES LYON, Sheriff for Henry County. Wit: DAVID LANIER, WILLIAM HORD, THOMAS STOVALL. Proved 28 May 1792.

Pages 351-352: 2 Nov 1787. HUGH MCCAIN of Guilford County, North Carolina to ANDREW RAY of Henry County, Virginia sells and conveys land on the waters of Marrowbone Creek containing 211 acres for the sum of one hundred fifty pounds...said land was purchased by MCCAIN of GEORGE LUMPKIN bounded by GEORGE HAIRSTON, THOMAS JAMISON, GOODWIN MAYSE, DAVID MAYSE and JOHN REDD. Signed: HUGH MCKAIN. Wit: THOMAS JAMISON, JAMES LARIMORE, ALEXANDER JOYCE. Proved May Court 1792.

Pages 352-353: 28 Jan 1792. WILLIAM GRAVES for the sum of twenty five pounds sells unto JOSEPH MARTIN all and every part of his father's estate which was willed to the said WILLIAM GRAVES. His father was WILLIAM GRAVES, SENR. Should the Courts of Henry County before the decease of his mother MARY GRAVES rule that the will is not lawfull, then the estate to be equally divided between the heirs of his father. Signed: WILLIAM GRAVES. Wit: WILLIAM (X) TOOMBS, BRICE MARTIN, JR.

Pages 353-355: 4 July 1792. Deed of Trust. SAMUEL HUGHES of Henry County to SAMUEL CALLAND of Pittsylvania County in the amount of one hundred twenty six pounds, fifteen shillings, a penny and a half penny that the said SAMUEL HUGHES is justly indebted to SAMUEL CALLANDS. Therefore assigns the following: a tract of land on Turkey Cock Creek containing 200 acres, which the said HUGHES purchased of SAMUEL JOHNSON, 10 head cattle, 1 bay mare 10 years old, 1 sorrel mare 8 years old, 1 black mare 4 years old, sorrel colt 1 year old, 17 head sheep, 1 pr mill stones, his stock of hogs, 2 feather beds and furniture, together with all household and kitchen furniture and all plantation tools. Date due: 1 March 1794. Signed: SAMUEL (X) HUGHES. Proved July Court 1792. Wit: SAMEUL TOMPKINS, JR., SAMUEL JOHNSON, JOSEPH REYNOLDS, BOWKER SMITH.

Pages 356-357: 3 July 1792. SAMUEL JOHNSON of Henry County to SAMUEL HUGHES of the same for the sum of one hundred fifty pounds sells a tract of land containing 200 acres on Turkey Cock Creek. Signed: SAMUEL JOHNSON. Wit: SAMUEL CALLAND, BOWKER SMITH, SAMUEL TOMPKINS, JR. Payment received 3 July 1792. Proved July Court 1792.

Page 358: 13 July 1792. Bond of JOHN OLDHAM with JOHN REDD his security...JOHN OLDHAM hath undertaken to build a bridge 12 feet wide across

Beaver Creek near the mouth of said creek sufficient for a loaded wagon and to keep same in repair for a term of seven years to be completed before 25 Dec 1793. Signed: JOHN OLDHAM, JOHN REDD. Wit: GEORGE HAIRSTON, JOHN COX, JOHN SALMON. Proved July Court 1792.

Pages 358-359: 31 July 1792. Bond of JAMES REA and GEORGE HAIRSTON his security. The said JAMES REA has obtained authority of the Court of Henry to perform marriages.

Pages 359-360: 4 Apr 1787. WILLIAM SWANSON of Henry County to WILLIAM PACE of the same, for the sum of two hundred fifty pounds sells a parcel of land being 162 acres on the south side of Smith River. Signed: WILLIAM SWANSON. Wit: DAVID LANIER, JOHN PACE, THOMAS ADAMS,JR., NEWSOM PACE, DANIEL RAMEY. Proved July Court 1792. . .Possession given 4 Apr 1787.

Pages 361-363: 5 Sept 1792. WILLIAM ROBERTSON of King William County, Virginia to PETER HAIRSTON of Stokes County, North Carolina for the sum of three hundred fifty pounds sells and conveys land in Henry County, Virginia on the south side of Smith River containing 742 acres being part of a 1,142 acre tract granted WILLIAM ROBERTSON (which I have deeded the residue of 400 acres to JAMES REA). Land goes to a branch near the place where the Baptist baptize near the Meeting House to a main branch that leads thru JAMES REA'S plantation and down a branch called the north fork of the Marrowbone Creek joins Doctor GEORGE GILMORS line. Signed: WILLIAM ROBERTSON. Wit: GEORGE HAIRSTON, ABNER (X) REA, THOMAS GRAVES, ABSALOM REA. . .MEMO: Part of the 742 acres is claimed by WILLIAM RICE and part by NATHAN HALL, should these claims be considered to be valid I, PETER HAIRSTON shall not have any recourse for damage against WILLIAM ROBERTSON. Signed: GEORGE HAIRSTON attorney for PETER HAIRSTON. Proved 24 Sept 1792.

Pages 363-364: 13 Apr 1792. Deed of Trust. DAVID LANIER to GEORGE HAIRSTON and JOHN ALEXANDER in the amount of five hundred fifty pounds secures with nine negros to wit: CATE, JEFF, BOB, CHARLES, ISBEL, JUDE, CHANEY, JANEY and EASTER also 10 head horses, a wagon, 25 hd cattle, 6 feather beds and furniture, all household furniture of all descriptions. Condition is that the said DAVID LANIER pay or cause to be paid a certain Bond he owes to FREELAND

& LERAX and for a considerable sum of money which the said GEORGE HAIRSTON, JOHN ALEXANDER and JOHN KING are bound as security. Signed: DAVID LANIER. Wit: BENJAMIN LANIER, JOHN LANIER, JOHN ROWLAND. Proved 24 Sept 1792.

Pages 364-365: 4 Sept 1792. GEORGE HAIRSTON of Henry County to JOHN PACE of the same, for and in consideration of two hundred pounds sells and conveys a tract of 150 acres on the north side of Smith River. Signed: GEORGE HAIRSTON. Proved Sept Court 1792.

Pages 365-366: 14 June 1792. DAVID WEATHERFORD of Henry County to JOHN HAMMONDS of the same for fifty pounds sells a 60 acre tract of land it being part of the Mill Tract, with the Mill thereon on both sides of Leatherwood Creek...20 acres on the west side and 40 acres on the east side of the Creek. Signed: DAVID WEATHERFORD, MARY WEATHERFORD. Wit: JOHN (X) HARDY, THOMAS MARSHALL, JOHN LAFAYE, MOSES (X) WILSON, FRANCIS GILLEY.

INDEX

Compiled by

Marguerite Palmer Mitchell

And

Leona Benice Mitchell

ACHOLS, Abner 71
ACUFF, Cain 40,41,73,75,111
  John 40,41,45,57,68,74,75
  John, Jr. 40,41,45,68,72
  John, Sr. 40
  Sarah 40,41
  William 41,45,73,75
ADAMS, ... 82, 105
  Absalom 10,52,72,74,84
  Edward 60,88,99,115
  George 92,106
  Hanah 32
  Isaac 30,32,71
  Jacob 5,6,10,43,57,64,65,66,72,73
  Jacob, Jr. 64,66,71,73,102,103
  John 98,106,115
  Mary 43
  Peter 93
  Richard 30,32,72,73
  Sarah 101,107
  Sylvester 34
  Thomas 30,32,36,41,71
  Thomas, Jr. 36,48,59,120
  Thomas R. G. 60,71
  William 28,30,32,57,66,71,73,74,101,106,107,115
AKIN, Nicholas 72,75,87,112
ALEXANDER, Daniel 36
  Jean 30,33
  John 8,36,49,63,80,87,115,120,121
  John Martin 63
  William 8,30,33
ALLEN, Erasmus 71
  George 48
  Hanah F. 48
  Samuel 22,23,33,40,49,61,73,75
ALLET, Eliase 94
  George 94
  Joseph 94
ALLEY, Ann 25
  Erasmus 60
  Nicholas 25,26
AMBROSE, Joseph 75,77
AMOS, Martin 62,103
  William 7,39,41,44,62,72,74,86,106
ANDERSON, David 57
  John 10
  Robert 76
  William 29
ANDREW, Merry 53
ANGLIN, Philip 73,95
ANTHONY, Bowling 90
  James 6,14,21,26,38,44,47,68,70,73,75,82,89,99,104,108,111,112,114
  Elizabeth 14,90
  Joseph 14,18,21,26,38,47,72,75,82,114
  Mark 90
ARDEN, Abraham 4
ARMSTRONG, James 89,92,102,104
ARNOLD, Henry 67
  William 3,104

ATKINS, Jesse 75,79
ATKISSON, Jesse 40,56,70,72,78,93,95
AUSTIN, William 83
BAKER, Edward 28,33,42,44
  Elijah 112,113
  Elizabeth 33
  James 8,9,10,17,56,85,87,95,96,97,98,104
  John, Senr. 95
  Rebeccah 95
  Richard 14,20,33,43,83
BALLINGER, Achillis 56,68,70,75,76,78,83
BANKS, William 30,32,43,71,73,77,96
BARKER, Charles 53
  James 53,68
  John 73,102,103
  John, Sr. 65
  Michael 72,73
BARKSDALE, Henry 74,75
  John 8,18,75,90
BARNARD - BERNARD
  Charles 39,41,44,73,85,92,93
  William 47,117
BARNETT, Abner 34,39
  Richard 58
BARNOT, Charles 75
BARROTT, Francis 71,73
  John 49,72,73
  Shadrack 71,73
BARTEE, William 72,74
BARTLETT, James 64,69,72,73
BARTON, ... 17
  David 20
  Thomas 93
BASSETT, Nathaniel T. 72,75
BATES, John 41
BAUGHAN, Aristiphus 90
BAUGHN, Henry 75
BAYS - BAYSE
  Ellinor 39
  Peter 42,72,73
  William 22,65
BEAVERS, James 29
BECKNELL, William 118
BEHELERE, ... 14
BENDER, John Wildrick 78
BIRCH - BURCH
  Garrot 12
BIRD - BYRD
  Francis 23
  James 11
  John 16,18,29,74,88,108,109,110
  Mary 16
  Molly 29
  Samuel 11,13,16,88
BIRKS - BURKE
  Rowland Horsley 12,16
  Sarah 12
BISHOP, Widow 39
BITTING, Anthony 6,26,47,68
  Martha 26
BLACK, Quilles 72
BLACKLEY - BLAKEY
  Acquilla 43,74,89

BLACKLEY - BLAKEY (cont.)
  George 82,92
  Joseph 112
  Margaret 68,92
  Quil. 101
BLANKENSHIP, William 13
BLANTON, James 44
BOATMAN, Richard 72,74
BOLDIN, James 74
BOLLING - BOWLING
  Christopher, Senr. 29,104,112
  James 45,71
  John 73,75
  Joseph 54,71,73
  Samuel 18
  Thomas 57,71,85,110
  William 72,74
BOLTONS, Thomas 2
BOOTH, John 45,67,70,117
BOULDIN - BOULDING
  Joseph 49,76,80
BOWLES, James 115
BOWLIN, Thomas 108
BOWMAN, Widow 39
BOYD, James 102
  John 102,103
  Joseph 102,103
BRADBERRY, Richard 43
  Sarah 47
  William 72
BRADLEY, Joseph 75
BRANHAM - BRANNUM
  William 67
BRAMMER, Edmund 100
  John 41,58,72,74,75,103
  John, Jr. 39
  John, Sr. 100
BRETHARD - BRETHEART
  William 61,73,75,89
BREWER, James 78
BRIANT, Elias 75
  Josiah 46
BRIENTS, ... 101
BRISCOE, Ann 24
  John 24
BRISTOW, Benjamin 71,106,115
  William 22,42,56,65,71,97,99,104,115
BRITTIAN - BRITTON
  George 31,71,74,108
BROADY, Joseph 73
BROCK, Allen 69
  Sarah 39
BROSHEARS, Ann 65
  Phillip 65
BROWN, Augustine 72
  Davis 44
  John 40
  Stark 29,38,75,112
  Tabithia 112
  William 55,57,70,75,110,111
BUCKLEY - BUCKLES
  Samuel 71,88,116
BUNCH, David 86,88,110,111
  Martin 86,88,110,111
BURCH, Jereard 68
  John 106
  John, Jr. 67,70
  John, Sr. 106

1

BURCH (cont.)
  Susan 106
BURCHETT, Daniel 113
  John 92
BURGE, Woody 8,72,75
BURGESS, David 76
  John, Jr. 76
  John, Sr. 76
BURKE, ... 12
BURNETT - BURNET - BURNIT
  Catherine 31
  Charles 31,72,74,86,111
  Griffin 61
  William 61,85
BURRES, Charles 101
BUSH, Thomas 8
BUTLER, Henry 38,79
BUTTERWORTH, Benjamin 67
BUZZARD, Philip 50
CAHILL, John 55
CALDWELL, David 91
CALLANDS, Samuel 119
CALLEY, John 71
CALLAWAY, ... 101
  James 7,45,46
CALVIN, John 50
CAMERON, Cassenerh 46
  Jesse 46,71,73,77
  John 32,71,72
  Joseph 77
  Susannah 46,77
CAMPBELL - CAMELL
  David 94
  James 80,96
  William 36,37
CANNON, Benjamin 75,86
  Samuel 95
CARLIN, Daniel 91,118
CARTER, George 54,58,71,73,
    102,103
  John 48
  Stephen 117
  William 58,67,71,73,83,
    103
  Widow 39
CASEY, Daniel 7
CAVE, Enie 43
  Robert 43
CAVORN, John 84
CAYTON - CATON
  Cornelius 118
  Jacob 68,86,118
  Peggy 118
  William 86
CHADWELL, David 42,71,81,
    97,98,104,110
  Elizabeth 97,98,104
CHANDLER, Joseph 30,58,59,
    71
  Thomas 117
CHAPMAN, Thomas 45
CHARLES, James 101,102
CHAVERS, Adam 39
CHEADLE, John 93
CHEWNING, Thomas 35,68
CHILDRESS, John 109
CHILES, Nancy 11
  Rowland 11,22,43,65,74,
    75
CHOAT, Ann 21
  Isham 16,21
CHOICE, ... 2
  Tully 11
CHEWNING - CHOWNING
  Thomas 35,68
CLACK, David 81
  Samuel 81
  Spencer 29
CLANCHE - CLONCH
  Jeremiah 11,22,101
CLARK, David 54,89
  Henry 18,38,73,75
  John 72,74
  Samuel 42,43,110

CLAYBROOK, James 100,105
CLOUD, Isaac 79
  Joseph 7,64
  William 71,73
COCKRAN - COCKRAM - COCKRUM
  David 53,100
  Edward 31,34,36,117
  Mary 31
  William 13
COGAR, Nicholas 64,75
COLE, James 88
  Walter King 8,17,18,30,
    33,41,68,80,107,115
COLLEY, John 23
COLLIER - COLYAR
  Charles 5,10,14
  John 56,60,118
  Richard 1,11,12,44
COLLINS, John 112
CONWAY - CONNAWAY
  Betty 12
  John 64,74,111,118
CONLEY, James 74
CONWAY, ... 116
COOK, Benjamin 11,17,18,23,
    25,31
  Harmon 22
  James 98
  John 17,18,24,25
  Joseph 17,18,25
  Judith 24
COOKSAY - COOKSEY
  William 14,15,28,72,74
COOLY, Ann 16
  James 16
COOPER, Benjamin 84
  James 44
  John 88,91,47,68,71,73
  Joseph 4,26,44
  Sarah 26,96
  Thomas 6,14,18,36,38,39,
    44,54,60,74,85,86,89,
    90,96,99,113,114,115
COOTS, William 118
COPLAND, Charles 108
  Elizabeth 113
  Peter 62,108
  Richard 108,112,113
CORN, George 87,104
  Jesse 15,53,62,71,74,
    85,92,93
  John Peter 51,62
  Joseph 110
  Peter 104
  Samuel 104
CORNWELL, Peggy 89
  Richard 20,74,89
  William 56,72
COULY, Jacob 68
COWDEN, James 3
COX, Charles 34,71,100
  Francis 34,45,72,82,87,
    116
  Frankey 110
  Jacob 49
  James 37,77,99
  James, Jr. 60
  John 4,18,20,27,36,37,
    61,64,100,110,116,120
  Mary 27,87
  Russell 60,71,110
  Samuel 54,64
  Tunstall 34,64,110,116
  William 9,37,86,100,105,
    117
  William St. 117
  Winifred 37
CRADDOCK, Isham 84
CRAIG, Thomas 75
CRAIN, William 116
CREASEY, John 116
CREWS, Thomas 6
  Susannah 6

CRITCHFIELD - CRUTCHFIELD
  Samuel 22,65,74,75,81,
    85,98,104
CRITZ, Hamon 6,71,73,77,78
  Hamon, Jr. 71
  Hamon, Sr. 56,66
  Jacob 32,56,70,71,73
CROMWELL, William 74
CROUCH - CROUCHER
  Samuel 31,32,71
CROWLEY - CROLEY
  James 65,66,72
CRUTCHER, Samuel 6,73
CRUM, John 94
CUMMINS - CUMMINGS
  Joseph 53
  Susannah 91
  Thomas 61,114
CUMPTON, Boner 24
CUNNINGHAM, Ann 31
  John 4,12,18,20,24,25,
    31,32,38,68
  Thomas 84,91,110
  William 68,76
DALTON, Robert 22
DANDRIDGE, William 51
DANIEL, Edward 88,103
  John 58,72
  Mary 58
DAUGHORTY
  Hugh 27
  Mary 27
  Michal 27
  Sarah 27
DAVIDSON - DAVISON
  Golden 83
  Richard 79
DAVIS, Charles 72,74
  John 10,17,71,74,88,112
  Joseph 15
  Lewis 61
  Richard 113
DAY, John 53,71,73,102
DAWSON, ... 107
  John 105
  Thomas 105
DEACONS, Richard 47
DEAL, William 84
DELOZEAR, Jesse 112
DENNIS, Josiah 37,45
DENNY, James 39,41,44,73,74
DENT, Waller or Walter
    73,75
DENSON, William 48
DEPRIEST, Tabithia 35
DICKERSON, Charles 90
  David 60,90
  James 42,43,102
  Jean 42,43
  John 9,32
  Nelson 90
  Obediah 94
  Thomas, Jr. 30,117
  Thomas, Sr. 57,90
DICKINSON, ... 12
DIKES, James 109
DILLARD, John 3,6,23,27,28,
    31,36,39,46,50,52,55,
    61,70,73,75,78,81,86,
    90,93
  Sarah 27
DILLEN - DILLON - DILLION
  Benjamin 72,75
  Benjamin, Sr. 116
  Henry 73,116
  Henry, Sr. 75
  Joseph 81
  Randolph 106
  Samuel 14
DILLENDER, Jacob 35,86
DILLINGHAM - DILLENHAM
  1
  John 53

DILLINGHAM - DILLENHAM
(cont.)
  Joshua, Joshaway 26,53,
    55,70,74,109
  Michael 38,48,53,71,90,
    113
  William 13
DODSON - DOTSON
  Charles 72,73
  Elizabeth 48,69.70
  George 69,70.71,72
  George, Sr. 104
  Lamboth 48,71,79.93
  Lamboth, Jr. 48
  Thomas 69.72,73
  William 74
DOGGETT, Chatten 10
  Thomas 10,28
DONATHAN, Elijah 58,59
  Rachel 58
DOTSON, George 40
DORREL, John 42,65
DOYAL, Francis 22
  John 22,34
DUNCAN, Charles 55
  Jane 84
  John 59,71,84,94
DUNKIN, John 72
DUDLEY, Thomas 93
DUNIVANT, Thomas 44
DUNN, ... 106
  Michael 37
  Waters 41,106
  William 41
DURHAM, Gregory 5,21,22,72,
    75,84,102
  Nat. 88
DURST, Samuel 33,47
DYER, George 58,117
  Phillip 58
  Rachel 58
  Thomas 17,22
EADES - EADS
  Abraham 71,73
  Bartlet 32
EARLS, Thomas 60
EARLY, Jeremiah 13,45,46
  John 45,46,109
  Joseph 45
EASLEY, John 79
  Mary 82
  Miller Woodson 7,71,73,
    82
  Warsham 71,73,79,81
EASON, Samuel 37
EAST, Eussan 26
  James 20,21,24,26,30,35,
    46,47,48,49,73,75,98,
    107
  James, Sr. 26,32,46
  John 44,60,63,115
  Joseph 26,32
  Mary 47
  Thomas 60,63,80
EASTES see ESTES
ECHOLS, Abner 75,107
EDWARDS, Ann 25,53
  Arthur 25
  Edmund 12,117
  Elizabeth 12
  Isham 71,105
  James 24,34,71,74,86,105
  John 108
  Letty 105
  Nancy 25
  Thomas 1,2,19,24,32,33,
    71,75
  Thomas, Jr. 1,2
  Thomas, Sr. 35,108
  William 1,2,53,105
  William, Sr. 1,2
ELKINS, Caty 34,46
  James 34,39,46,58,73,101

ELKINS (cont.)
  Jesse 71
  Ralph 40,50
  William 21,27
ELLIOTT, Samuel 106
ESTES, Ann 23
  Bottom 29
  Elisha 29,93
  Elisha, Jr. 29
  Elisha, Sr. 28
  Joel 23,44
  Millicent 93
  Robert 93
  William 11,38
EVANS, George 71
  William 16,17,52
FAGAN, William 74
FARGUSON - FERGUSON
  Joseph 41,42,112,113
  Patience 113
FARRAR, Richard 8
FARRELL - FERRELL
  John 19,72,73
FARRIS, Charles 33,71
  Charles, Jr. 107,115
  Charles, Sr. 107,115
  Edy 115
  Jacob 18,38,72,74
  Josiah 28
FAULKNER - FALKNER
  William 75
FEE, Henry 15,48,49,93,115
  Rachel 15
  Thomas 15,49,115
  William 15,49,50,115
FERGUS, John 24,25
FEWSON, William 101
FINN, William 66
FIPHER see PHIFER
FISHER, Jabus 81
FITZGERALD, Frederick 49,
    50
  Harvey 7,64,104
  Isham 10
FLETCHER, George 28
  John 65,66,72,74
FLOWERS, Thomas 5,15,33,75
FOLEY, Barbery 62,63
  Bartholomew 62,63
  Bartlett 11,73,74
  Luke 15,72,74
FONTAINE, ... 4,95
  John 49,80,92,109
FORD, Andrew 78
FORSICE - FOSSIE - FORSIL
  John 45,82
  John, Jr. 45
FORTNER, Jonah 91
  Jonas 91
  John 91
  William 71,91
FOSTER, Charles 30,39,73,
    75,97,101,107
  Charles, Jr. 30
  John 27
FRANCE, Daniel 26
  Homon 81
  Henry 4,23,40,72,74,109
  John 71,73
  Mary 81
  Peter 71,73
  William 54,97
  William, Sr. 71
FRANUS, Joseph 79
FRANKLIN, Lewis 103
FRASHURE - FRAZIER
  Alexander 33,98,104
  Robert 33,75
  Thomas 50
  William 97,98,104
FREELAND & LENOX 120,121
FRENCH, William 6,20,46,96
FULCHER, George 35,77

FULKERSON, Frederick 15,16,
    49,50,71,73,82,107
  James 16
FUSON - FEWSON
  Elizabeth 47
  John 33,47
  John, Jr. 33
  William 97
GALLAWAY, James 96
  Robert 96
GARDNER, William 5,15,72,
    74,85,100
GARNER - GARNOR
  Thomas 73,75
GARNOGAN, John 28
GARREOTT, Benjamin 71,73
GASLOBY, Daniel 71
GIBSON, William 28
GILLIAM, Charles 109
  Deverix 43,66,72,73,88,
    95
  Eady 43,66
  Peter 4
GILLESPIE - GALLASY
  John 21
GILLEY, Charles 114
  Elizabeth 114
  Francis 34,60,72,110,114,
    117,121
  Francis, Jr. 110
  Francis, Sr. 34,60
GILMOR, George 120
GLASS, Thomas 14
GOLDSBAY, Daniel 41,48,79,
    93
GOING, John 84,97
GOODMAN, Charles 62,63
GOODSON, John 37
  Thomas 37
  Thomas, Sr. 37
GOODWIN, Joseph 31,74,79,
    104,105
GOWING, James 9
GRASBY, John 75
GRAVELY, John 71,106
  Joseph 37,68,70,71,74,
    110
GRAVES, William 3,73,75,86,
    119
  Mary 86,119
  Peyton 24
  Polly, Jr. 86
  Thomas 85,120
GRAY, ... 106
  William 72,75
GREEN, James 27
  William 70
GREER, Moses 10
GRIGGS, John 72,74,110
GRIFFIN, William 72,74,107
GRIMIT - GREMET
  John 20
  Robert 52
GRIMES, Francis 75
GRISHAM, Thomas 90
GROGAN, Henry 36,105
  John 36,71,74,100
GROOM, Anne 47
  Zackahiah 47
GRYMES, John Dawson 105
GUFFEY - GUFFEE
  Henry 5,15,72,74
GUSSETT, John 50,73,75
HAILE - HAIL - HALE
  James 53,74,102
  Rachael 33
HAILEY - HALEY
  Barnett 118
  David 87
  James 29,45,71,75
  John 45,57,73,74,89,111,
    113,118
HAIRSTON, Elizabeth 63,63

HAIRSTON (cont.)
  George 14,19,22,26,29,
    30,31,33,35,36,41,42,
    46,48,50,51,56,58,59,
    62,63,65,68,69,72,74,
    76,77,79,80,84,86,88,
    92,96,98,108,111,112,
    113,114,115,116,119,
    120,121
  Peter 120
  Robert 92
  Samuel 41,44,45
HAIZE, William 79
HALE, James 72,102
HALL, Isham 13,24
  John 36,37,39
  Nathan 20,21,34,39,53,
    58,59,74,75,97,120
  Randolph 21
  Robert 83
  Sarah 39
  Thomas Row. 53,58,59,
    96
HALLADAY - HOLLIDAY
  Robert 9
HAMILTON, George 41
  Mary 41
  Thomas 72,75
HAMMOCK, Daniel
HAMMIT, William 32,69
HAMMON - HAMMONS - HAMMOND
  6
  John 88,121
  Thomas 13
  William C. R. 88
  William Robertson 32,33,
    41
HAMPTON, Robert 57
HANBY, ... 79
  Jonathan 48,54,58
HANCOCK, Benjamin 71,73,86
  John 86
  Joseph 62,63,97
  Lewis 15,62,86
  Major 86,93
  William 85,92
HANDY, Joseph 75
HANLEY, John 48
HARBOUR, Adonijah 55
  Catherine 64
  David 15,75
  David, Sr. 40,62
  Esaias 56,61,64,91
  Elisha 64,103,106
  Isaac 73
  Iseau 75
  Joel 56,57,64,75,91
  Moses 73,103,106
  Talmon 56,57,61,64,77
  Thomas 6,73,75,81
HARD, Stephen 82
HARDIE, Joseph 43
HARDING, Elutrus 7
  William 7,14
HARDMAN, John 2,27,59
  William 7,21,27
HARDY, John 121
HARMER, George 18
  John 8,41
HARRIS, George 32
  George Fuller 33
  Henry 16,73,75,80
  John 15,25,118
  Samuel 20,42
  Sarah 20
  William 20,22,75,101
HASTEN, Charles 5
HASKINS, William 10
HATCHER, Archer 61
HAWKINS, Benjamin 28
  James 3
HAYS - HAYSE
  William 28,48,71,93

HEARD, George 13
  Jesse 4
  John 14,16,18,26,29,83
  Stephen 14,24,82,83
  Stephen, Jr. 83
  William 7,16,18,74,92
  William, Sr. 75
HELTON see HYLTON
HENDERSON, Elizabeth 7
  John 7,15,19,56,57,61,
    72,91,100,103,106
HENDRICK, John 40
HENRY, Dorthea, Dorothy 49,
    96
  Patrick 46,49,63,64,80,
    96,106,110
HENSLEY, William 91
HERON, Andrew 102,103
HEWLETT, William 65
HIBBER - HIBBERT
  Charles 5,6,70,74,75,83,
    84
  Lydia 84
HICKEY, Jacob 43
HICKMAN, William 95
HICKS, Benjamin 26,58,59
  James 58,59,111
  Miles 22,59
HIGGINBOTTOM, Mary 9
  William 9,89
HILER, David 108
HILL, Francis 12
  Manning 82
  Reuben 69,70,73
  Swinfield 20
HILTON see HYLTON
HINTON, William Robert 63
HOBART - HOBARD
  Harrison 33,54,69,87
HODGES, Moses 8
HOLLAND, Ben 37
  John 19
  Peter 7
  Sarah 19
  Thomas 73,75
HOLLANDSWORTH, Isaac 83
  Thomas, Jr. 50
HOLLAWAY, ... 7
HOLLIDAY, John 52
HOLMES, John 38,47,72
HOLT, Edmond 34
  Francis 66
  John 71
HOMES, John 74
HOOKER, ... 12
  John 71,72,92
  Robert 28
  Samuel 58,59
HORD, John 26,30,84,97,98,
    103,104,105,110,113
  Justiania 112
  Mordecai 8,36,37,38,49,
    72,75,110,111,112,113
  Ruth 84,113
  Stanwix 38,97,98,103,
    104,110,111,112
  Susannah 26
  William 90,103,110,111,
    112,113,114,118
HUBBARD, Benjamin 71,74,90
  Eusebus 2
  Durrett 17
  James 29
  Joel 97
HUCHERSON, Elkanah 18
HUDGINS, John 71
HUDSON, Hall 5,67
  Joshua 83
  Obediah 59,71,73
HUFF, Mary 7
  Thomas 6,81
HUGHES, Archelaus 4,48,54,
    72,74,85,91,109

HUGHES (cont.)
  A. 77,92,96,97,111
  Beveridge 67,72,74
  Leander 97,109,114
  Robert 67,103
  Samuel 119
HUDSPETH, Robert 14,15,78,
    92,102,107
  Thomas 102,107
  William 71,102,107
HUMPHREYS, Morris 12,49,50,
    72,75,95
  Sarah 50
HUNTER, Alexander 17,33,35,
    37,38,42,56,68,73
  El. 111
  John 6,18
  J. W. 114
  George 18,19
  Martha 17
  William 18,19,32,118
HURD, William 38
HURT, Joseph 15,72,74,85
  Moses 85
HUTCHINGS - HUTCHERSON
  Charles 23
  Frederick 48
  John 48,73
  Sarah 23
  Thomas 107
  William 23
HUTET, William 49
HYLTON, John 10,25,28
  Newman 67
  Samuel 84
INGRAM - INGRUM
  James 16,56,73,77,99,101
  John 42,43,73,74
INNES, Hugh 11,13,18,29
  James 99
IRVIN, ... 18
ISAM - ISOM
  William 33,40,49,73
ISHAM, James 83
  William 72
IVIE - IVEY
  Elisha 59,72,75
  Martha 59
JACKSON, Daniel 111
JAMES, Edward 38
  James 44
  John 77
  Spencer 44,73,96
JAMISON - JAMERSON
  Hannah 80
  John 3,73,75,80,117
  Thomas 26,36,48,62,75,
    80,88,92,119
  Thomas, Jr. 80
  William 72,74,105
JENKINS, Lewis 24
JENNINGS, Miles 54,78,79,
    89,90
  Susannah 89,90
JERVIS - JARVIS
  Thomas 48,82,98
JOHNSON - JOHNSTON
  Betty 12,68,76
  David 71,74,110
  James 58,59,68,76
  Samuel 4,12,30,45,55,57,
    68,73,74,76,78,83,119
JONNYKIN - JOURNKIN
  John 55
JONES, Armstead 41
  Ambrose 26,38,75,90,99,
    112,113
  Benjamin 89,92
  Buckner 105
  Felding 8
  Henry 8,40,41,45,72,74,
    87,115
  Hugh 17

JONES (cont.)
  John 38,49
  Joseph 41,116
  Robert 17,22,41
  Thomas 7,11,17,25
  William 99,104,112
JORDON - JURDEN
  Samuel 82
  Thomas 91,94
JOYCE, Alexander 26,36,43,
    48,58,59,65,71,76,119
  Frances 65
  Joseph 34
  William 88
JURDENS, ... 11
KEARBY, Richard 15
KEATON - KEETON
  Jacob 71,100,117
  William 53,65
KEATH, James 43
KELLY, Bennett 68
  John 13,68,104
  William 13,29
KENDRICK - KINDRICK
  John 5,6,15,33,67,103
  Preston 31,71
KANNON, Benjamin 71
KENNON, Benjamin 32,46,98,
    107
KERBY, Richard 15,19
  Sarah 15,19
KEY, Martin 8
KING, John 36,48,71,121
  Joseph 10,18,38,39,75,
    80,81
  Stephen 38,61,65,74,75,
    111,113
  Samuel 79
  Walter 66
  Zackeriah 95
KINSEY, Benjamin 78
  Benjamin, Jr. 78
  John 25
KIRBY - KERBY - KEARBY
  Jesse 10,17
  John 10
  Richard 106
KOGER - COGER
  Elizabeth 79,82
  Henry 72,73,114
  Jacob 39
  John 20,73,75,79,82,83
  Nicholas 5,73,81,91
LACKEY, Adam 33,40,49
  John 74,75,101
LAFEYE, John 121
LANDERS, James 89
LANDRETH, Benjamin 56
LANE - LAIN - LAYNE
  Dutton 1,24,47,49,71,75
  Samuel 85,92
LANIER, Benjamin 80,117,121
  David 11,19,26,41,49,58,
    59,63,72,80,96,104,109,
    118,120,121
  John 121
  Mary 80
  Samuel 36
  Washington 26,71,99,102
LANKFORD, James 5
  Nicholas 4
  Robert 4
LANSFORD, Henry 108
LARIMORE, Hugh 95
  James 119
LAW, Thomas 16
LAWLESS, Augustine 38,74,
    116
  Austin 72
LAWRENCE-LARRANCE-LAURANCE
  Henry 68,76
  Martin 5,67,72,74
  William 68,76

LAWSON, David 54
  John 44
LAYNE, Dutton 24,65
LEAK, Peter 1,21,35,72,85,
    86
  Thomas 60,71
LEE, John 58
LETCHWORTH, Thomas 45,60
LEVISTONES, John 85
LIMING, John 93
LINDSAY, Elizabeth 5
  Mary 6
  John 5,23,27,28,31,35,
    82,109
LITRELL, Michael 57,65
  Nathan 57
LLOYD - LOYD
  Benjamin 108
  James 89
  John 64,77
LOCKHART, Richard 112
  Thomas 6,53,72,73
LOMAX & COMPANY 46,106,112
LONG, William 14
LORTON, Robert 76,109
LOWE, Alice 40
  Thomas 40
LOVELL - LOWELL
  Markham 73,75,82,92
  William 21
LUCK, Mary 38
LUMPKIN, George 80,119
LUMSDEN, John Jr. 4
LYALLS, Joe 60,76
LYNCH - LINCH
  Becky 62,95
  William 61,62,72,73,95
LYNE, Edmund 8,116
  Henry 29,38,39,51,53,55,
    57,61,65,80,84,87,110,
    115,116
LYON, Col. James 7,25
  Humberston 87,102
  James 9,22,29,38,39,51,
    63,72,75,80,82,87,118
  Stephen 7,34,35,63,72,
    91,95,96,97,104
MABRY - MABERRY
  George 39,41,44,72,74,
    91,94
  George, Jr. 78
  Isaac 23
MAC BRIDE, James 23
MAGWIER, Aleyond 13
MAGRUDER, Blizard 34
MAJORS, James 29
MANENS - MANES
  Jacob 9
  Richard Tucker 44
MANKINS, James 7,72,73,104
MANNEN, John 86
  William 102
MANNER - MANOR
  Richard 71,72
MANNING, John 72
MANNION, John 27
MAQUIRE, William 110
MARCUM, John 7
  Josiah 7
MARR, ... 79
  John 14,15,50,51,52,56,
    59,62,69,70,71,74,77,
    79,83,92,95,99,105,
    107,109
  Maj. John 27
  Susanah 79
MARROW, Thomas 49
MARSHALL, Thomas 121
MARTHELY, Joseph 45
MARTIN, Boman 42
  Brice 26,27,38,88,116
  Brice, Jr. 119
  Brice, Sr. 115

MARTIN (cont.)
  Joseph 70,89,104,109,111,
    112,113,115,116,119
  Martin 107
  Susanah 89,99
  William 11,42,86,89
MASON, James 7,13,14,83
  Robert 9,16,17
MASTERS, James 74
  John 31,75
MASTIN, James 89
MATHEWS, John 51,72,73
  Thomas 47
MATLOCK, Charles 20,33
  William 20
MAUPIN, Jesse 38
MAVITY, Mary 7
  William 7
MAY, Caleb 108,109
  Elizabeth 65
  James 3,24,65,72
  John 24,65,72,75
  William 24
MAYO, William James 85,92,
    93
  Valentine 64,73,74
MAYS - MAYSE
  Abraham 42,43
  David 42,55,71,88,119
  Goodwin 71,88,119
  Henry 36,54,55,71,74
  James 48,75
  Sarah 43
  Sherod 55,71
MAXEY, Sampson 68,104
  Susan 104
  Walter 30,44
MEAD, Robert 96
  William 17,96
MEDKIFF, Ruthy 9
  Thomas 8,9
MEDLEY, John 53,84
MEGEE see also MC GHEE
  Holden 33,102
MELTON, James 2,3
  Nancy 2,3
MELY, John 102
MENEFEE, Milley, Jr. 20
  Milley, Sr. 20
MEREDITH, ... 116
  Bradley 62
  James 74,87,88,110,111
  Junor 63
MERRY, Morrah 9
MILLER, John 56
  John Frederick 50
  Martin 50
  Thomas 23,28
  Thomas, Jr. 25,28
  Thomas, Sr. 25
  William 28
MILLS, William 109
MINISS, Dorothy 105
MINN, John 56
MINTER, John 13,45,61,64,73,
    75,111,118
MITCHELL, Elizabeth 86,116
  John 45,74,116
  Ralph 5,6,9,40
  Richard 54,74,86
  William 45,54,72,114
MOBLEY, Samuel 74
MOON, Alexander 44
MOORE, Alexander 115
  Benjamin 55
  Rodham 14,64,72,74,95
  William 23,44,55,71,85,
    86,97,98
MORGAN, John 34,92
  Mary 92
MORRAK, David 75
MORRIS, Ezekiel 58,78
  John 73,75

5

MORRIS (cont.)
  Joseph 26,35,46,71,74,
    84,86
  Mary 86
  Samuel Coleman 21,22,35,
    46,47,71,74,78,79,86
MORRISON, James 62,72,74
  Thomas 86
MORROW, Thomas 15,19,72,74,
  106
MORTON, James 45,60,73,75
  John, Sr. 117
  Joseph 78,83
MOSLEY, Samuel 41,116
MULLINS, William 11,18,75
MURPHY, James 73,75
  Jesse 71,88
MURRELL, Benjamin
  Thomas 67
MC ALEXANDER, Alexander 94
  Jenny 94
  John 94
  William 94
MAC BRIDE, Daniel 118
  James 39,71
  Sarah 118
MC CAIN, Hugh 119
MC CLANE, Thomas 101
MC CRAW, James 46
  Jacob 45,89
MC CULLOCK, Alexander 45,
  108
MC DANIEL, Michael 80
MC DONALD, Isaac 57,64,71
MC GOWAN, John 102
MC GHEE-MEGEE-MAGEHEE
  Holden 33,102,103
  John 62,95
MC GUFFEY, Henry 33
MC GUIRE, Anderson 106
  William 110
  Zackeriah 61
MC KINNEY - MC KINSEY
  Daniel 75
  James 3
  Kinney 59,63,66,75
MC MILLIAN - MC MILLION
  John 39
  Paul 89
MC WILLIAMS, Hugh 75
  James 16,74
  John 109
NANCE, John 40,111
  Reuben 21,45,55,57,64,
    73,75,110,112
  Sally 13
  William 40
NASH, Marvel 94
NEAL, Benjamin 47,69,71,72
  Elizabeth 47
NEVILLS, John 72
NEWMAN, Daniel 71,72,103
  John 103
  Joseph 72
NICKHAM, John 37
NICOLD-NICULS-NICHOLS
  John 35,57
NICHOLAS, John 82,83,106
  Robert 82
NITE, John 93
NOE, ... 101
  Gidion 107
  Samuel 62,63
NORRIS, G. T. 33
  John 29,80,109,117
NORTHCUT, Francis 57
  Nathan 57
NORTON, John 35,71,73,77,
    83,112,113,115
  Nehemiah 74,106
NOWLAND - NOWLIN
  John 4
  Samuel 107

NOWLING, James 39,84,96
NUCOLDS, John 71
NUCOM 75
NUNN, Elizabeth 24
  Ingram 7
  Joseph 27,71
  Thomas 7,10,17,37,38,46,
    61,56,73,80,93
OFFICER, James 86,110
OAKLEY, Thomas 71
OAKES, James 74,90
  John 92
  William 92
OLDHAM, Elizabeth 109
  John 45,71,74,87,109,
    119,120
  Mary 19,105,106
  Thomas 105
OLIVER, John 78
O'NEAL, Edward 103
OSBORNE, John 80
PACE, Elizabeth 108
  Joel 60,71
  John 30,33,44,54,74,79,
    107,108,115,120,121,
  Newson 7,54,93,108,120
  William 120
PACKWOOD, Samuel 73,75,100,
  118,145
PARKER, John 53
PARKS, Mary 117
  William 117
PARR, Arthur 81
  John 71,82,87
  John, Jr. 72,73
  John, Sr. 51,73,81
PARIOTT, Nathaniel 13
PARRY, Thomas 106
PARSLEY, Richard 52,53,75
PATTERSON - PATTSON
  Jarrett 23
  Samuel 23,44
PAYNE, Abm. 71
  Reubin 11,41,42,88,115
PEDIGO - PEREGOY
  Edmond
  Edward 59,74
  Elizabeth 52
  Joseph 52,53,74
  Robert 52,53,57,74
  Robert, Jr. 52
  Robert, Sr. 52
PEGOR, Edmund 71
PELFER - PELFREE
  John 75,87
  John, Jr. 87
  William 87
PENN, Abram. Abraham 10,18,
    25,27,30,31,32,39,42,
    43,51,52,59,60,66,78,
    85,87,89,95,102,103,
    107,117
  George 28,31,32,60,62,
    69,83,84,85,95,98,114
  George, Jr. 79
  Lucinda 60
  Philip 28,31,47,69,71,
    73,109,135
  Ruth 18,59
PENNINGTON, Isaac 79
PEREGAN, Jacob 28, 35,43
PERKINS, Const. 51,92
  Christopher 72,74
  David 91
  Peter 64,87
  William 75
  William, Jr. 91
  William, Sr. 39
PERRY, James 99
  Samuel 28,33,44,72,99
PERRYMAN, Anna 100
  Benjamin 17
  Richard 13,17

PERRYMAN (cont.)
  Robert 99,100
PHIFER, James 30
  Joseph 38,53
PHIPS (FEPS)
  James 20
PHILLIPS, George 68,70
  John 45
  Thomas 115
PHINN, William 66
PIGG, Elizabeth 36
  James 58,69,71,72
  Richard 36
PHILPOTT, B. W. 95
  John 20,33,71,74
  Samuel 20
  Zackeriah 90
PHINN see FINN
PIGG, James 89,94
  Paul 34
PILGRIM, Michael 50
  Thomas 38
PILSON, Kelley 44
  Richard 66,71,74
PINKARD, Charles 23
PITTMAN, James 28,72,75
POLSON, Andrew 72
POORS, George, Jr. 73
  George, Sr. 71
  William 43,54
POSEY, Benjamin 9,20,74,
    104,105,114
  Bennett 24,83
  Hunphrey 54,75,87
  Susanah 105
  Thomas 54,87,98,104
POTEET, James 34,39,72,84,
  100
  James, Sr. 100
  James, Jr. 100
  John 100
POTTER, Thomas 24
PRATER - PRATOR
  Nehemiah 71,73,93,94
  Thomas 38
PRESTON, John 6,57,65,66
PRICE, Barnet 101
  Bernard Moore 101
  Joseph Showers (Shores)
    21,22,25,29,51
  Lucy 101
  Showers 29
  Salley 101
  William 43,100,101
  William Barber 43,100
PRUNTY, James 2,29
  Robert 2,16,29
  Thomas 9,22,25,32,33
PRYOR, James 105
  John 14,15,27
PULLAM - PULLIAM
  John 58,72,80
PYRTLE, John 38,75,84
  John, Jr. 88
  John, Sr. 88
  John P. 110,111,113
QUARLES, David 108
  William 105
RAINEY, Judith 88
  Mathew 31,32,33,41,76,
    77,88
  Stephen 33
RAKES, Charles 53
RANDALS - RANDEL
  John 69
  Weniford 69
RANDOLPH & COMPANY 106
RAMEY, Daniel 9,46,49,74,
    76,115,120
  Sanford 115
RAMSEY, John 11
  George 11
  Mary 11

RANDELL - RANDELLS
    John 58,70,72,104,108
RANDOLPH, ... 7,10
    Thomas Mann 6,18,46,51,
        85
RANEY, Mathew 71,74
RATLIFF, Silas 59,71
RAY see REA
REA, Abner 120
    Absolom 120
    Andrew 11,12,43,71,88,93,
        95,100,117,119
    James 74,120
    John 60,99,107
    Sally 11
READ, John 5,48
    Samuel 38,75
READER, William 93
REAMEY - RAMEY
    Daniel 8,19
    Sanford 44
REDD, John 18,53,60,62,70,
        74,75,80,82,92,113,
        114,117,119,120
REED, John 27
    William 98
REEVES-RIEVES-REIVES
    Frederick 25
    George 33,73,75,97,113,
        118
REDMAN, Ignatious 71,73
REIORS, George 85
RENNO, John 11,75,99
    Stephen 11,59,74,99
RENTFRO, ... 7
    Jesse 17,22
    John 10,13,21,22,51
    Moses 25
REUBIN, ... 87
REY, John 21
REYNOLDS - RUNNOLDS
    Archalus 80
    Bartlett 71,93,94
    Bartus 80
    David 79
    George 36,47,117
    Jesse 5,57,65,71,73,80
    Joseph 56,57,119
    Mary 19,79
    Millenton 80
    Moses 71,72,79,80
    Reuben 80
    Richard 19,91,116
    Susannah 47
RICE, Daniel 6,32
    John 44,54
    Judy 32
    Mary 90
    William 74,90,104,120
RICHARDS, Patty 101
RICHARDSON, Aaron 10
    Amos 2,3,4,10,14,29
    Amos, Senr. 31
    Benjamin 14
    Daniel 10,11,17,18,25,44
    Elizabeth 17
    John 14,74,102
    Lucy 31
    Martha 4
    Mary 33,46
    Thomas 34,36,46,47,73,
        75,87
RICKLE - RICKELS
    Fred 88
    John Frederick 40,41
    William 8,31,33,40,41
RICKMAN, Peter 61
RIGG - RIGGS
    Charles 72,75
RIVES, Frederick 24
ROBERTS, ... 117
    Ea. 8
    Gabriel 31,90

ROBERTS (cont.)
    James 4,51,90
    John 85,91
    Joseph 61,85
    Salley 76,77
    Samuel 33,76,77
    Samuel S. 76,77
    William 117
ROBERTSON - ROBERSON
    Archibald 14,59
    John 44
    William 41,71,74,120
ROGERS - RODGERS
    Clem 102
    David 64,72,75,102
    George 54,72,73
    Henry 25
    James 2,4,17
ROSE, Caroline Matilda 82
    Hugh 82
ROSS, Charles 104
    Daniel 107
    David 80
    John 34
ROW, Thomas 39
ROWARD - ROWARKE
    Ames 48
    David 58,69,74,95
ROWDIN, Abram E. 42
    Abraham 11,74
ROWLAND, Baldwin 20,80,113
    George, Sr. 20,44
    John 20,41,63,80,87,121
    Mary 27,58,81
    Michael 44,45,62
RUBLE, Thomas White 118
RUNNOLDS, George 47
RYAN, Darby 17,41,64
    John 81
    Joseph 81
    Nathan 30,44
    Obedience 27,79
    Philip 44,58,75,76,79,
        81
    William 4,23,44,88
SALESBURY, Jeremiah 24
SALMON, Drury 34,71,73
    Elizabeth 31
    Hezekiah 38
    John 10,11,18,20,26,27,
        29,31,38,39,50,70,72,
        75,80,81,110,111,116,
        117,120
    Rowland 39
    Thaddeus 27,31,45,81,116
SANFORD, George 71,75
    James 40,75
SAUNDERS, Peter 21,46
SCAIFE, William, Jr. 81
    William, Sr. 81
SCALES, Joseph 72,75
    Nathaniel 38,72,74
    Nicholas 105
    P. 38
    Polley 109
SCRUGGS, Julius 75
SENTER, Stephen 101
    Tandy 101
SHARD, Hannah 13
    James 12,13,40,50,75
SHARP, James 73
    Jamima 58
    John 4,40,58,72
    William 40,52,58,71,73
SHAW, Isias 33
    Josiah 1,35,36,55,58,59
SHELTON, Ann 35
    Anney 64
    Capt. 39
    Cuthbert 59
    Eliphaz 5,9,49,64,67,72,
        73,93
    Elizabeth 6,88,93

SHELTON (cont.)
    Ezekiel 93
    Hezekiah 72,74,105
    James 5,6,50,70,105
    Palatiah 23,34,35,62,64,
        96
    Ralph 58,59,64,71,73,92
    Ralph, Sr. 5,71
    Samuel 64,70,71,75
    Thomas 64
    William 21,35,50,51,70,
        72,86
SHEWMATE see SHUMATE
SHIELDS, John 34
SHUMATE, Samuel 40,87
SIMMONS - SIMMINS
    John 11,27,59,65
    Shockly 31
SIMMS - SIMS
    Charles 72
    Ignatious 54,74,75
    James 49
    Parish 49
    Sabra 54
SKILMAN, Christopher 23,29
SMALL, John 39,41,44
    Mathew 73
SMALLMAN, John 54,98
SMITH, ... 18,51
    Anthony 51,97,99
    Bartlett 72,73
    Benjamin 92
    Bowker 119
    Bradley 71,75,78,93
    Caleb 59,74
    Charles 85,97
    Daniel 38,59,73,74,97,
        118
    Edward 45,60,72,74,78,83
    Elijah 78
    Harbourd 19
    Hobart 72,73
    Henry 7,72,73
    Jamima 6
    John 54,55,62,97,99
    Josiah 6,20,31,70,97
    Isaac 20,32
    Mary 32,59,60
    Munford 89
    Sally 77,96
    Sarah 95
    Stephen 46
    Thomas 30,72,73,77,95,96
    William 3,6,60,91,104
    William, Sr. 19
    Zackariah 28,71
    Zadock 59,60,71,72
SOUTHERLANE, Elizabeth 2
SOWELL, Elizabeth 27
    Joseph 77,78
    Mary 78
    William 27,71,73,82
SPANGLE, Daniel, Jr. 25,28
    Daniel, Sr. 25,28
SPEARS, Nicholes 8
SPENCER, James 6,23
    John 72,73,95
    William 62
SPERIDAN, Philip 33
SPRAGINS, Matitizah 96
SPROUSE, Charles 45
STAMPS, John 23,75
    Parthaney 23
STANDEFER, Israel 24
    James 24
    Jacob 24
    William 17
STANDLEY, John 75
    Moses 58
STALLING - STARLING
    Ann 9
    Jacob 9,76

STAPLES, John 3,6,20,23,45,
   46,55,61,70,74,77,85,
   91,97,99
   Samuel 18,65,70,74,88,
   95,103
STEVENS - STEPHENS
   Ann 31
   Dudley 106
   John 76,77
   Leanner 47
   Sampson 47
   William 21,31,33,36,47,
   71,74,88
STEWART, Mordecai 18
   Thomas 106,117
STINET - STENNET
   Benjamin 33,40
STOCKTON, John 58
   Richard 39,72,74,89,108,
   111,112
   Robert 6,18,21,55,57,66,
   79,86,88,111,113
   Robert, Jr. 113,117
   Thomas 103
STOKES - STOCKS
   John 38,44,73,75,99,112
   William 70,82
STONE, Eusebous 37,38,42,
   73
   Micajah 100
   Richard 100
   Sabert 18
   Stephen 18
   Thomas 71,73,91
STORM, Cornoold 20
   Peter 20
STOUT, Catherine 29
   James 13
   Joseph 29
STOVALL, Brett 23,32,65,
   96,119
   Joseph 33,55,65,66
   Madam 30
   Mary 32
   Thomas 36,41,73,75,77,
   83,90,95,96,100,111,
   114,115,117,118
STOVER, Jacob 52
STREET, Anthony 42,56,79
   Butler Stone 106
   Joseph 16,28,42,72,99
   Milley 16
STRODE, William 46
   stults, Adam 72,75
SULIVANT - SWILLIVANT
   Daniel 71
   John 69,71
SUMPTER, Elizabeth 81
   George 9,10,81
   Gl. 113
   Henry 52,73,75,84,85,
   106
   John 113
SWAN, Johnathan 3
SWANSON, William 120
SWEENY, Edmond 77
TACKETT, William 34
TALBOT, Ezekiel 77
   Mathew 25
TANZEY, William 83
TARRANT - TARRENT
   Carter 66,68
   James 34,35
   John 35
   Reuben 56
   Reuben, Jr. 60
   Samuel 37,57,60,72,74
TATE, Henry 7
TATUM, Edmond 49
   Edward 9,40,54,70,72,74,
   91,102
   Isham Brawder 34

TAYLOR, Daniel 20,83,99
   George 13,15,40,48,50,
   54,71,73,78,79,93
   Isaac 25
   James 28,39,51,57,59,
   65,71,72,75,80,84,115
   James, Jr. 79
   John 24,28,72,73
   Joseph 71,73
   Josiah 78,79
   William 28,71,73
TENNESON-TENISON-TENASON
   Thomas 28,62
   Saphaniah or Tafeniah
   or Zapheniah 22,65,
   101,107
TERRY, Elizabeth 92
   Jasper 37
   Thomas 28,29
THOMAS, Augustine 15,16,73,
   75
   Charles 58,59,96
   Henry 16
   Milley 3
   Nancy 90
THOMASSON, Fleming 112
THOMPSON, Dick 70
   James 50
   Mary 93
   William 93
TITTLE, Anthony 73,84,85,
   107
   David 85,101
   George 101
   Patty 101
   Peter 73,101
TOMBS - TOOMS
   Edmond 118
   William 71,74,118,119
TOMPKINS, John 89
   La., Jr. 83
   Samuel 34
   Samuel, Jr. 89,119
TOWNLEY, Joseph 73
TOWNWELL, Joseph 74
TRAMELL, Dennis 37
   Dennis Baker 37
TRENT, Bryant 14
   Henry 13
   William 13
TUGGLE, John 94
TUNSTALL, George 60,90
   William 8,60,85,108
TURNER, Adam 66,81
   Francis 7,66,73,75
   James 66
   Jeremiah 74,118
   John 34
   Josiah 100
   Larkin 75,81
   Shadrack 118
   William 73,75,118
VAN MEAPOLL, Jean 13
   John 13
VANDERGRIFF, Leonard, Sr.
   38
VAUGHAN, Aris 75
   Fanny 92
   Henry 11,92
   Hundley 22
VENABLE, Richard 36
VERNON, Thomas 102
VESS, Catherine 88,104
   Peter 88,100
   Samuel 84,88,100,103,
   104
VINSON, Elisha 73,74
VOURN, Rubin 59
WADE, Ballinger 78,79,80,
   89,93
   Bartlet 46
   Jonadab 86

WALDEN - WALDIN
   Aaron 42
   Benjamin 56
   Elisha 90
   Joseph 42,72,74,91,98,
   99,107,108
   Moses 42,75
   Nathan 42,56
   Rachel 99
   William 12,42
WALKER, Elisha 34
   James 60,98
   Meredith 17
   Samuel 55,72
WALLEN, John 116
WALLER, Ann 87
   George 10,21,25,26,27,
   38,59,63,73,74,87,104,
   115
   George, Jr. 55,87
   John 18,38,60,72,75,87,
   110
WALTON, George 4,49,50,58,
   115
   Robert 38,49,50,64,115
WANN, William 102
WARD, John 67,77,91,94,97
   William 69
   William W. 42
WARDEN, Robert 42,56,72,73
WARREN, Davis 16
   Elizabeth 16
   William 16,92
WASH, John 60,72,74
WATKINS, George 81
   Isaiah 33
   Willis 33
WATSON, David 12,71,74
   John 26,47,50,73,75,81,
   93
   Dr. John 39
   Richard 53
   Robert 52,53
   Samuel 53
   Michael 73,75
WATTS, William 31
WEAKLEY, ... 12
WEALCH, Richard 74
WEATHERFORD, David 106,121
   Mary 121
WEAVER, John 38,75,99
WEBB, Jacob 10
   Merry 79,106,114
   Morrah 9
   Morris 63
   Theodrick 10
WELCH, Richard 28,71,92
WELLS, Barnaba 30,66,110,
   117
   John 20,30,39,45,56,73,
   75,117
   Mathew 12,29,30,117
   William 93
WEST, Robert 77
WHEAT, John 90
WHEELER, Luke 80,96
WHITRITTS, William 21
WHITLOCK, Thomas 54
WHITSETT, Eleanor 88,92
   William 68,82,88,92
WHITT, Silvanus 3
WILKINS, Elizabeth 112
   Thomas 3,71,74,112
WILLIAMS, David 59
   Garrot 83
   James 55,57,73,74
   Robert 36,80
   Widow 57
   William 92
WILLIAMSON, ... 115
   Robert 114
WILLINGHAM, Jesse 11

8

WILLIS, David 11,18,74,88
   John 9,23
   Phebe 23
   William 69
WILLS, Isaiah 22
   John 4
WILSON, Aaron 110
   Daniel 108
   Harris 7
   James 55,65,102,106,110
   John 106
   Joshua 28
   Moses 76,77,121
   Richard 42,60,71
   Robert 95
   Shadrack 29
   Thomas 117
   William 43,50,92
WIMBISH, John 4
WINN, John 87
WINNINGHAM, John 99
WINSTON, Edmund 35,83
WITT, David 3,23,71,75,76
   Jesse 1,21,22,35,46,75,
     84
   John 33,50,54,55,56,57,
     73
   Silvanus 3
   William 50,54,73,74,84
WOLVERTON, Andrew 65,71,73
WOMACK, Abra. 68
WOOLARD - WOOLLARD
   William 98,107
WOOD - WOODS
   12
   Elliott 87
   James 44
   John 60
   Robert 3
   William 3,30
WOODY, William 72
WRIGHT, John 22
YOUNG, Elizabeth 48
   James 2,3,30
   William 48

SLAVE INDEX

Abraham 97
Archer 63
Andrew 35
Aggy 45
Armsted 57
Adam 60
Anthony 37
Anderson 95

Betty 27
Bob 45,61,63,120
Betsy 36
Benjamin 56
Blacksmith 81
Bess 37
Barbary 90

Charles 63,120
Cate 63,120
Cornwal 95
Chlo 43
Cloe 45
Chaney 63,120

Deaner 43
Dianah 45,110
Daniel 55,79

Easter 120
Elizabeth 95
Esther 90
Ester 63

Frank 55
Frazer 63

George 43,57
Gilbert 90

Hampton 81
Hanah 113
Harry 45,95
Henry 37,43,45

Isabel 63,120
Isack 95

Jack 43,91,95
Jessie 45
John 63
James 43
Jane 63
Janey 120
Jude 23,63,120
Judah 45
Juda 55
Jeff 63,120
Jinney 43
Judith 113
Jacob 81,113
Jusy 81

Kate 45
Kadrick 45

Latt 36,90
Liza 83
Lott 23
Lucy 27,36,57

Martin 72
Major 29
Mingo 23
Margery 36
Mandrey 37
Milley 37
Mildred 45
Moses 90

Ned 45

Old Jude 43

Peggy 37
Phillis 58,63,76
Peter 37,45,80
Ploth 63
Phebe 90

Randall 36
Randolph 37
Rose 41
Reuben 57

Sal 43,81
Sam 43
Set 43
Sarah 90
Shadock 95

Tazey 26

Will 27,45,82,113
Winney 37

www.ingramcontent.com/pod-product-compliance
Lightning Source LLC
Chambersburg PA
CBHW031423290426
44110CB00011B/498